LONDON'S SECRETS
MUSEUMS &
GALLERIES

A Guide to Over 200 of the City's Top Attractions

Robbi Atilgan & David Hampshire

T0159520

Survival Books • Bath • England

First published 2013

Copyright © Survival Books 2013
Cover design: Di Bruce-Kidman
Cover photo: Nude Woman with Necklace, Picasso (Tate Modern)
© Mark Colliton (markcolliton.com)
Maps © Jim Watson

Survival Books Limited
Office 169, 3 Edgar Buildings
George Street, Bath BA1 2FJ, United Kingdom
☎ +44 (0)1935-700060
✉ info@survivalbooks.net
🖳 www.survivalbooks.net

British Library Cataloguing in Publication Data
A CIP record for this book is available
from the British Library.

ISBN: 978-1-907339-96-7

Printed in Singapore by International Press Softcom Limited

Acknowledgements

The authors would like to thank all those who helped with research and provided information for this book, unfortunately too many to list here. Special thanks are due to Jenni Lloyd (Estorick Collection), Hannah Talbot (Courtauld Gallery), Peter Read for research and editing; Alex Browning for proof-reading; David Woodworth for final proof checking; Di Bruce-Kidman for DTP, photo selection and cover design; Jim Watson for the superb maps; and the authors' partners for continuing with the pretence that writing is a proper job (that pays a proper salary).

Last, but not least, a special thank you to the many photographers who provided images (listed on page 318) – the unsung heroes – whose beautiful images add colour and bring the museums and galleries to life.

NOTE

Before visiting anywhere mentioned in this book, it's advisable to check the opening times, which are liable to change without notice.

St Jerome in the Wilderness, Albrecht Dürer , National Gallery

Towards Pink, Kandinsky (Courtauld)

Contents

2. CITY & EAST LONDON 94

3. NORTH LONDON   140

4. WEST LONDON 188

5. SOUTHWEST LONDON 210

6. SOUTHEAST LONDON 242

Readers' Guide

The notes below refer to the general information provided for each museum/gallery and other information 'boxes'.

♦ **Address:** Includes the phone number and website (if applicable). You can enter the postcode to display a map of the location on Google.

♦ **Opening hours:** These can change at short notice, so confirm by telephone or check the website before travelling. Note that the last entry is usually at least 30 minutes before the closing time. Some venues close for private or official events, and smaller galleries have no permanent exhibitions and are open only during exhibitions.

♦ **Cost:** Many museums – such as national museums and galleries – offer free entry but charge a fee for special exhibitions. Ask about concession and family rates if not indicated. Many museums have lower fees for groups, either per head or a fixed rate, which must usually be pre-booked (particularly for small museums). Groups may also be able to visit at times when museums are closed to the general public. Major museums allow you to buy tickets online, thus circumventing queues, and prices may also be slightly lower. Museum cafés and shops often allow free public access.

♦ **Transport:** The nearest tube or rail stations are listed, although in some cases there may also be a lengthy walk. You can also travel to most venues by bus and to some by river ferry. Some museums are best reached by car, although parking can be difficult or impossible in many areas. Most venues don't provide parking, particularly in central London, and even parking nearby may be a problem (and expensive!). If you need to travel by car, check the parking facilities beforehand.

♦ **Amenities:** Facilities such as a restaurant or café, pub, shop, library, garden, park, etc. are noted. Most museums have a WC, although not all are wheelchair accessible.

Access

Many museums housed in old buildings don't provide wheelchair access or may allow access to the ground floor only. Wheelchairs are provided at some venues, although users may need assistance. Contact venues if you have specific requirements (see also Artsline, 🖳 artsline.org.uk).

♦ **Food & Drink:** All major museums and galleries provide cafés and/or restaurants, many of which are excellent. Where applicable we have also made alternative suggestions. Some venues provide a picnic area or you can usually eat a packed lunch in a nearby park or square.

♦ **Allow:** The time required to see collections varies considerably, from less than an hour for a small gallery to a number of days for national museums. If your time is limited it's advisable to check a museum's website and decide what you most want to see. Don't forget to allow time for travelling, coffee/tea breaks and lunch.

♦ **Don't Miss:** This highlights an unusual exhibit, an important piece of art or a 'must-see' attraction.

Introduction

London is one of the world's great art and cultural centres – many claim it's the art capital of the world – with more popular museums and galleries (some 250, excluding commercial galleries) than any other city. It's also home to seven of the world's top 50 most-visited museums and art galleries, beating rival cities such as New York and Paris. The London art scene is a lot like the city itself – diverse, vast, vibrant and in a constant state of flux – a cornucopia of traditional and cutting-edge, majestic and mundane, world-class and run-of-the-mill, bizarre and brilliant. From old masters to street art and everything in between, London has it all in spades.

Not surprisingly, everyone wants to see the world-class national collections, such as the British Museum and National Gallery, but once you've explored the Egyptian galleries and admired Van Gogh's *Sunflowers*, what next? Well, then it's time to seek out smaller but equally captivating collections, such as the Wallace Collection and the Dulwich Picture Gallery; absorbing 'specialist' museums like Sir John Soane's eclectic house of

National Gallery

treasures, Dennis Severs' enchanting house and the fascinating Brunel Museum; and controversial, thought-provoking (even shocking) modern art at the Saatchi Gallery and Tate Modern. London has something for everyone. Furthermore, many museums and galleries are housed in magnificent historic buildings – either purpose-built or former grand homes – which are works of art in their own right.

Also, don't overlook the treasure trove of smaller 'secret' museums (not to mention the plethora of interesting local history museums), many of which are known only to insiders and locals; some are tucked away in the suburbs, but are well worth the extra effort involved to explore them.

Best of all, most national museums offer free entry (although there's a suggested donation to help defray running costs), as do many others. In fact over half the places featured in this book are free! No other city in the world offers free access to so many museums.

London is also one of the world's most dynamic

The Plains of Heaven, John Martin (Tate Britain)

Bacchus and Ariadne, Titian (National Gallery)

centres for contemporary art, with an abundance of commercial art galleries catering to all tastes and forms of modern art. Enterprising galleries and artists' spaces have burgeoned across the capital, and, in turn, have attracted artists from of all corners of the globe to live and work in the city. Most galleries stage regular free exhibitions, including artist retrospectives and showcases for new talent, and visiting them is a great way to get a feel for the changing arts scene and spot the Next Big Thing! Although the majority of commercial galleries are situated in central London, don't neglect other areas, particularly East London, which has become one of the city's most vibrant art hubs in recent years.

As that great man of letters Samuel Johnson once said, "When a man is tired of London he is tired of life; for there is in London all that life can afford." It's hard to imagine anyone tiring of the capital's museums and galleries, where there's always something new, unexpected or unexplored to capture your imagination and fire your enthusiasm.

So, whether you're an art lover, a culture vulture, a history buff or just looking for something to entertain the family during the school holidays, you're sure to find inspiration in London. All you need is a comfortable pair of shoes, an open mind – and this book!

Robbi Atilgan & David Hampshire
January 2013

Discobolus (British Museum)

CENTRAL LONDON

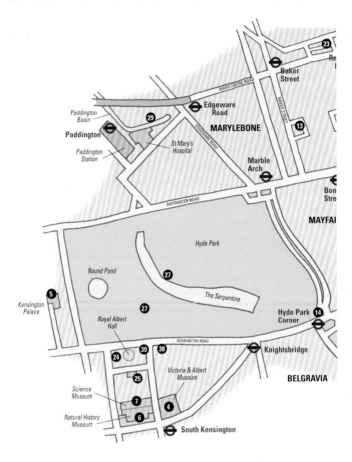

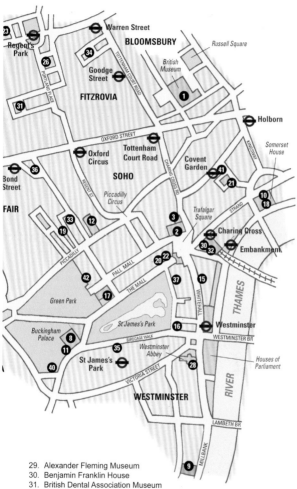

1   BRITISH MUSEUM

Address: Great Russell Street, WC1B 3DG (☎ 020-7323 8299,
🖳 britishmuseum.org).

Opening hours: Sat-Thu, 10am to 5.30pm; Fri 10am till 8.30pm (most galleries).
The Great Court opens at 9am. Closed 24-26th December and 1st January,
and from 5.30pm on Good Fridays. Galleries may be temporarily closed for
refurbishment, so check beforehand.

Cost: Free. There's a fee for some temporary exhibitions.

Transport: Tottenham Court Road, Holborn, Russell Square and Goodge
Street tube.

Amenities: Restaurant, two cafés, four shops, wheelchair access.

The British Museum is a London landmark and both the city's most popular museum (attracting some 6m visitors annually) and the third most-visited museum in the world after the Louvre and New York's Metropolitan Museum. It provides an almost overwhelming smorgasbord of human history and culture stretching across centuries and continents, one that's best appreciated in small bites. The museum has a permanent collection of some 8m objects – although only around 1 per cent is on show at any one time – housed in almost 100 galleries.

The British Museum grew from the private collection of curiosities bequeathed to George II by physician and scientist Sir Hans Sloane (1660-1753). Sloane's collection comprised around 71,000 objects including books, manuscripts, natural history specimens and antiquities. The museum was established by Act of Parliament in 1753, and opened in 1759 in Montagu House in Bloomsbury, on the site of the current building. It was the first national public museum in the world, and set a precedent by offering free entry to 'all studious and curious persons'.

 ALLOW...

The British Museum covers over 92,000m² (990,00ft²) and it's impossible to see it in a day (or even a week). It's better to concentrate on one or two departments at a time. But if time is short, the museum's website (🖳 britishmuseum.org) is invaluable. As well as allowing you to explore 2m objects online, it provides themed object trails and suggested itineraries if you have only a few hours to spare.

The museum has grown over the last two and a half centuries in an

Reading Room

Tomb of Nebamu

attempt to keep pace with its ever-expanding collection, which has been swelled by numerous bequests and by discoveries by colonial adventurers from Asia Minor to the South Sea Islands. The magnificent building you see today – a quadrangle with four wings and a Greek revival façade, based on the temple of Athena Polias at Priene in Asia Minor (Turkey) – was designed by Sir Robert Smirke and completed in 1852. There have been many additions since, including the cast iron circular Reading Room which housed much of the British Library until its move to St Pancras in 1997. Its removal made way for the Great Court, Norman Foster's spectacular glass structure which opened in 2000 and is the largest covered public square in Europe.

Start your tour in the Great Court, where information desks provide floor plans and itineraries, including the award-winning BBC collaboration, *A History of the World in 100 Objects*, which tracks human evolution from Stone Age tools to a solar-powered lamp. If your time is limited you can opt for a 40-minute 'eyeOpener' tour of a chosen department or hire one of the multimedia guides (£5) and explore at your own pace. Note that the Montague Street entrance at the rear (north side) of the British Museum can be much less crowded than the main entrance, and is a quick way to access the Egyptian and African rooms.

The main departments and highlights are as follows:

Ancient Egypt (rooms 4, 61-66): The largest collection of Egyptian

Egyptian Column

Upstairs, the perennially popular collection of 140 mummies and mummy cases and other objects offers insight into the Egyptians' preoccupation with the afterlife. One of the most studied is the Mummy of Katebet from Thebes, which dates back to 1300-1280 BC; this elderly woman was mummified with a scarab beetle for protection and a mummy statue to act as her servant.

Don't miss the Sphinx of Taharqo, a ruler of Kush around 700 BC, which was found in Upper Nubia (Sudan) and has a distinctively African face.

Ancient Greece & Rome (rooms 11-23, 69-73): One of the world's most inclusive assemblies of antiquities from the classical world, from the Greek Bronze Age (around 3200 BC) to the reign of Emperor Constantine I (4th century AD). It also encompasses the Cycladic, Minoan and Mycenaean cultures, plus elements of two of the Seven Wonders of the Ancient World: the Mausoleum at Halicarnassus and the Temple of Artemis at Ephesus.

The biggest draw is the so-called Elgin Marbles, a group of iconic sculptures removed from the Parthenon in the early 19th century and bought by the British government in 1816. Put aside their much debated relocation

antiquities outside Cairo. Room 4 contains the blockbuster sculptures, including the authoritative bust of Ramesses II (1250 BC) and the Sarcophagus of Nectanebo II (360 to 343 BC), which was once rumoured (wrongly) to have contained the body of Alexander the Great. The most important object is the Rosetta Stone, a large slab of granite featuring writing in three scripts – Greek, everyday Egyptian and hieroglyphics – which enabled linguists to decipher the hieroglyphic code.

Elgin marbles

China's Terracotta Army Exhibition, 2007-8

and instead enjoy their intricate and lifelike detail, in particular the reclining statue of Dionysos and the head of the noble Selene horse.

Smaller but no less impressive are the collections of jewellery, bronzes, Greek vases and Roman glass. Look out for the bronze statue of a Minoan bull leaper from Crete, a gold coin said to have belonged to King Croesus and the elegant Portland Vase, made from Roman cameo glass.

 FOOD & DRINK

Court Restaurant: Fine dining and afternoon tea under the Great Court's glass roof.
  Court Cafes: Fill up on sandwiches and snacks between exhibits.
  Museum Tavern: Decent pub grub in a historic hostelry opposite the main entrance to the museum.

Middle East (rooms 6-10, 34, 52-59): These collections represent the great ancient civilisations of the Near East – the area between the Mediterranean and modern-day Iraq.

The museum possesses by far the world's largest and most important collection of Mesopotamian antiquities outside Iraq. The flagship pieces are the massive winged human-headed lion statues from the biblical city of Nimrud and the alabaster bas-reliefs which depict scenes from ancient Nineveh. The Royal Lion Hunt reliefs are among the museum's most important possessions.

Smaller but still significant are the Flood Tablet found at Nineveh, which tells part of the story of Gilgamesh – and has parallels with the biblical story of Noah – and the Royal Game of Ur, a board game from 3,000 BC unearthed in the Royal Cemeteries at Ur in southern Iraq.

The Oxus Treasure is a collection of precious metal items from the first Persian Empire, which includes an intricate gold chariot and vessels shaped like fish, while another room houses Islamic art: pottery, inscriptions and Iznik tiles.

Prehistory & Europe (rooms 40-51): This collection covers a geographical area from Spain to the

Black Sea and from Scandinavia to North Africa, and a timescale stretching from earliest man – some objects date back 2m years – to the present day. It's particularly strong on life in Britain under the Romans, featuring armour, mosaics and even a party invitation inscribed on a stone tablet! Some of the most ornate objects are from hoards – buried treasure unearthed centuries later – and include a ceremonial helmet from the 7th century (Sutton Hoo), gorgeous silver tableware used by Romans (Mildenhall Treasure) and the Bronze Age Mold Cape made from beaten gold.

Objects range from the rudimentary – a swimming reindeer carving from a mammoth's tusk – to the flamboyant. The Royal Gold Cup, solid gold and lavishly decorated, was the proud possession of several European monarchs.

Royal Gold Cup

the region's religions, such as the 1st-century BC Buddhist limestone reliefs from Amaravati in India, and a vast collection of Chinese paintings, porcelain, lacquerware and jade. One of the most pleasing jade objects is an incredibly lifelike terrapin, which probably belonged to a Mughal emperor in 17th-century India. Equally charming are the detailed burial figures which were recovered from the tomb of a Chinese soldier from the Tang dynasty (around 700 AD). The collection also boasts the most complete collection of Japanese pre-20th-century art in the Western world, from Samurai armour to tea sets.

 DON'T MISS!

The Lewis Chessmen are a set of characterful chess pieces made from walrus tusk and whale tooth, which were unearthed on the Scottish Isle of Lewis in the 1830s. They are thought to date from 12th-century Norway and would once have kept Viking warriors amused. See them in the Medieval Europe gallery (room 40).

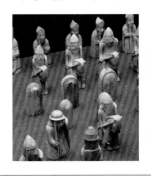

Asia (rooms 33, 67, 92-94): The broadest collection in terms of countries covered, this department features over 75,000 objects. Highlights include sculptures and paintings celebrating

Africa, Oceania & the Americas (rooms 25, 26-27): A diverse and compelling collection which gives a glimpse of the indigenous peoples of three continents. Visit the Sainsbury African Galleries to view masks, sculptures and the amazing Benin Bronzes, detailed brass plaques from the royal palace of the Kingdom of Benin (in present day Nigeria) depicting sophisticated courtly life in 15th-century Africa. The Americas collections feature objects from Inca, Mayan and Native American cultures. Many have an animal theme, such as the otter-shaped pipe from 1st-century Ohio and the elegant ballgame belt from Veracruz in Mexico with the face of a toad and a grisly secret – losers in this ceremonial game often lost their heads as well.

gold statue of Kate Moss, Marc Quinn

Prints & Drawings (room 90): The museum has about 50,000 drawings and over 2m prints dating from the 15th century to the present day. It's one of the largest and best print room collections in existence, ranking alongside the Albertina in Vienna, the Paris collections and the Hermitage, and a selection is displayed in room 90.

Enlightenment Gallery (room 1): Opened in 2003 to celebrate the 250th anniversary of the museum, this is dedicated to discoveries made during the Age of Enlightenment (1680-1820), when our thirst for knowledge was at its keenest. Objects reflect the exciting new disciplines of the age – religion and ritual, trade and discovery, archaeology, art history, classification, the decipherment of ancient scripts and natural history – and many were collected by the museum's founder Sir Hans Sloane. They range from the delicate Sloane astrolabe, a map

of the heavens first used in medieval times, to a flint hand axe dating back some 350,000 years and discovered in London in the late 1600s.

The Wellcome Trust Gallery (room 24): This room displays objects from places as diverse as New Zealand, Ghana and the Pacific islands on the theme of Living and Dying, and is

Apollo

Enlightenment Gallery

dominated by one of the largest objects in the museum: the four-ton basalt statue from Easter Island known as Hoa Hakananaia'a ('Stolen or Hidden Friend'). Once a potent symbol of ancestor worship, the statue was one of many discovered by Captain Cook, and was later transported to England on board the HMS Topaze – with the permission of the islanders – in 1868.

There are many more rooms to explore, including one devoted to money – a coin collector's nirvana – and another dedicated to clocks and watches, while The Changing Room (room 2) features a rotating selection of objects from the main collection.

The British Museum is famous for its landmark exhibitions, such as the Treasures of Tutankhamun, which had visitors queuing around the block in 1972, and The First Emperor: China's Terracotta Army which brought some of Emperor Qin Shi Huang's 3rd-century terracotta warriors from Xi'an to London in 2007. But the free exhibitions are also well worth exploring. In 2012 and 2013, these included a virtual autopsy of a 5,000-year-old Egyptian mummy; Renaissance to Goya, presenting Spanish art from the mid-16th to the early 19th century; and the highly acclaimed The Horse: from Arabia to Royal Ascot, examining the history of equine influence on civilisation since 3500BC.

Once you've completed your tour(s), the British Museum's shops are an irresistible diversion, selling everything from beautifully illustrated books to a rubber duck in the shape of a sphinx!

The British Museum

NATIONAL GALLERY 2

Address: Trafalgar Square, WC2N 5DN (☏ 020-7747 2885,
🖥 nationalgallery.org.uk).
Opening hours: Daily, 10am to 6pm (9pm Fridays). Closed 24-26th December and
1st January.
Cost: Free. There's a fee for some temporary exhibitions.
Transport: Charing Cross tube/rail.
Amenities: Restaurant, two cafés, three shops, wheelchair access.

Hay Wain, Constable

One of the finest collections of Western European art in the world, the National Gallery is the second most-visited museum in the UK and a must-see for anyone interested in art. It boasts more than 2,300 works of art, dating from the 13th century to 1900 – from Botticelli's *Venus and Mars* to Constable's *The Hay Wain*. It's a museum for contemplation rather than interaction, and one that deserves to be dipped into time and again.

Despite its grand frontage, the National Gallery (NG for short) was always intended to be a people's gallery. The founders chose Trafalgar Square for its location – the rich could ride up from the west in their carriages, and the East End's poor could get there on foot – and entrance has been free since its inception. That said, it's one museum that really deserves your donations as without gifts and bequests it wouldn't exist.

Unlike other European countries, which nationalised their royal art collections for public consumption, the British government had to buy its paintings. Its first purchase was a private collection of 38 paintings from John Julius Angerstein in 1824 which cost £57,000; a huge investment, although it pales in comparison with the £95m the NG paid for two Titians in recent years. The only place to display Angerstein's paintings was in his former

The Wilton Diptych, 1395-9

home in Pall Mall and that's where they stayed, along with other acquisitions, until a decision was made to build a gallery on the site of the former Royal Mews overlooking Trafalgar Square.

The building was designed by William Wilkins who may have lacked the foresight to realise the sheer number of paintings it would be required to display. It opened in 1838 and the first director, Sir Charles Lock Eastlake, appointed in 1855, soon expanded the collection by making frequent buying trips to Italy and attracting further bequests. Some gifts, including over 1,000 works left to the nation by the artist Turner, couldn't

be accommodated and ended up in other locations. This led to the creation of a gallery on Millbank – now Tate Britain – dedicated to British art. The National Gallery continued to expand, most recently with the addition of the Sainsbury Wing, the Postmodernist extension which opened in 1991.

The National Gallery's paintings are grouped chronologically and displayed in four wings. The Sainsbury Wing hosts medieval and early works, while the 16th-century Renaissance paintings are housed in the West Wing. The North Wing to the rear is home to 17th-century works and the East Wing has 18th- and 19th-century paintings,

The National Gallery

Venus and Mars, Botticelli

including the British School. The NG's map is colour-coded and easy to navigate, and the website version is interactive so you can see at a glance which paintings are in which room.

 ALLOW...

Allow plenty of time to take in the paintings – you can make sketches although taking photos is banned – as each of the four wings could easily occupy you for a day. If you cannot spare the time, the website suggests 30 'must-see' paintings and lets you take a virtual tour. There are daily one-hour guided tours which leave from the Sainsbury Wing at 11.30am and 2.30pm, or use the NG's multimedia touch screen system, ArtStart, to plan your own tour and print a free map.

It's impossible to list the full collections here, just as it is to see them all in a day, but the following is a taster of what's on view.

Sainsbury Wing: Early Italian, Dutch and German Schools (1250 to 1500). The collection includes works by Uccello, van Eyck, Lippi, Botticelli, Dürer and Bellini, among others. Many were intended as icons and altar pieces, and the monochrome interior of the rooms (51-66) is the perfect foil for the paintings' jewel-like colours. Overriding themes are the life of Christ and the saints, although from the 1400s onwards characters from mythology – notably Venus – were popular subjects, and portraits of the painters' contemporaries begin to appear. Highlights include:

♦ *The Wilton Diptych* by an unknown artist was painted in 1395-9 as an altarpiece for Richard II. It's one of very few to survive from medieval England.

♦ *The Battle of San Romano* and *Saint George and the Dragon*, both by Uccello. The latter has a

The Boulevard Montmartre at Night, Pissarro

Sunflowers, Vincent van Gogh

fairy-tale quality with the fearsome dragon held on a leash by the princess.

◆ *The Arnolfini Portrait* by van Eyck. This famous but homely portrait of a nobleman and his wife illustrates the artist's incredible use of light. The wife isn't pregnant but rather is holding up her skirts as the fashion decreed.

◆ *The Virgin of the Rocks* by Leonardo da Vinci is one of two versions; the other hangs in the Louvre.

◆ *Venus and Mars* by Botticelli shows Mars in post-coital slumber, to the amusement of the satyrs.

◆ *The Painter's Father* by Dürer is an honest but affectionate study.

 FOOD & DRINK

National Dining Room: The best of British fine dining with prices to match.
Café in the Crypt, St Martin-in-the-Fields: Just across Trafalgar Square, open until 8pm – the Les Routiers London Cafe of the Year 2012.

West Wing: Renaissance Italian, Dutch and German Schools (1500 to 1600). Works by Leonardo, Michelangelo, Raphael, Titian, Holbein and Brueghel among those on display in rooms 2 to 14. The stars of the show are undoubtedly the Italian Renaissance painters. This was the era in which the skill of the artist began to win as much appreciation as the subject matter, as the great and the good commissioned art for art's sake. Highlights include:

◆ *The Ambassadors* by Holbein which is notable for the incredible detail of objects surrounding its subjects, such as the Turkish carpet, and the skull which appears distorted unless viewed from a certain angle.

◆ *The Raising of Lazarus* by del Piombo, from Angerstein's collection, was the first painting to enter the gallery in 1824.

◆ *The Entombment* and *The Manchester Madonna* by Michelangelo are the only works by the artist in the National Gallery; both are unfinished.

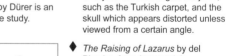

- *The Madonna of the Pinks* by Raphael is a tender depiction of the young Virgin Mary amusing baby Jesus with a bunch of carnations.

- *The Family of Darius before Alexander* by Veronese depicts a triumphant Alexander with the family of the Persian king; most of the subjects wear Venetian attire.

- *Bacchus and Ariadne* by Titian. Among the gods and satyrs, you can spot a King Charles spaniel – a popular pet in Titian's time.

North Wing: Dutch, Flemish, French, Italian and Spanish Schools (1600 to 1700). The 17th-century artists represented in rooms 15-32 and 37 include Caravaggio, Rubens, Poussin, Van Dyck, Velázquez, Claude, Rembrandt and Vermeer. This is the era in which artists began to impose their own style onto traditional subject matters, while the subjects they painted shifted from religious themes to everyday scenes, still lifes and landscapes. Highlights include:

- *Seaport with the Embarkation of Saint Ursula* by Claude – a fabulous seascape.

- *Self Portrait at the Age of 34* by Rembrandt shows the artist at the peak of his career.

- *A Peepshow with Views of the Interior of a Dutch House* by Samuel van Hoogstraten is an early attempt at presenting a scene in 3D.

- *Samson and Delilah* by Rubens presents a sensual retelling of the Old Testament tale featuring an unsuspecting Samson at the mercy of voluptuous Delilah.

- *Equestrian Portrait of Charles I* by Anthony Van Dyck is more than 3m high and would have dwarfed its subject. Charles was only 5ft 4in (163cm) tall and was often painted on horseback to increase his stature.

- *The Supper at Emmaus* by Michelangelo Merisi da Caravaggio perfectly captures the disciples' shock when they realise they're eating with the resurrected Jesus.

East Wing: British, French and Italian Schools (1700 to 1900). The latest

The Fighting Temeraire, JMW Turner

paintings are in rooms 33-36 and 38-46, and include works by Canaletto, Goya, Turner, Constable, Ingres, Degas, Cézanne, Monet and van Gogh. This is the time when artists began to rebel against conformity and form new art movements. The Impressionist and Post-impressionist rooms are always popular, as are those displaying the best of British paintings. Highlights include:

◆ *The Hay Wain* by Constable. This was first exhibited at the Royal Academy in 1821 where it failed to find a buyer, although it was much appreciated in France.

👁 DON'T MISS!

One of the gallery's more controversial paintings, *The Toilet of Venus* by Velázquez (see below) was completed between 1647 and 1651. Also known as *The Rokeby Venus*, it's one of very few nudes to be painted by a Spanish artist for fear of reprisals by the Inquisition! In 1914 it was famously slashed by a suffragette, Mary Richardson, in protest at the arrest of Emmeline Pankhurst.

◆ *The Fighting Temeraire* by Turner shows the last of the victorious Trafalgar fleet on her way to be scrapped; she appears ghostly in Turner's misty light.

◆ *Whistlejacket* by Stubbs depicts the Marquess of Rockingham's racehorse in all his temperamental splendour.

◆ *The Stonemason's Yard* by Canaletto shows an unexpected view of the Grand Canal in Venice and is full of detail, from a woman spinning thread on a balcony to a mother rushing to comfort her fallen child.

◆ *The Water-Lily Pond* by Monet. The National Gallery is fortunate to have 18 Monets, including *The Beach at Trouville* and *Irises*.

◆ *The Umbrellas* by Renoir. This wonderful Parisian street scene was left to the gallery by Sir Hugh Lane, who died in the sinking of the Lusitania in 1915.

◆ *Sunflowers* by Vincent van Gogh. Possibly the world's greatest still-life painting, it's one of several sunflower paintings by the artist who had to work early in the morning before the blooms began to wilt.

There's a lot more going on, including temporary exhibitions, concerts, workshops and talks, most of which are free. It's hard to get out of the National Gallery, however, without spending money in the shop which sells prints and posters of its entire works, alongside art books and other goodies.

The Toilet of Venus, Velázquez

NATIONAL PORTRAIT GALLERY 3

Address: St Martin's Place, WC2H 0HE (☎ 020-7306 0055, 💻 npg.org.uk).
Opening hours: Daily, 10am to 6pm (9pm on Thursdays and Fridays). Closed 24-26th December.
Cost: Free. There's a fee for some temporary exhibitions.
Transport: Leicester Square tube.
Amenities: Restaurant, café, bar, two shops, wheelchair access.

Whether you're seeking artistic inspiration or voyeuristic pleasure, you'll find it in the National Portrait Gallery, where a unique collection of portraits shows famous and influential British people from the last 500 years – from Henry VIII to Winston Churchill – captured in paintings, sculpture, drawings and photography.

Established in 1856, the National Portrait Gallery (NPG) was the first of its kind in the world. It was the forerunner of today's *Hello!* magazine in that it allowed the public to see the people who had shaped their world, although it was born out of a desire to educate and inspire, rather than titillate and amuse.

The NPG was founded by Philip Henry Stanhope, Thomas Babington Macaulay and Thomas Carlyle, all of whom are immortalised in stone above the main entrance. Its first portrait was one of William Shakespeare which was donated by Lord Ellesmere. The man in charge of the gallery was an illustrator, George Scharf, who managed the collection for 40 years until just before its move to its permanent home.

As the collection grew, it was shifted between several locations until the philanthropist William Henry Alexander donated £80,000 for a permanent museum to be built in St Martin's Place, next to the National Gallery. The architect Ewan Christian designed the building in rather fanciful Florentine style, and it opened to the public in 1896. The site has been extended twice: the Duveen Wing was opened in 1933 and the Ondaatje Wing in 2000.

Michael Parkinson, Jonathan Yeo

 ALLOW...

It's possible to see the highlights of the National Portrait Gallery in a day but it takes a little planning. Start off in the Digital Space on the ground floor and make use of the Portrait Explorer, which helps you find out what's currently on display and follow a themed tour or plan your own route. The entire primary collection can be viewed on the Portrait Explorer and it also allows access to much of the reference collection. Audio guides are available in several languages and cost £3.

The NPG owns over 300,000 images, including some 11,000 portraits, although it can only display some 1,400 at any one time. Others are exhibited in its three regional galleries, and many are archived. The primary collection is laid out chronologically over three floors. The top floor displays from the Tudor up to the late Regency period, while the first floor presents Victorians, Edwardians and 20th-century folk. Contemporary portraits are on the ground floor; interestingly, the gallery has only displayed portraits of living figures since 1969.

The following is a brief guide to some of the highlights, albeit a subjective one. Note that some may be removed when you visit. The website provides an up-to-date room-by-room guide to what's currently on display.

Tudors & Stuarts (1485-1714, rooms 1-8): Many of the people portrayed here are familiar, from Holbein's powerful 'cartoon' of Henry VIII, which became the blueprint for how we now see him, to the shifty-looking image of Richard III. There's a plump Cardinal Wolsey, a pensive Thomas Cranmer, later burned at the stake, and several of Henry's ill-fated wives, including a lovely study of Anne

Diana, Princess of Wales, Mario Testino

King Henry VIII, unknown artist

Boleyn, described as having 'eyes which were black and beautiful'. Elizabeth I is at her most regal in the 'Ditchley Portrait' by Marcus Gheeraerts the Younger. It was completed around 1592 when Elizabeth was approaching her 60s although in it she looks around 35!

Other royal portraits include several paintings of Charles II, from a plump baby grasping a King Charles spaniel by the ear to a grumpy and dissolute man painted a few years before his death. There's an unfinished sketch of James II by Sir Peter Lely, a renowned court painter, and a flattering full-length one of Queen Anne.

Significant subjects from this period include John Bunyan, Samuel Pepys, Sir Issac Newton and Ben Jonson, whose appearance is incredibly modern compared to his peers. Here, too, you can see the famous

Chandos portrait of Shakespeare that began it all, though some experts have questioned whether it really is a picture of the Bard.

> ### 👁 DON'T MISS!
>
> One of the strangest paintings is an anamorphic portrait of Edward VI by William Scrots, usually on show in room 1. The deliberately distorted perspective is a way for the painter to show off – view the painting from a particular angle and it magically corrects itself.

Georgian & Regency (1714-1837, rooms 9-20): These rooms present the movers and shakers of the 18th and early 19th centuries, including artists, scientists, politicians and royals. One room is devoted to the be-wigged Whigs of the Kit-Cat club, painted by

Queen Elizabeth II, Dorothy Wilding, 1952

There are some fascinating ensemble pieces, including one of abolitionist Granville Sharp and his family giving a concert on a Thames barge – clearly a joyous occasion. In complete contrast, *The Death of the Earl of Chatham* by John Singleton Copley is a moving historical document recreating the collapse of William Pitt the Elder in the House of Lords; it required sittings by 55 of the Earl's peers.

Regency subjects include two dashing portraits of George

Sir Godfrey Kneller. Other highlights include Sir Christopher Wren, satirists Jonathan Swift and Alexander Pope, the latter crowned with a Roman laurel wreath, William Hogarth's self-portrait and Handel holding a score of the *Messiah*. The courtesan Kitty Fisher is painted with a bowl of goldfish, which may be a comment on the effects of celebrity in Georgian times.

IV and a vivid recreation of the 'trial' of his popular wife, Queen Caroline of Brunswick, whom the king wished (but failed) to divorce. There are studies of Lord Nelson and Lady Hamilton, and the Duke of Wellington. The romantics are well represented, with portraits of poets Wordsworth, Keats and Percy Bysshe Shelley, and Lord Byron in Albanian dress. Subjects from the dawn of the Industrial Revolution include George Stephenson and John Loudon McAdam, inventor of tarmac.

Victorians & Edwardians (1837-1910, rooms 21-29): This is one of the largest collections, reflecting the age in which the gallery was founded. Queen Victoria's coronation portrait shows her looking young and apprehensive, although *The Secret of England's Greatness* portrays a much more assured Victoria presenting a Bible to

 FOOD & DRINK

Portrait Restaurant: Great food and a panoramic view of Nelson's Column and Big Ben in this rooftop restaurant. A two-course lunch starts from around £25.

Portrait Café: Reasonably priced sandwiches and drinks in the basement café with its signature glass roof.

a grateful African man! There's more empire-building in the Statesmen's Gallery, with its great many busts and oils of politicians, and it's a pleasant surprise to find the be-whiskered cricketing legend WG Grace tucked in among them.

Victorian arts are represented by a fresh-faced Charles Dickens, a pugnacious William Makepeace Thackeray, a painting of Edwin Landseer modelling one of the lions for Nelson's Column and complementary portraits of Robert Browning and Elizabeth Barratt Browning side by side. One of the most charming paintings is of Anne, Emily and Charlotte Brontë, painted by their brother Branwell; it was lost for many years before being rediscovered on top of a cupboard in 1914!

These galleries are a roll call of accomplishment, from Michael Faraday to Isambard Kingdom Brunel. There are several likenesses of Charles Darwin, including one in which he's cheekily caricatured as an ape. The portraits become less posed in the later part of the century – look for Robert Louis Stephenson, captured in a single setting by William Blake Richmond as the pair drank coffee and told ghost stories.

20th Century (1914-1990, rooms 30-32): Important figures from the two world wars figure highly here. *Statesmen of World War I* by Sir James Guthrie is a group painting which shows Churchill surrounded by Lloyd George, Kitchener and other great men of the age. There's also a sketch for Graham Sutherland's 'bulldog' portrait which Churchill hated; his wife destroyed the original!

There are many images of the Queen, including Cecil Beaton's timeless monochrome photographs from the '50s and '60s. One of the loveliest is *Conversation Piece at the Royal Lodge* by James Gunn, which revealed a new informality as George VI enjoys tea with his wife and daughters.

With so many familiar faces summing up a turbulent century it's hard to pinpoint the best portraits, but look out for a young Dylan Thomas

Shakespeare, John Taylor

Winston Churchill, Ambros McEvoy

Portrait Restaurant

– painted by his friend Augustus John – and Kingsley Amis wreathed in smoke from his pipe, Aleister Crowley adopting a mystical pose and Anna Neagle oozing Hollywood glamour. The portrait of writer-turned-farmer Beatrix Potter makes her look like one of her cuddly animal characters. *Carry On* star Sid James scowls out of a TV screen, Paul McCartney is captured in vibrant colour, while a black and white photo by Peter Rand catches Richard Branson in his pre-Virgin student days.

Contemporary Portraits (rooms 35-36, 38 and 41): These walls are lined with celebrities, from actors and writers to sportsmen and comedians, plus the odd politician. Worth seeking out are portraits of footballer David Beckham and director Mike Leigh, as well as actors Ian McKellen, Helen Mirren and a curiously disembodied head of Michael Caine. Some rooms are set aside for themed exhibitions, while others host major events, such as 2012's 'The Queen: Art and Image', which presented some of the NPG's 712 images of Her Majesty, and the annual BP Portrait Award, an open-entry competition for portraitists which takes place each summer. There's a fee for some exhibitions but many are free.

There are a range of special events, including talks, drop-in sketching sessions and guided walks. Many take place during the late shift (Thursdays and Fridays until 9pm) when there's a bar and live music or DJs providing the soundtrack. Be warned: the NPG has an excellent gift shop and book shop, and you're unlikely to leave empty-handed.

Lucian Freud, self-portrait

VICTORIA & ALBERT MUSEUM 4

Address: Cromwell Road, SW7 2RL (☎ 020-7942 2000, 🖥 vam.ac.uk).
Opening hours: Daily, 10am to 5.45pm (Fridays selected galleries remain open until 10pm). The National Art Library, Prints & Drawings and RIBA Architecture study rooms are closed on Mondays. Closed 24-26th December.
Cost: Free. There's a fee for some temporary exhibitions.
Transport: South Kensington tube.
Amenities: Two cafés, two shops, wheelchair access.

The Victoria and Albert Museum (usually abbreviated to the V&A) is the world's leading museum of art and design. Its immense and eclectic investment in decorative art takes in glass and ceramics, textiles and costumes, metalwork and jewellery, domestic items and furniture – and the museum is also rich in fine art. Its permanent collection numbers over 2.2m objects, of which around 60,000 are displayed at any one time. They are divided into five main themes – Asia, Europe, Materials & Techniques, Modern and Exhibitions – and displayed in 145 galleries.

The V&A has the reputation of being a maze and one that's constantly evolving. An intensive programme of refurbishment to update the entire museum for the 21st century has seen entire galleries remodelled, new ones opened and others closed. Work is on-going and it's advisable to check the V&A's website or call ☎ 020-7942 2211 if you have your heart set on seeing a particular exhibit or gallery. You can track down specific objects via the excellent online archive (🖥 collections. vam.ac.uk).

The museum was established in 1852, after the Great Exhibition. Prince

ALLOW...

Like London's other great galleries and museums, it's impossible to 'do' the V&A in a day, but it's easy to dip into the sections which most interest you. To help you find your feet, there are free one-hour introductory tours leaving the Grand Entrance several times a day – see website for details.

people, and was assisted by Henry Cole – inventor of the Christmas card – who became the museum's first director. Five years later, the collection moved to its current site and was officially opened by Queen Victoria in June 1857. Not only was the collection world class, but the building was also a work of art (see the Ceramic Staircase below) and much copied.

Albert was one of the Exhibition's organisers and was disappointed that Britain, while excelling in manufacturing, missed out on design prizes. He wanted a museum of applied arts that would inspire and educate

Throughout the next four decades, buildings were added and extended and in 1899 work began on a new building by Aston Webb, which now provides the museum with its distinctive façade. When Queen Victoria laid the foundation

The Ceramic Staircase, Frank Moody

Sacred Silver & Stained Glass Gallery

stone on 17th May that year – her last official public appearance – the Victoria and Albert Museum was born.

> ### 👁 DON'T MISS!
>
> Tipu's Tiger is a mechanical organ designed in the form of a tiger mauling a British officer. It was commissioned around 1795 by Tipu Sultan, ruler of Mysore, and when the handle is turned you can hear the tiger's growls and its victim's cries for help! See it in room 41.
>
>

From the outset, the V&A was seen as a 'practical' museum, one which documented its evolution by preserving current pieces as well as historical objects. It has any number of must-see items, including the ornate Ardabil Carpet from Persia (Iran), the oldest dated carpet in the world (1539), and the massive Great Bed of Ware (1590) which at more than 3m (10ft) wide was able to accommodate up to 15 sleepers at a time – such was its notoriety, it even merits a mention in Shakespeare's *Twelfth Night* and Lord Byron's *Don Juan*. But you will need many visits to take in all the V&A's diverse delights. Some of the main subject areas are described below.

Architecture: Four centuries of architecture are represented in the V&A's display, created in collaboration with the Royal Institute of British Architects (RIBA). Drawings, models and photos are on show, including work by British greats such as Adam, Nash and Wren. Don't miss the outtakes from original buildings, including a pillar from the Alhambra Palace in Spain.

Asia: The collection of Asian art comprises over 160,000 objects, including pottery, jade, Buddhas and kimonos. The Jameel Gallery of Islamic Art has the abovementioned Ardabil Carpet, as well as a stunning tiled fireplace from 18th-century Istanbul. Chinese art takes in objects from the Ming, Qing and Tang dynasties, and includes earthenware tomb guardians and a 2,000-year-old horse's head made from jade, as well as modern Chinese art. The Nehru gallery of

Delft Flower Pyramid

Indian art features religious sculptures – Hindu, Buddhist and Jain – jewel-encrusted spoons used by Moghul emperors and glorious textiles.

British Galleries: Refurbished and reopened in 2001, these 15 galleries are among the most visited. They present four centuries of design from 1500 to 1900, and include work by such icons as Grinling Gibbons, Josiah Wedgwood, Thomas Chippendale and William Morris. There are reconstructions of period rooms, some of them rescued from demolished houses, including the parlour from 2 Henrietta Street circa 1727-28, designed by James Gibbs, and the Norfolk House Music Room, St James's Square, which dates from 1756. Other notable items include Henry VIII's lavishly gilded writing desk, a life-size sculpture of the composer Handel by Louis-François Roubiliac, and Arts & Crafts furniture by Charles Rennie Mackintosh. Exhibits are supported by computer interactive displays, objects which you can handle and video screens.

Ceramics & Glass: The V&A has the largest collection of ceramics in the world, from Delft and Meissen to Worcester and Royal Doulton, while its glass includes Venetian and Tiffany glass and stunning stained glass windows. Highlights include the Möllendorff Dinner Service of Meissen porcelain which was designed around 1762 by Frederick II the Great, King of Prussia, and features nymphs and satyrs cavorting on the cruet sets.

Fashion & Textiles: The costume collection contains over 14,000 outfits from 1600 to the present day, from medieval vestments and 19th-century corsets to statement pieces by modern designers. Important items include the wedding suit of James II, elegant ball gowns from the '50s, and a collection of 178 Vivienne Westwood costumes. The V&A has over 53,000 textile samples, dating back to the 1st century AD. Look out for the Devonshire Hunting Tapestries from the 15th century, woven in the Netherlands and depicting in incredible detail Flemish nobility hunting deer, otters and bears.

Fashion and Textiles

Samson Slaying a Philistine, Giambologna

Furniture: Clocks, musical instruments and all manner of chairs, cabinets and commodes make up this 13,000-strong collection. Most of it is British, although there are reconstructions of elegant European rooms, such as the Boudoir of Madame de Sévilly straight from 1780s Paris. The Melville Bed gives the Great Bed of Ware a run for its money in the must-see stakes: it's an extraordinarily opulent four-poster draped in crimson hangings and looks as comfortable today as when it was made for a Scottish earl in 1700. Contrast it with streamlined '60s designs, such as Peter Ghyczy's yolk-yellow Egg Chair on show in the Contemporary galleries.

Jewellery & Metalwork: Over 6,000 items of jewellery, including pieces by Fabergé and Lalique, are on display, much of it in the William and Judith Bollinger Gallery. Historic pieces include diamond-studded ornaments worn by Catherine the Great and the 'tutti frutti' bandeau of rubies, sapphires and diamonds bought by Lady Mountbatten from Cartier in 1928. Metalwork encompasses gold, silver, bronzes, enamels and even ironwork – one of the largest objects in the V&A is the Hereford Screen, an 11m wide structure of timber and cast iron embellished with brass and copper, which once stood in the chancel of Hereford Cathedral. The Whiteley Galleries shimmer with their vast collection of silver, historic and contemporary, secular and religious, and the V&A also houses the famous Gilbert Collection of gold, silver, mosaics, snuff boxes and miniatures.

Medieval & Renaissance: A remarkable collection of treasures from 300 to 1600, including sculptures by Donatello, Leonardo da Vinci's notebooks and the Becket casket, an enamelled box said to contain the bones of the medieval martyr Thomas à

Silver Galleries

Becket. Don't miss the intricately carved frontage of Sir Paul Pindar's house dating back to 1600, which miraculously escaped the Great Fire of London,

Painting & Photography: Though not a fine art gallery as such, the V&A has many fine paintings. British artists are well represented with works by Constable, Turner and Landseer to name but a few; Europe by Botticelli, Van Dyck, Degas, Rembrandt and many others. Major crowd-pullers include the seven Raphael Cartoons which were commissioned by Pope Leo X as designs for tapestries to hang on the wall of the Sistine Chapel, beneath the ceiling of Raphael's great rival Michelangelo. They now belong to the Royal Collection, and were loaned to the V&A by the Queen.

Sculptures: Beautifully displayed in modern light-filled galleries, the V&A's sculpture collection numbers some 22,000 pieces, including over 20 works by Rodin which the sculptor gave to the V&A in 1914, as acknowledgement of Britain's support of France in World War One. Especially interesting are the Cast Courts, which host Victorian plaster copies of some of the world's most celebrated sculptures, from Trajan's Column – cut in half to fit the room – to Michelangelo's David. The latter has a specially commissioned fig leaf which could be hooked onto his manhood to save Queen Victoria's blushes when she visited the courts! He no longer wears it but it's preserved in a glass case to the rear of his plinth.

The above highlights only scratch the surface of the V&A which has a great many more elements, including the National Art Library with over 750,000 books, the Contemporary galleries which feature the cream of 20th-century design ideas, and the many temporary exhibitions which take place each year.

Of course, few can resist the gift shop which sells books, posters, fabrics plus jewellery, clothes and home ware, reproductions of exhibits and new cutting-edge designs.

FOOD & DRINK

V&A Café: Hot dishes, sandwiches and cakes served up in the original Morris, Gamble and Poynter Rooms which were the first museum 'cafes' in the world. The ornate tiling is said to be modelled on Prince Albert's dairy.

Garden Café: Drinks and snacks in a quiet corner of the John Madejski Garden.

stained glass window, Steinfeld Abbey, Germany (1540-1542)

KENSINGTON PALACE 5

Address: Kensington Gardens, W8 4PX (☎ 0844-482 7777, ⌨ hrp.org.uk/ kensingtonpalace).

Opening hours: Daily, 10am to 6pm (5pm from November to February). Closed 24-26th December.

Cost: £14.50 adults, £12 concessions (over 60s, students), children (under 16) free when accompanied by an adult.

Transport: High Street Kensington or Queensway tube.

Amenities: Restaurant (Orangery in Kensington Gardens), café, two shops, gardens, wheelchair access.

Kensington Palace has been a residence of British royals since 1689 – before Buckingham Palace was built – and has a fascinating historical and archaeological heritage. For many people, it's inextricably linked with the late Diana, Princess of Wales and the vast sea of floral tributes spreading out from the gates following her death in 1997. Fittingly, her son Wills and his bride Kate (the Duke and Duchess of Cambridge) live there now. Current residents also include the Duke and Duchess of Gloucester, the Duke and Duchess of Kent and Prince and Princess Michael of Kent.

Kensington Palace (or KP as it became known during Diana's time) began as a Jacobean mansion, built in the early 17th century for the Earl of Nottingham and purchased by William III and his wife Mary II in 1689 as an escape from damp and dirty Whitehall. Sir Christopher Wren enlarged it by adding pavilions to each corner and also reoriented the building to face Hyde Park.

 ALLOW...

Three hours should be time enough to explore Kensington Palace, but allow extra time if you also wish to look around the gardens.

The couple didn't live long enough to enjoy their palace – Mary died in 1694, William in 1702 – and their successor

King's Gallery

Queen Anne did little to the house, although she lavished attention on the gardens. George I embarked on a major rebuild with Sir John Vanbrugh in 1718 and commissioned William Kent to decorate the new rooms, but it was his son George II who benefited and the palace was a principle royal residence during his reign. After his death in 1760, it became a home for less important royals and courtiers who lived at the King's 'Grace and Favour'. Edward VIII once called it an 'aunt heap' because of the number of his older relatives residing there.

👁 DON'T MISS!

Over the fireplace in the King's Gallery is a wind dial dating from the time of William III. Made in 1694 by Robert Morden, it's connected to a weather vane on the roof by chains and pulleys and showed the King (quite literally) which way the wind was blowing, allowing him to plan military campaigns. Amazingly, it's still working today.

One of its most famous inhabitants was Princess Victoria, who was born at the palace in 1819 and brought up there in solitude until her accession to the throne in 1837. She later moved to Buckingham Palace, but her affection for her former home ensured that Kensington Palace was restored and

opened to the public at the end of the 19th century.

Managed by the charity Historic Royal Palaces, KP was relaunched as an attraction in 2012, following a £12m transformation project, which included the creation of new 'routes' to provide a more logical path though the sometimes confusing jumble of rooms. The state apartments have also been given a thematic twist with multi-medium installations, interactive theatre and costume displays. The result may be a bit Disney but it should keep children and teens entertained. The main attractions include the following:

Victoria Revealed: The first of four new 'routes' through the palace, this takes visitors through some of the rooms where Victoria lived, recreated to reflect her era. These include the bedroom she shared with her mother and the Red Saloon where she held her first Privy Council meeting as an 18-year-old queen. The design was inspired by her journals, and the rooms feature personal objects such as her

Queen Victoria's bedroom

ceiling detail

King's Staircase

dolls, wedding gown, baby clothes and mementoes of Prince Albert.

Three more 'routes': *The (Very Public) Private Life of the Queen* (covering the reigns of William III, Mary II and Anne), *The Curious World of the Court* (George II) and *It's Not Easy Being a Princess* (Princesses Diana and Margaret) were due to be launched in 2013.

The Queen's State Apartments: These private rooms were created for Mary II and used by her successors, including Queen Anne. They include the Queen's Gallery, which was the backdrop for Mary's huge collection of oriental porcelain, the Dining Room with its 17th-century panelling and the Closet which features portraits of Anne and her much-loved husband George of Denmark. Visitors are taken on a journey though the rooms by Anne's son Prince William, once heir to the Stuart throne, who supposedly danced himself to death on his 11th birthday.

The King's Staircase: Providing the entrance to the King's Apartments, this is notable for the life-size paintings of George I's court by William Kent. The vast crowd peering over the painted balustrade includes not just courtiers and ladies-in-waiting, but also the king's two Turkish servants, Mahomet and Mustafa, and Peter, the 'wild boy' who was found in woods near Hanover and brought to live at court. Look up at

the ceiling to see a self-portrait of Kent admiring his handiwork. Not everyone was a fan – one 18th-century art critic described some of Kent's paintings as a 'terrible glaring show'.

The King's State Apartments: These grand rooms recreate life in the Georgian era and visitors can join in an interactive card game to experience the social manoeuvring that was an essential part of courtly life. The most important room is the Cupola Room, with its blue and gold ceiling and an eye-catching centrepiece: a clock dating from 1793 by Charles Clay and John Pyke which once played tunes by Handel, who was a regular guest at George II's court. This is also where the infant Victoria was christened using a punchbowl from the Tower of London.

Other rooms include the Presence Chamber, where formal receptions took place – a gilded armchair once owned by George II's son Frederick takes the place of a throne – and the Privy Chamber which is decorated with another of Kent's murals, this time depicting the gods Mars and Minerva reclining on a cloud. In the Council Chamber you can see what people wore in these splendid rooms.

The King's Gallery: At 29m (96ft) long, this is the largest of the palace's state rooms and looks much as it did in George I's time. It was designed for exercise and to display royal works of art. The walls are hung with paintings from the Royal Collection, while the ceiling displays scenes from the tales of Ulysses by Kent.

The Gardens: Transformed by Charles Bridgeman in the 1720s to include the Serpentine and the Round Pond, Kensington Palace Gardens are one of the capital's most tranquil spots. Explore at your leisure or take a free, hour-long tour during the summer months, held on Tuesdays, Thursdays and Saturdays at noon and 2pm. They take in the secluded Sunken Garden and other horticultural (and historic) highlights, and can be booked at the palace.

 FOOD & DRINK

Orangery Restaurant: From Shetland salmon to Cornish yogurt, thoroughly British fare served up in Queen Anne's greenhouse.

Palace Café: Light refreshments, sandwiches and cakes with a view of the gardens and the Wiggly Walk.

The Orangery

Sunken Garden

NATURAL HISTORY MUSEUM   6

Address: Cromwell Road, SW7 5BD (☎ 020-7942 5000, 🖥 nhm.ac.uk).
Opening hours: Daily, 10am to 5.50pm, plus a late session until 10.30pm on the last Friday of the month. Closed 24-26th December.
Cost: Free. There's a fee for some temporary exhibitions.
Transport: South Kensington tube.
Amenities: Restaurant, two cafés, snack bar, three shops, garden, wheelchair access.

From dinosaurs to diamonds, the Natural History Museum is one of London's most enthralling destinations – and especially popular with children. Covering all aspects of life and earth sciences, it doesn't just preserve the past but also seeks to preserve our planet by providing a hub for research and education.

The museum began as a collection of specimens given to the nation by Sir Hans Sloane in 1753. They were originally displayed in the British Museum, where they were overshadowed by the mummies and 'marbles', until a new superintendent of natural history, Richard Owen, was appointed in 1856 and lobbied for the building of a separate museum. Designed by Alfred Waterhouse, the Natural History Museum opened in 1881, although it didn't formally split from the British Museum until 1992.

The museum is one of the most architecturally pleasing in Britain: a Romanesque confection clad in terracotta tiles. The design incorporates reliefs and sculptures of creatures both living and extinct – look out for the dodo and pterodactyls – as well as detailed ceiling panels depicting plants from around the world. The central hall is truly impressive, and it's easy to understand why Victorian visitors described the museum as 'the animals' Westminster Abbey'.

More manageable than the British Museum or the V&A, the Natural History Museum still has a challenging number of galleries to take in. It has some 70m items grouped in five main collections – botany, entomology, mineralogy, palaeontology and zoology – laid out over five floors. To

Diplodocus

make exploration easier, there are four colour-coded zones, each dedicated to a different theme. All include interactive displays that entertain and educate by answering questions you'd never thought to ask, such as 'What might you find in a crocodile's stomach?' and 'How do you tell the age of a whale?'

From Dinosaurs to Man (Blue Zone): This zone contains the most-viewed section of the museum – the Dinosaurs gallery, where an animatronic T. rex roars a greeting to visitors from its pit and you can get up close to dinosaur skeletons and a nest full of hatchlings. Just as impressive is the life-size, skeleton-model of a blue whale which hangs from the ceiling of the Mammals gallery; weighing 10 tons, it dwarfs even the dinos. Other mammals on display include elephants, lions, polar bears, a duck-billed platypus and the skull of a woolly mammoth.

There are fish, reptiles and marine invertebrates galore, including a Komodo dragon, a spooky vampire squid and the intricately coiled skeleton of an Indian python, while the Human Biology gallery reveals the most complex animal of all – us! Don't miss the giant baby who helps visitors experience life in the womb. Also take time to see the 'Images of Nature' gallery, which has over 100 drawings, paintings and photographs of the natural world.

 ALLOW...

The time it takes to see the museum depends on your interests and how crowded it is but you should allow at least a day. Unless you're a parent, avoid weekends and school holidays, when it can take an hour just to get inside! Queues are often shorter at the Exhibition Road entrance. During summer holidays you can jump the queue into the Dinosaurs gallery by booking free tickets in advance by phone or online.

Birds, Bugs, Fossils & Minerals (Green Zone): Beginning in the central hall which is dominated by the 32m (105ft) replica skeleton of a Diplodocus – 'Dippy' for short – who grazed the earth some 150m years ago, this area takes in the other inhabitants of our planet: animal, vegetable and mineral. The marvellous collection of Birds includes the legendary dodo while the aptly-named Creepy Crawlies gallery is a celebration of insects, spiders, crabs and centipedes. You can step inside a termites' tower and build your own arachnid!

baby in womb

👁 DON'T MISS!

The Power Within (Red Zone) lets you experience violent natural events in 'scientific' safety. Here, you can watch lava erupt from underneath a volcano, and stand in a Japanese supermarket during a computer regeneration of the Kobe earthquake.

Our Place in Evolution looks at our earliest ancestors, including the skull of a Neanderthal who lived 400,000 years ago, while Ecology explores the earth's environment. It resists the temptation to lecture visitors by presenting the subject in a very visual way, from a giant leaf factory to the recycling of a rabbit. The Minerals gallery displays its rocks and stones in Victorian oak cabinets, giving a sense of how the museum appeared to early visitors. The rarest and most beautiful finds are kept safe in the Vault: don't miss the unique medusa emerald (on display until July 2013) or pieces of meteorites from Mars and the moon.

Planet Earth (Red Zone): These galleries present the story of our planet, past, present and future – from the Big Bang to current environmental issues. It's best entered from Exhibition Road, into a vast hall lit by constellations and up into a giant globe (by escalator). From here you can examine the remains of creatures from the distant past, including a dinosaur's footprint, admire the glittering treasures beneath Earth's surface – which include a chunk of 'kryptonite' – and find out how wind, water and our weather systems are creating constant change.

Darwin Centre and the Wildlife Garden (Orange Zone): The newest part of the museum is the Darwin Centre, housed in an eight-storey

Charles Darwin

entrance to the Red Zone

main entrance hall

cocoon. Named after Charles Darwin, its cutting edge design protects the immense collection of specimens and provides space for scientists to work. Visitors enter at the top and meander down through its myriad collections of plants, insects and microscopic creatures, guided by 'virtual' curators. Highlights include daily free tours of the Zoology Spirit Collection (book in advance), a zoo-full of specimens preserved in glass jars, many collected by Darwin, including sharks and giant squid.

Outside, the Wildlife Garden offers a complete contrast to the overcrowded museum. Open from 1st April to 31st October (10am to 5pm), it's a living exhibition which shows the potential for wildlife conservation in the inner city. It portrays a range of British lowland habitats – including fen, reed bed, hedgerow, woodland and meadow – and attracts dragonflies, moorhens, moths, foxes, robins, marsh marigolds, primroses and even grazing sheep.

In addition to the main attractions, the museum hosts four temporary exhibitions each year – in 2012 these included 'Scott's Last Expedition' and 'Animals Inside Out'. There are frequent special events, many aimed at young visitors, and several gift shops, including one entirely devoted to dinosaurs!

🍴 FOOD & DRINK 🍴

The Restaurant (Green Zone): Freshly-prepared food, drinks and puddings, including vegetarian dishes, dairy-free food, gluten-free dishes and a kids' menu.

Deli Café (Red Zone): Veggie options and child-sized portions.

Central Hall Café (Blue Zone): Good for cakes and snacks.

Picnic Area (Green Zone basement): Bring your own lunch and buy drinks from the snack bar.

SCIENCE MUSEUM   7

Address: Exhibition Road, South Kensington, SW7 2DD (☎ 020-7942 4000,
🖳 sciencemuseum.org.uk).

Opening hours: Daily, 10am to 6pm (7pm during school holidays and weekends in summer – check website). Closed 24-26th December.

Cost: Free. There's a fee for some attractions, such as the flight simulator and IMAX cinema, and for some special exhibitions.

Transport: South Kensington tube.

Amenities: Restaurant, two cafés, shop, wheelchair access.

If you think science is boring or baffling, the Science Museum will change your mind. Forget test tubes and telescopes, this museum presents a clear and compelling record of man's achievements in all scientific fields – communications, engineering, medicine, transport and more – in an entertaining environment that appeals to all the senses.

Like the Victoria and Albert Museum across the road, the Science Museum was born out of the Victorians' insatiable curiosity and passion for learning. Both institutions were founded in the wake of the Great Exhibition of 1851, and at first the scientific collections shared a building and name – the South Kensington Museum – with the V&A's art and design exhibits. The Science Museum didn't become an independent entity until 1909, and it was another two decades before it moved to its current site.

The building's core, the East Block, was designed by Sir Richard Allison, who is said to have modelled its three-story open-plan interior and surrounding galleries on a department store. It opened in 1928 and changed very little

until 2000, when the Wellcome Wing opened as a platform for contemporary science and technology.

 ALLOW...

The website suggests how long you should allow for each gallery in its 'Galleries and Exhibitions' pages, although you need a couple of days to do justice to the whole museum. There are daily tours of specific areas, such as the Spaced Out and Flight gallery tours, or if time is short you can download the 'World of Wonders' trail to see seven of the museum's major draws.

Today, the Science Museum provides a seamless link from before the Industrial Revolution through to the 21st century and beyond. It has assembled a priceless collection of over 300,000 items, from steam engines to space modules, and visiting it feels like taking a ride on a machine that's in perpetual motion.

The exhibits are laid out over seven floors and blend displays of objects with hands-on interactives. There's too much to include here in a floor-by-floor listing but some of the highlights are listed below:

Apollo 10 Command Module

Atmosphere (second floor): Climate science made simple in a gallery designed to resemble Earth's atmosphere, where touchscreen games make serious issues such as climate change into enjoyable challenges. Ideal for greens and restless teens.

Challenge of Materials (first floor): A look at how we manufacture, use and dispose of different sorts of stuff – metal, plastics, cardboard and so forth. Get a close-up view of a bullet-proof vest and a cardboard chair.

Computing (second floor): This gallery presents a brief history of information technology, looking back to a time when a single computer (less powerful than today's PCs) filled a room! Don't miss the Difference Engine No. 2, built by museum boffins in 1991 to Charles Babbage's original plans – it's displayed alongside half of the great man's brain!

Energy Hall (ground floor): See massive

Corliss Steam Engine

engines at full steam, such as James Watt's pioneering rotative engine (1788) and another that powered 1,700 looms in a 1900s Burnley mill. Another exhibit, **James Watt and our World**, allows visitors to step into the great man's workshop and see how his inventions have changed our lives.

👁 DON'T MISS!

The world's oldest surviving steam locomotive, known as Puffing Billy, which first hauled coal from Northumberland to the River Tyne nearly 200 years ago. Puffing Billy can be admired in the Making the Modern World gallery on the ground floor.

Exploring Space (ground floor): Rockets, satellites and a piece of moon rock are displayed in this exploration of space travel since 1957. The stars of the show are the Black Arrow satellite launch rocket from 1971 and a replica of the Eagle lander which took the first men to the moon in 1969.

Flight (third floor): The planes which hang from the rafters of this huge hall include a model of the Wright Brothers' plane from 1903, the Gypsy Moth which Amy Johnson piloted to Australia in 1930, and a Hawker Hurricane that flew in the Battle of Britain. There are also more than 100 models, plus engines (including one that powered Concorde) and flight paraphernalia. A flight simulator offers visitors the chance to fly with the Red Arrows and then take the controls – see website for prices.

Health Matters (third floor): An exploration of medical technology, including a '50s iron lung and a home dialysis machine used in the '60s, plus interactives to help you monitor your own health.

Launchpad (third floor): Aimed at 8 to 14-year-olds, this is the ultimate hands-on experience where young visitors can experience science first hand in 50 interactive exhibits, whether building a bridge, freezing their shadow or making instant ice.

Making the Modern World (ground floor): This huge exhibit presents milestones in our development, from

Future Face

the world's oldest surviving steam locomotive to the Apollo 10 space capsule. Among the most fascinating exhibits are Charles Babbage's original Difference Engine (1832), the forerunner of today's computers, and the first model constructed of DNA (1953), which won its makers Francis Crick and James Watson the Nobel Prize.

Measuring Time (first floor): This exhibit spans the history of time-keeping, from sundials to wristwatches. Star billing goes to the Wells Cathedral clock, the second-oldest in England, which has been ticking away since 1392.

Secret Life of the Home (lower ground floor): The stories behind the everyday objects we take for granted. Learn how a washing machine works, try to outwit a burglar alarm and marvel at Thomas Crapper's Valveless Waste Preventer, No. 814 – one of the earliest flushing toilets.

The Science and Art of Medicine (fifth floor): A collection of 5,000 medical objects revealing the history of medicine across the world. It includes treasures from Ancient Egypt, Greece and Rome as well as traditional medicine from Africa and the East. Objects range from the beautiful to the bizarre, such as the 19th-century

female urinal made from delicate Spode china and the 1940s reusable condom!

There are more medical exhibits in the **Veterinary History** section (fifth floor), while **Glimpses of Medical History** (fourth floor) provides visitors with a ringside seat to reconstructions of medical procedures such as a 14th-century dissection and childbirth in a Victorian home.

The Science Museum hosts many temporary exhibitions, talks and workshops, most of which are free. But if you want to view a film in the new IMAX 3D Cinema, charges apply. The shop is worth checking out for its games and gadgets, while the Dana Centre provides an adults-only space for lectures and events on scientific issues.

 FOOD & DRINK

Deep Blue: The museum's main eatery, serving up salads, burgers and grills, with reduced-price portions for under-12s.

Picnic Area: You can eat your own food on the first floor, or if the weather's good, take your sandwiches to nearby Hyde Park.

STATE ROOMS, BUCKINGHAM PALACE   8

Address: Buckingham Palace, SW1A 1AA (☎ 020-7766 7300, 🖥 royalcollection.
org.uk/visit/buckinghampalace).
Opening hours: Daily, 9.45am to 6.30pm in August and September (dates vary, so
phone or check website for details).
Cost: £18 adults, £16.50 over 60s/students (with valid ID), £10.25 under 17s, under-
5s free, £47 families (2 adults and 3 under 17s). Ticket includes entrance to special
exhibitions and an audio tour.
Transport: Green Park or Hyde Park Corner tube or Victoria tube/rail.
Amenities: Café, shop, gardens, wheelchair access.

The official London residence of the British monarch since 1837, Buckingham Palace stands in splendid isolation at the top of the Mall, one of the most iconic sights in the capital. Until recently the only way to get inside was by invitation – to a banquet, investiture or one of the famous garden parties – but since 1993 the state rooms have been opened to the public in summer when the Queen and her family decamp to Balmoral.

The palace was originally built as a townhouse for the Duke of Buckingham in 1705. It was purchased in 1761 by George III as a residence for his wife Queen Charlotte, but it was their son George IV who commissioned John Nash to transform it into a palace. Nash's design was truly extravagant, incorporating a dome and a massive entrance arch – by the time of the king's death in 1830 costs had soared to £600,000. Nash was taken off the job and the work was completed by Edward Blore who relocated Nash's arch – it now stands at one corner of Hyde Park as Marble Arch – and added the east wing and front balcony. This is the image of Buckingham Palace which we see today.

The palace became the principal royal residence in 1837 when the young Queen Victoria moved in. It was further extended during the 19th century, and in 1913 the Mall façade

State Dining Room

was faced with Portland stone by Sir Aston Webb.

🕑 ALLOW...

A tour of the state rooms takes up to two and a half hours. You can combine it with the other two major royal attractions – the Royal Mews and the Queen's Gallery – with an inclusive ticket costing £31.95 for adults, £29.25 concessions and £18.20 children aged five to 16 (see ▢ royalcollection.org.uk for more information).

Today, the palace has 775 rooms, including 19 state rooms, 52 royal and guest bedrooms, 188 staff bedrooms, 92 offices and 78 bathrooms. The tour takes in just the state rooms: the public rooms in which guests and dignitaries are received and entertained on state, ceremonial and official occasions. It doesn't include the private apartments where the Queen and her family reside or areas where less formal entertaining and audiences take place.

The state rooms' décor reflects the taste of previous monarchs, in particular George IV from whose former residence at Carlton House many important pieces of furniture and works of art were relocated. There's a treasure trove of pieces from the Royal Collection, including paintings by Canaletto and Van Dyck, Canova sculptures, fine furniture and priceless trinkets at every turn.

Tours start in the courtyard behind the east wing, which gives visitors a chance to admire the warm Bath stone of Nash's original palace frontage. Once inside, your route should take in the following rooms:

The Grand Staircase: Designed by Nash and constructed from Carrera marble, this provides a wonderfully theatrical entrance. The eye is drawn to a massive glass dome, which allows light to flood in and flicker off the intricate gilt-bronze balustrades. The white and gold colour scheme was introduced by Edward VII, but the portraits which line the stairs to 'receive' visitors are of Queen Victoria's family.

The Throne Room: This is hung with red silk and topped with an elaborate white and gilt ceiling. The thrones were made for the Queen and Prince Philip for her coronation in 1953 and behind them are gilt trophies which represent the Four Seasons – they may once have decorated Carlton House. This grand room is used only on the most special of occasions, such as the Jubilee celebrations, and is where the Duke and Duchess of Cambridge's wedding photos were taken in 2011.

> ### 👁 DON'T MISS!
>
> The Table of the Grand Commanders is made from Sèvres porcelain, and features portraits of great leaders, including Caesar, Hannibal and Alexander the Great. It was commissioned by Napoleon and presented to George IV by a grateful Louis XVIII in 1817, two years after the Battle of Waterloo. It now stands in the Blue Drawing Room.

The Throne Room is approached by a ceremonial route which includes the **Guard Room** – complete with white marble statues of Queen Victoria and Prince Albert in Roman costume – and the **Green Drawing Room**, which was Queen Charlotte's Saloon. It displays

a wealth of Sèvres porcelain, much of which was obtained from the French royal family during the French Revolution.

The Picture Gallery: At the very heart of the suite of state rooms, this 47m (154ft) corridor was designed by Nash to show off George IV's art collection. The paintings are subject to change but include works by such masters as Rembrandt, Van Dyck, Rubens and Claude. The art theme is underlined by four marble chimneypieces, incorporating female figures holding palettes and brushes, each with a garlanded medallion of Titian, Leonardo da Vinci, Dürer and Van Dyck.

This room is where the recipients of honours congregate before their investiture in the 38m (123ft) long **Ballroom** at the southern end of the state suite.

The Blue and White Drawing Rooms: One of the finest Georgian interiors in the palace, the **Blue Drawing Room** takes its name from

White Drawing Room

The Grand Staircase

the blue flock wallpaper which was added by Queen Mary in the early 20th century. Portraits of George V and Mary stare down at their creative opulence from either side of the fireplace.

The **White Drawing Room** is clad in white and gold damask and has a spectacular convex ceiling by Nash. Look out for the ebony-veneered cabinets at each end of the room; the one in the northwest corner conceals a hidden door which allows the royals to make a discreet entry into (or exit from) the state rooms. The two drawing rooms are linked by the **Music Room**, with its great bow window overlooking the palace's gardens.

Buckingham Palace has the largest private garden in London and while visitors cannot wander through it at their leisure, the exit route takes in a half mile stroll through the garden and offers a view of the rear of the palace, something which few people see.

As well as the state rooms, there's usually a special exhibition to see – in 2012 the theme was Royal diamonds. Time your visit right and you can also take in the Changing the Guard which takes place daily at 11.30am during summer.

 FOOD & DRINK

Garden Café: Take tea on the palace's West Terrace overlooking the lawn. Sadly, a picnic isn't an option as food and drink aren't allowed inside the state rooms.

Victoria: There are dozens of quick places to eat in and around nearby Victoria railway station.

The Throne Room

Blue Drawing Room

TATE BRITAIN 9

Address: Millbank, SW1P 4RG (☎ 020-7887 8888, 🖥 tate.org.uk).
Opening hours: Daily, 10am to 6pm (10pm on Fri). Open on Bank Holidays but closed 24-26th December.
Cost: Free, except for special exhibitions.
Transport: Pimlico or Vauxhall tube.
Amenities: Restaurant, three cafés, two shops, wheelchair access.

This is the original Tate gallery, which was opened in 1897 to provide a dedicated home for British art. A major rebranding in 2000 saw its modern art moved down the River Thames to Tate Modern at Bankside (see page 250) while Tate Britain, as it's now known, majors on historic and contemporary art.

The gallery's permanent collection dates from 1500 to the present day, and is one of the most comprehensive of its kind in the world. It includes a priceless display of works by Turner, as well as Gainsborough, Hogarth, Constable, Stubbs, Bacon, Moore, Hockney and many more, and attracts some 1.5m art lovers annually.

The Tate was originally created to house a collection of British art owned

👁 DON'T MISS!

Although best known for his misty seascapes and luminous landscapes, one of JMW Turner's most captivating paintings is his *Self-Portrait*. Painted in 1799 when he was just 24, it depicts an earnest young man already making his name in the art world; he had just been elected as an Associate of the Royal Academy.

by sugar magnate Sir Henry Tate (of Tate & Lyle fame). When he offered it to the nation in 1889, there was no room for it at the National Gallery so it was decided to open a new National Gallery of British Art. This was built on the site of the old Millbank Prison and opened in 1897, displaying 245 works in eight

The Bath of Psyche, Lord Leighton

long sculpture galleries, new rooms and, in 1982, the award-winning Clore Galleries, designed by James Stirling to house the Turner collection. The Manton Entrance and Linbury exhibition galleries were added in the '90s, and in 2010 work began on a 20-year renovation scheme to upgrade the older parts of the building. Expect some facilities to be closed while all this goes on.

 ALLOW...

You'll need at least a day to take in the highlights of Tate Britain's permanent collection, although you could easily spend most of it admiring the Turners. For a quick taster, take advantage of the free guided highlights' tours which last 45 minutes and leave the top of the Manton stairs at 11am, noon and 3pm, with a Turner tour at 2pm.

The main body of the permanent collection is displayed in three chronological areas: historic, 20th-century and contemporary art. There are also Focus rooms which allow for more in-depth studies of specific artists and subjects. The gallery's policy of constantly updating its displays to keep them fresh means that artworks move around frequently, rooms are reorganised and themes change, so it's impossible to give a room by room guide to the museum's highlights, and you should check the website before you visit. But if you're lucky, you should see some of the following:

Key Works from the Historic Collection: This spans four centuries, from Tudor portraits through 18th-century landscapes to the Pre-Raphaelites, and is displayed in a central gallery on the upper floor. It's a 'who's who' of British art, with works by Gainsborough, Hilliard, Hogarth, Lely, Millais, Reynolds, Rubens, Stubbs and Van Dyck, among other masters.

rooms from British artists dating back to 1790. It soon became known as the Tate Gallery, although the name only became official in 1932.

The building, designed by Sidney RJ Smith, resembles a temple with its grand porticoed entrance and central dome. It has been greatly remodelled and extended over the last century, to include

Highpoints include Hilliard's bejewelled portrait of *Queen Elizabeth I*, Sir Nathaniel Bacon's *Cookmaid with Still Life of Vegetables and Fruit* and Reynolds' gorgeously attired *Suzanna Beckford*. Hogarth's *O the Roast Beef of Old England* leaves little doubt as to his opinion of the French, while his self-portrait, *The Painter and his Pug*, reveals a softer side. Another favourite is *The Cholmondeley Ladies*, an almost cartoon-like depiction of two women in bed each holding a baby; both subjects and painter are unknown.

The Bridge of Sighs, Turner

Elsewhere, the bucolic pleasures of Stubbs' *Haymakers* and Gainsborough's *Wooded Landscape with a Peasant Resting* contrast with Siberechts' moody *Landscape with Rainbow, Henley-on-Thames*, and with Danby's terrifying *The Deluge*, which interprets the Biblical Flood as a fearsome tsunami. Artists from the Victorian era include Millais (*The Boyhood of Raleigh*), Martineau (*The Last Day in the Old Home*), Rossetti (*Beata Beatrix*) and Waterhouse (*The Lady of Shalott*). The Pre-Raphaelites, especially, are perennially popular.

A Walk Through the 20th Century: On both sides of the central gallery, a series of rooms charts more recent development in British art. What's amazing is how rapidly it reinvented itself during just a few decades – compare the winsome appeal of John Singer Sargent's *Carnation, Lily, Lily, Rose* from 1885 with Mark Gertler's geometric *Merry-Go-Round* painted just 30 years later.

This diverse collection spans all manners of styles, from Gwen John's *Nude Girl* and Sickert's Impressionist *Brighton Pierrots*, via Christopher Wood's *Zebra and Parachute* and Paul Nash's surreal *Totes Meer (Dead Sea)*, inspired by the wreckage of World War Two planes, to Francis Bacon's *Study of a Dog* (very different from Hogarth's pug) and Gilbert & George's *Red Morning Trouble*.

Look out for work by Sir Stanley Spencer and Lucien Freud (a huge-eyed *Girl with a Kitten* as well as his infamous nudes), Peter Blake and Graham Sutherland. One of the most moving

Servants, Hogarth

paintings is Chris Ofili's *No Woman, No Cry* from 1998, a tribute to the murdered London teenager Stephen Lawrence.

There are also some seminal sculptures, such as Henry Moore's *Woman* and Barbara Hepworth's gorgeously tactile *Three Forms*.

Contemporary Collection: Titled The Space Between, this features the most current works, many of which would be just as at home in Tate Modern. Highlighted artists in 2012 include Alison Wilding, Sarah Lucas, Robert Holyhead and Rachel Whiteread among others.

Turner Collection: Thought by many to be Britain's greatest ever painter, Joseph Mallord William Turner has the Clore Galleries almost entirely to himself (although he shares a corner with John Constable). Faced with rooms full of Turners it's hard not to be overawed by the scope of his landscapes and his understanding of light. Famous paintings on display include *Norham Castle, Sunrise*, *London from Greenwich Park*, *Snow Storm: Hannibal and his Army Crossing the Alps* and *The Shipwreck*.

Constable's works include *The Sea Near Brighton* and *Flatford Mill*. The Clore Galleries are also home to the Tate's Prints and Drawings Rooms.

The main galleries are only part of the story at Tate Britain and it's worth checking the temporary exhibitions in the Focus rooms and on the museum's top floor. Many temporary exhibitions are free, although there's usually a charge to see the blockbusters. A major retrospective on LS Lowry is planned for 2013.

FOOD & DRINK

Rex Whistler Restaurant: British classics in an arty setting and worth a visit just to see Whistler's massive mural, *The Expedition in Pursuit of Rare Meats*.
Pizza Express: Classic pizzas and dough balls at 25 Millbank, just two minutes' walk from the Tate.

The Tate hosts the annual Turner Prize, named after the painter and presented to a visual artist aged under 50. It's the most publicised and controversial of the art prizes, having attracted exhibits as diverse as a garden shed (Simon Starling) and an unmade bed (Tracey Emin). Shortlisted artists go on display, usually at Tate Britain, in the autumn.

Ophelia, Millais

COURTAULD GALLERY 10

Address: Somerset House, Strand, WC2R 0RN (☎ 020-7848 2526, 🖳 courtauld.ac.uk).

Opening hours: Daily, 10am to 6pm (9pm on a few selected Thursdays – see website). Closed 25-26th December.

Cost: £6 adults, £5 concessions (seniors, part-time and international students), free for under-18s, full-time students, the unemployed, Friends of The Courtauld and National Art Pass holders. Mondays £3 all day.

Transport: Temple, Embankment or Covent Garden tube and Charing Cross tube/rail.

Amenities: Café, shop, wheelchair access.

Although somewhat overshadowed by London's national galleries, The Courtauld Gallery contains a gem of an art collection, situated at the heart of The Courtauld Institute of Art, one of the world's leading centres for the study of art history and conservation. The Gallery is housed in the North Wing of Somerset House, a spectacular 18th-century building designed by William Chambers (1723-1796) and once the home of the Royal Academy of Arts.

Until 2000, Somerset House was home to the Registrar General of Births, Marriages and Deaths. It's now a centre for the visual arts and hosts open-air concerts and film screenings, as well as art exhibitions. During summer months, 55 fountains dance in Somerset House's magnificent Edmond J. Safra courtyard, while in winter it becomes one of London's favourite ice rinks.

 FOOD & DRINK

The Courtauld Gallery Café: Serving delicious light meals, snacks and drinks.

Tom's Kitchen: British brasserie serving classics, such as seven-hour cooked lamb and macaroni cheese with truffles, from Michelin-starred chef Tom Aikens.

Tom's Terrace: Coffee, cocktails, sharing plates – and some of London's most captivating views.

The Gallery's celebrated collection of paintings ranges from the early Renaissance to modernist works of the 20th century, with a splendid array of Gothic and medieval paintings, plus Renaissance masterpieces by artists such as Cranach. Baroque highlights include a comprehensive display of iconic paintings by Rubens.

The core of the art collection was assembled by Samuel Courtauld (1876-1947), who donated his extensive collection of mainly French Impressionist and post-Impressionist paintings in 1932, which was further enhanced by gifts in the '30s. Art lovers have been donating to The Courtauld

Self-Portrait with Bandaged Ear, Van Gogh

over subsequent decades and, in total, the Gallery owns some 530 paintings and over 26,000 drawings and prints. The collection includes such masterworks as Manet's *A Bar at the Folies-Bergère* and a version of his *Déjeuner sur l'Herbe*; Renoir's *La Loge*; landscapes by Claude Monet and Camille Pissarro; a ballet scene by Edgar Degas; and major works by Cézanne. Other paintings include Van Gogh's *Self-Portrait with Bandaged Ear* and *Peach Blossoms in the Crau*; Gauguin's *Nevermore* and *Te Rerioa*; as well as important works by Seurat, Henri 'Douanier' Rousseau and Toulouse-Lautrec.

The collection extends into the 20th century with works by Modigliani, Matisse, Kandinsky and the Bloomsbury group, alongside masterpieces of German Expressionism and modern British art. The Gallery also contains an outstanding collection of drawings and prints, and fine sculpture and decorative arts from Europe and the Middle East. Italian Renaissance wedding chests are displayed alongside marble reliefs and an outstanding collection of Renaissance maiolica (tin-glazed earthenware). The Courtauld also houses an extensive collection of Iznik and Spanish lustreware ceramics, and superb items of Islamic metalwork, including pieces by the master craftsman Mahmud the Kurd. Furthermore, there's a priceless sculpture collection, with works by Henri Matisse, Auguste Rodin, César, Frank Dobson, Henry Moore, Barbara Hepworth, Antony Caro and Philip King.

The website provides an excellent guide to the Gallery's collection, as well as an interactive map which allows you to take a virtual tour through some of the rooms. You'll also find information about temporary exhibitions, entrance to which is included in the ticket price. In addition, public lectures, short courses and lunchtime talks allow visitors to share in the wealth of expertise at The Courtauld, which includes Brian Sewell, Anita Brookner and even Hammer Horror actor Vincent Price among its numerous alumni.

👁 DON'T MISS!

The Courtauld's world-class collection of paintings by Baroque master Rubens includes *The Family of Jan Brueghel the Elder* (1613-15), a charming portrait of his good friend and fellow artist together with his wife and children. The two painters often worked together, Rubens painting the figures and Brueghel the animals.

The Family of Jan Brueghel the Elder, Rubens

QUEEN'S GALLERY, BUCKINGHAM PALACE 11

Address: Buckingham Palace Road, SW1A 1AA (☎ 020-7766 7301,
🖥 royalcollection.org.uk/visit/queensgallerylondon).
Opening hours: Daily, 10am to 5.30pm. Closed 25-26th December and during
some state visits (phone or see website).
Cost: £9.25 adults, £8.50 over 60s/students, £4.65 under 17s, under 5s free, £23
families (2 adults, 3 under 17s).
Transport: Green Park or Hyde Park Corner tube, Victoria tube/rail.
Amenities: Shop, wheelchair access.

Together with the State Rooms and Royal Mews, the Queen's Gallery is one of the major draws at Buckingham Palace, particularly if you're an art lover. The British Royal Family owns one of the largest and most important art collections in the world, containing over 7,000 paintings, 40,000 watercolours and drawings, and around 150,000 old master prints, plus photographs, tapestries, furniture, ceramics and other works of art. Its value has been estimated at £10bn but it's quite literally priceless.

The collection was begun by Henry VIII, although little remains from his time; much was sold off on Cromwell's orders after Charles I's execution. It was re-created after the Restoration in 1660 and by George III and IV and Victoria and Albert. The Queen doesn't actually own the collection; she keeps it 'in trust for the nation' and it's displayed in her palaces or loaned to major museums.

The Queen's Gallery was built out of the ruins of a former private chapel at the Queen's instigation to display the Royal Collection. It opened in 1962, and was greatly extended and updated by John Simpson in preparation for the Golden Jubilee in 2002. His Doric entrance portico is very much in keeping with Nash's designs for Buckingham Palace, although some of the new interiors have been described as 'fussy'. There are three display rooms – the Pennethorne, the Nash and the Chambers galleries – which are sometimes combined for special exhibitions.

Paintings form the backbone of the Royal Collection and reflect the tastes of individual royals. There are over 200 works from the Dutch school, including six Rembrandts and an important

Vermeer, *The Music Lesson*, dating from 1665. Italian paintings also predominate, including more than 50 paintings and 140 drawings by Canaletto, who was hugely popular in England during the mid-18th century. There are also important paintings by Caravaggio, Claude, Cranach, Gainsborough, Holbein, Lanseer,

Charles I, Van Dyck

Queen Victoria, Heinrich von Angeli

Michelangelo, Tintoretto and Van Dyck, who was court painter to Charles I, as well as more than 600 drawings by Leonardo da Vinci.

A huge assembly of (mainly French) furniture is scattered around the royal residences, and some is displayed in the gallery, along with sculptures, tapestries and rare porcelain, including possibly the world's largest collection of Sèvres porcelain. There are Fabergé eggs, jewelled caskets, candelabra and clocks, and much more. Some of the more unusual items include a gilded terracotta bust of a laughing boy, thought to be Henry VIII, by Mazzoni

👁 DON'T MISS!

The collection includes a number of paintings by the Flemish artist Anthony Van Dyck (1599-1641), who – as the leading court painter to Charles I – had a huge influence on English art. Among his most notable works are *Charles I with M. de St Antoine* (1633) and *Triple Portrait of Charles I* (1636).

(1498), a gold tiger's head from the throne of an Indian sultan, and the prototype for the Victoria Cross. There are also some fascinating black and white photographs – try to find the one of Obaysch the hippopotamus taking a nap at London Zoo.

What you will see when you visit very much depends on what's on display. The gallery can only show around 450 items at a time, and some are displayed at other royal residences, such as Windsor Castle or the Queen's Gallery at Holyroodhouse in Edinburgh, although you can view a lot of the Royal Collection online.

Most tours end up at the gift shop which has plenty of suitably regal souvenirs.

⏰ ALLOW...

A tour of the Queen's Gallery takes around one hour. Ask a warden to stamp your ticket and you can return any time in the next 12 months free of charge. This applies to all four attractions managed by the Royal Collection Trust: Buckingham Palace, Clarence House, The Queen's Gallery and the Royal Mews. See 🖳 royalcollection.org.uk for details.

ROYAL ACADEMY OF ARTS 12

Address: Burlington House, Piccadilly, W1J 0BD (☎ 020-7300 8000,
🖳 royalacademy.org.uk).
Opening hours: Thu-Sat, 10am to 6pm; Fri 10am to 10pm. One-hour tours of the
John Madejski Fine Rooms, Tue 1pm, Wed-Fri 1pm and 3pm, Sat 11.30am. Closed
24-26th December.
Cost: Tours and some lectures are free. Fees vary for exhibitions (see website).
Transport: Green Park or Piccadilly Circus tube.
Amenities: Restaurant, two cafés, two shops, wheelchair access.

The Royal Academy of Arts (RA for
short) is an independent institution
run by eminent artists to promote the
creation and appreciation of visual arts.
It was founded in 1768 by George III to
educate, encourage and exhibit work
by contemporary British artists – at the
time, fashionable taste lent towards
traditional and continental art, and
home-grown artists had little chance
to shine.

Taddei Tondo, Michelangelo

👁 DON'T MISS!

The most cherished and charming
of the Academy's vast collection of
exhibits is Michelangelo's *Taddei
Tondo*. Created in Florence in 1504-
06, it's the only marble statue by
Michelangelo in Britain, and shows the
Virgin Mary and Child with the infant
St John the Baptist. It's displayed in
a purpose-built area on the Sackler
Gallery Landing.

The RA sought to change this by
holding an annual exhibition 'open
to all artists of distinguished merit' to
finance the training of young artists in
the Academy's Schools. The Summer
Exhibition (June to August) has
taken place every year since and is
the highlight of the Academy's year,
attracting thousands of applications.
It's an opportunity for unknown artists
to display their work alongside the
current Academicians, who include
such glittering names as David

Hockney, Anish Kapoor and Tracey
Emin.

In addition to the Summer Exhibition,
the RA holds regular temporary
loan presentations which boost its
international importance. These have
included such crowd pleasers as
'Byzantium 330-1453' (2008-9), 'The
Real Van Gogh: The Artist and His
Letters' (2010) and 'David Hockney RA:
A Bigger Picture' (2012).

Exhibitions take place in the
courtyard and rooms of Burlington
House. But many of the principal works
in the Academy's permanent collection
are displayed in the John Madejski
Fine Rooms which can be toured (free)
most days. The rooms feature works by
Royal Academicians past and present,
including Turner, Gainsborough,
Sargent and equine artist George
Stubbs, to name but a very few. You
can also view the RA collections online
(🖳 racollection.org.uk).

The RA is located in Burlington House (☎ 020-7493 0777, 💻 burlingtonhouse.org), one of London's finest Palladian buildings. Begun by Sir John Denham in 1665, it was sold two years later to Richard Boyle, 1st Earl of Burlington – from whom it derives its name – and has undergone many alterations since, including the monumental gateway to Piccadilly and the reconstruction of most of the principal interiors. Visitors are greeted by a statue of Sir Joshua Reynolds, the RA's first President, as they enter the courtyard.

In 1854, Burlington House was sold to the British government with a view to demolishing it. It survived and became home to a number of organisations, including the Royal Society of Chemistry, the Geological Society and the RA, which took over the main block in 1867. Free tickets are available for various societies' lectures.

The Academy's art school is the oldest in Britain. Past students include William Blake, Edwin Landseer and Sandra Blow. Today, 60 students study on a three-year postgraduate course. The RA receives no state funding and derives its income from exhibitions, sponsorship, trust funds, trading and its 'Friends'. The Friends of the Royal Academy is a charity founded in 1977; members' benefits include unlimited entry to exhibitions, use of the exclusive Friends Rooms – handy when the RA is heaving with visitors to major events – and a quarterly magazine.

FOOD & DRINK

The Restaurant at the Royal Academy: Enjoy tapas, afternoon tea or a three-course meal with menu by the ubiquitous Oliver Peyton and art by the Academicians.

42°Raw: Pristine café serving super-healthy, vegan-friendly food, including juices, soups and smoothies. Not a sausage sandwich in sight!

WALLACE COLLECTION 13

Address: Hertford House, Manchester Square, W1U 3BN (☎ 020-7563 9500, 🖥 wallacecollection.org).
Opening hours: Daily, 10am to 5pm. Closed 24-26th December.
Cost: Free, including temporary exhibitions.
Transport: Baker Street, Bond Street or Marble Arch tube.
Amenities: Restaurant, shop, wheelchair access.

This is one of London's best art collections, but it doesn't pull in the crowds, which is a pity – although those who do visit get to enjoy the paintings and other treasures in rooms that are sometimes almost devoid of visitors. It's also located in an attractive house built in 1776, pleasantly situated in Manchester Square, one of central London's smaller but best-preserved Georgian squares and well worth exploring.

The Wallace Collection is a tremendous grouping of fine and decorative arts dating from the 15th to 19th centuries, spread over 25 galleries. It has a lot of French 18th-century paintings, furniture (one of the finest collections of French furniture outside of France, including 22 pieces by André-Charles Boulle, who many consider to be the pre-eminent cabinet-maker of all time), Sèvres porcelain, arms and armour, and Old Master paintings. Best of all, it's free

to view so you can take it all in over several visits.

 DON'T MISS!

The Wallace Collection features one of the world's best-loved paintings: *The Laughing Cavalier* by Frans Hals. Painted in 1624, this Dutch Old Master is on display in the Great Gallery on the first floor. Seek it out and you discover that the subject is not a cavalier, nor is he laughing, though he demonstrates a slight smirk – the name was not coined until the late 19th century. But the attention to detail and bold use of colour are in a class of their own.

It's mainly the collection of the first four Marquesses of Hertford, particularly the fourth, Richard Seymour-Conway (1800-1870), who left it and the house to his illegitimate son (although he never acknowledged his paternity) Sir Richard Wallace (1818-1890). Sir Richard was also an important contributor to the

Laughing Cavalier, Frans Hals

stunning set of equestrian armour thought to date from 15th-century Germany. Other categories include bronzes, enamels, glass, majolica, miniatures, porcelain and sculpture – something to appeal to almost everybody. Look out for the Sèvres inkstand given by Louis XV to his favourite daughter, Madame Adélaïde. It incorporated two globes and the Crown of France, the latter concealing a bell which Madame Adélaïde used to summon her maid to collect letters she had written.

Refurbishment of the Great Gallery – home to many of the collection's Old Masters – was due to start in autumn 2012, so some paintings have been moved to other rooms, while others may be temporarily removed. Check Wallace Live, the online collection (wallacelive.wallacecollection.org/emuseumplus) before you visit.

collection and his widow bequeathed it to the nation in 1897 (it opened to the public in 1900). A condition of the bequest was that no object should ever leave the collection, even for temporary exhibition elsewhere, and no works can be stored off-site.

The collection contains around 5,500 objects and is split into six curatorial departments: Paintings and Miniatures; Ceramics and Glass; Sculpture and Works of Art; Arms and Armour; Sèvres Porcelain; and Gold Boxes and Furniture. The paintings collection includes work by such notables as Canaletto, Delacroix, Fragonard, Gainsborough, Hals, Landseer, Murillo, Poussin, Rembrandt, Reynolds, Rubens, Titian, Turner, Van Dyck and Velasquez. Notable paintings include Jean-Honoré Fragonard's frothily erotic *The Swing* and Rubens' glorious *Rainbow Landscape* which celebrates the Flanders countryside.

There's one of the world's best collections of arms and armour (European and Oriental), which includes a

---

FOOD & DRINK

The Wallace Restaurant: Another Oliver Peyton venue, serving up everything from oysters to scones in an attractive, tranquil glass-roofed courtyard.

Edgware Road: A short walk west brings you to an area famous for its Middle Eastern restaurants, including several incarnations of the excellent Lebanese chain Maroush.

blue and gold vase

APSLEY HOUSE   14

Address: 149 Piccadilly, Hyde Park Corner, W1J 7NT (☎ 020-7499 5676,
🖳 english-heritage.org.uk/daysout/properties/apsley-house).
Opening hours: April to October, Wed-Sun and Bank Holidays, 11am to 5pm;
November to March, Sat-Sun 10am to 4pm (see website for exact dates).
Cost: £6.50 adults, £5.90 concessions, £3.90 children aged 5-15, under-5s free.
Free for English Heritage members.
Transport: Hyde Park Corner tube.
Amenities: Shop, wheelchair access.

The residence of the Dukes of Wellington, Apsley House stands in solitary splendour at Hyde Park Corner and is both a museum and a private home. Grade I listed, it was built in red brick by Robert Adam between 1771 and 1778 for Lord Apsley, the Lord Chancellor, and acquired in 1817 by the Duke of Wellington, who faced the brick walls with Bath stone and added the Corinthian portico.

The interior has changed little since it was the home of the Iron Duke in the years following his victory over Napoleon at Waterloo. Many rooms were redesigned to reflect his growing status (he became Prime Minister in 1828). The house was a perfect setting for entertaining, including hosting an annual Waterloo Banquet to commemorate the famous victory, an event which continues to this day.

Waterloo Gallery

The 7th Duke gave the house and most of its contents to the nation in 1947. It's now run by English Heritage – the current Duke retains the right to occupy part of the property – and the dazzling interiors on public display are a magnificent example of Regency style. The art collection is one of London's most intriguing. There are over 200 paintings (some were part of the Spanish Royal collection, which came into the Duke's possession after the Battle of Vitoria in 1813 – they'd been plundered by Napoleon's brother Joseph), including works by Brueghel the Elder, Goya, Landseer, Rubens, Van Dyck and Velasquez.

On show also are many gifts that the first Duke received from European rulers in gratitude for his military campaigns, including porcelain, silver, trophies, uniforms and weapons.

 DON'T MISS!

You cannot miss Canova's colossal nude marble statue of Napoleon, posing somewhat inappropriately as Mars the Peacemaker, which stands 3.45m (11ft) tall in the stairwell in the centre of the house.

15 BANQUETING HOUSE

> **Address:** Whitehall, SW1A 2ER (☎ 020-3166 6154, 🖳 hrp.org.uk/banquetinghouse).
>
> **Opening hours:** Daily, 10am to 5pm. Closed Bank Holidays and 24th December to 1st January. It's sometimes closed for functions and events, so phone or check the website.
>
> **Cost:** £5 adults, £4 concessions, under-16s free.
>
> **Transport:** Westminster or Embankment tube or Charing Cross tube/rail.
>
> **Amenities:** Shop, wheelchair access.

One of the hidden delights of Westminster, this is the only surviving part of the Palace of Whitehall. Whitehall was the main residence of English monarchs in London from 1530 until 1698, when all except the Banqueting House was destroyed by fire.

DON'T MISS!

The building's major attraction is its richly painted ceiling, a masterpiece by Antwerp-based artist Peter Paul Rubens and his only surviving in-situ ceiling painting. Commissioned by Charles I, it celebrates the benefits of wise rule (!) and his father James I's flawed idea of the Divine Right of Kings. It's most fortunate that the ceiling survived the short period of Puritan rule that followed Charles' demise.

It's also significant in the history of English architecture for being the first building to be completed in the neo-classical style. It was designed by revolutionary architect Inigo Jones in 1622 in a style influenced by Palladio, an Italian Renaissance architect, who was himself influenced by Greek and Roman architecture. In the 19th century, Banqueting House was controversially refaced with Portland stone, although the details of the original façade were preserved. Today, the building is Grade I listed and cared for by the charity, Historic Royal Palaces.

The term 'Banqueting House' is something of a misnomer, as it was used not just for banquets but also for ceremonies, royal receptions and the performance of masques – a cross between a ball, an amateur dramatic production and a fancy dress party – which blended entertainment with political comment.

The most significant event to take place at Banqueting House was the execution of Charles I. Following his defeat during the Civil War, Charles was found guilty of treason and on 30th January 1649 he stepped from an upstairs window of the house onto a specially built scaffold where he was dispatched by an anonymous executioner.

Painted ceiling, Peter Paul Rubens

CHURCHILL WAR ROOMS 16

Address: Clive Steps, King Charles Street, SW1A 2AQ (☎ 020-7930 6961,
🖥 cwr.iwm.org.uk).
Opening hours: Daily, 9.30am to 6pm. Closed 24-26th December.
Cost: £16.50 adults, £13.20 concessions (over-60s, students, the disabled), children under 16 free.
Transport: Westminster or St James's Park tube.
Amenities: Café, shop, wheelchair access.

Sir Winston Churchill

This is one of five branches of the Imperial War Museum, and comprises the Cabinet War Rooms – an underground complex that housed a British government command centre during the Second World War – and a museum devoted to Sir Winston Churchill.

The Cabinet War Rooms were begun in 1938 and became operational in August 1939, shortly before the outbreak of war. They were the nerve centre of Britain's war effort, equipped with accommodation, offices, communications and broadcasting equipment, sound-proofing, ventilation and reinforcement. During the Blitz, the War Rooms were further protected by a massive layer of concrete known as 'the Slab', which was up to 5ft (1.5m) thick.

Around 30 of the historic rooms are on display, including the typing pool, the dormitories and Churchill's bedroom (although he preferred to sleep at 10 Downing Street). The Map Room and Cabinet Room were of particular importance, the former manned around the clock and producing a daily intelligence report. The rooms are almost exactly as they were when last used in 1945, the walls still plastered with maps covered in pins showing troop movements. In the Cabinet Room, 115 cabinet meetings were held, sometimes until after midnight – Churchill was noted for retiring late.

The Churchill Museum is innovative and interactive, using technology and multimedia to cover all aspects of Winston Churchill's long, varied life (1874-1965), private as well as public, downs as well as ups. You can hear his speeches, view his paintings and even read his love letters to his wife Clementine.

 ALLOW...

You're advised to allow at least 90 minutes for a visit, but in view of the number of rooms to explore, the amount of information to digest and the attractions of the on-site café – not to mention the high entrance price – many visitors stay for half a day or more.

17 CLARENCE HOUSE

Address: Stable Yard Road, SW1A 1BA (☎ 020-7766 7300, 🖥 royalcollection.org. uk/visit/clarencehouse).
Opening hours: Open in August for guided tours only (¾hr), Mon-Fri 10am to 4pm, Sat-Sun 10am to 5.30pm. Check website or phone for details and tickets.
Cost: £9 adults, £5 under-17s, under-5s free.
Transport: Green Park or St James's Park tube.
Amenities: Shop, garden, wheelchair access.

Clarence House is the official residence of the Prince of Wales (since 2003) and the Duchess of Cornwall, and the couple receive several thousand official guests annually from the UK and overseas.

Situated beside St James's Palace and sharing its garden, it was built between 1825 and 1827 to the designs of John Nash for Prince William Henry, Duke of Clarence, who lived here as William IV from 1830 until 1837. It was once the London home of Her Majesty the Queen (then Princess Elizabeth) and the Duke of Edinburgh following their marriage in 1947, and was the home of Queen Elizabeth, the Queen Mother, from 1953 until her death in 2002.

The house has been much altered, reflecting the changes in occupancy and use over almost two centuries. It was extensively refurbished for the Prince of Wales, although the rooms retain the ambience created by the Queen Mother, and much of her collection of works of art and furniture has been retained.

The five rooms open to the public are all on the ground floor: the Lancaster Room, the Morning Room, the Library, the Dining Room and the Garden Room. Here, you can view items from the Royal Collection and from the collection of Queen Elizabeth the Queen Mother, which is particularly strong in 20th-century British art, including important works by John Piper, Graham Sutherland, Walter Sickert and Augustus John. Also on display are superb examples of Fabergé, English porcelain and silver, particularly pieces relating to the Bowes-Lyon family.

 ALLOW...

A guided tour of Clarence House takes around 45 minutes and includes the five main rooms and adjoining spaces, as well as the formal garden at the front of the house which was created by Prince Charles in 2004-5 in memory of his grandmother.

EMBANKMENT GALLERIES, SOMERSET HOUSE   18

Address: Somerset House, Strand, WC2R 1LA (☎ 020-7845 4600,
🖳 somersethouse.org.uk).
Opening hours: Daily, 10am to 6pm; times vary for some exhibitions.
Cost: Check website or telephone for details.
Transport: Temple, Embankment or Covent Garden tube, or Charing Cross tube/
rail.
Amenities: Restaurant, two cafés, deli, shop, wheelchair access.

Somerset House is a spectacular neo-classical building in the heart of London, situated between the Strand and the Thames, and a centre of excellence for the arts. Well known for its seasonal attractions – open-air cinema screenings in summer, a spectacular ice rink in winter – it also hosts a number of galleries, including the Courtauld Gallery (see page 61) and the Embankment Galleries which opened in 2008.

The Embankment Galleries consist of two barrel vaulted galleries, plus a mezzanine floor which often serves as a catwalk for fashion shows – Somerset House is a host of London Fashion Week. They present a range of ideas-driven exhibitions which cover a cross section of contemporary art, from architecture and design to fashion and photography. The galleries are the venue for the annual 'Pick Me Up' graphic arts fair (March-April) and exhibitions have included 'SHOWstudio: Fashion Revolution', which brought fashion photographer Nick Knight's work to the gallery, and 'Dior Illustrated: René Gruau and The Line of Beauty', an exhibition of drawings from the master of illustration.

There's also a programme of free public displays in the Terrace and Courtyard Rooms, and the new East Wing Galleries, which opened in 2011.

Somerset House dates back to Tudor times and was used by monarchs from Elizabeth I to Charles II. The current building was completed by George III's architect Sir William Chambers, who began work in 1775, although the house wasn't completed to its current design until the mid-19th century. It's remarkable for its river views which inspired Canaletto among others.

DON'T MISS!

Discover some of Somerset House's 'Hidden Spaces and History' on one of the excellent free guided tours which take place on Thursdays (1.15 and 2.45pm) and Saturdays (12.15, 1.15, 2.15 and 3.15pm). Tickets are available from the Information Desk in the Seamen's Hall.

19 FLEMING COLLECTION

Address: 13 Berkeley Street, W1J 8DU (☎ 020-7042 5730,
🖳 flemingcollection.co.uk).
Opening hours: Tue-Sat, 10am to 5.30pm.
Cost: Free. There's a fee for private viewings (see website for details).
Transport: Green Park tube.
Amenities: Shop, wheelchair access.

The Fleming Collection is the finest assembly of Scottish art in private hands and the only dedicated museum granting public access to Scottish art all year round. It grew from an assembly of paintings gathered to decorate the new London premises of Dundee banking firm Robert Fleming & Co in 1968. The only guideline was that the art should be by Scottish artists or feature Scottish scenes, to emphasise the bank's heritage.

Scottish art was largely unknown outside of Scotland until the '80s; thus prices were relatively low, allowing the collection to grow quickly. It now comprises over 750 oils and watercolours from 1770 to the present day, including works by Raeburn, Ramsay and Wilkie. It's particularly noted for works by Scottish Impressionist William McTaggart and for a superb group of paintings by the Colourists, one of a number of Scottish groups who took their cue from Impressionist and Post-Impressionist art. Look out, too, for the domestic still lifes by Anne Redpath.

In March 2000, Flemings was sold to Chase Manhattan Bank. To avoid the collection being lost, the Fleming family funded the charitable Fleming-Wyfold Foundation to purchase it before the sale. In 2002 it moved to Berkeley Street where Gallery One on the ground floor shows temporary exhibitions, drawn from private and national collections, while the newer Gallery Two (upstairs) exhibits works from the permanent collection.

The main thrust of the Fleming Collection is now directed towards buying the work of young Scottish artists, and it remains a living and growing collection through further acquisitions.

DON'T MISS!

The Fleming Collection boasts some iconic paintings of the Highland Clearances – the forced expulsion of Highland crofters in the 18th and 19th centuries – including *The Last of the Clan* by Thomas Faed and *Lochaber No More* by John Watson Nicol.

INSTITUTE OF CONTEMPORARY ARTS 20

Address: The Mall, SW1Y 5AH (☎ 020-7930 3647, 💻 ica.org.uk).
Opening hours: Tue-Sun, 11am to 11pm. Galleries 11am to 6pm (Thu 9pm). Closed Mondays and 25th December to 3rd January.
Cost: Most exhibitions are free (see website for films and other events).
Transport: Charing Cross tube/rail.
Amenities: Café/bar, shop, wheelchair access.

The Institute of Contemporary Arts (ICA) is one of London's leading artistic and cultural centres, containing galleries, a theatre, two cinemas, a superb bookshop and a great bar. It's located within Nash House, part of Carlton House Terrace, a grand Regency period building on The Mall – a hidden gem in an unlikely location.

The ICA was founded by a group of radical artists in 1946 to challenge the foundations of contemporary art. Its founders wished to establish a space where artists, writers and scientists could debate ideas outside the traditional confines of 'retrograde institutions' such as the Royal Academy. After occupying a variety of 'temporary' locations, in 1968 the ICA moved to its present, splendid abode, which has become the home of British avant-garde.

In its early years, the Institute organised exhibitions of modern art, including Pablo Picasso and Jackson Pollock, and also launched Pop art, Op art, and British Brutalist art and architecture. Its history has included a who's who of artists and luminaries such as TS Eliot, Stravinsky, Elizabeth Lutyens, Ronnie Scott, Cartier-Bresson, Michael Foucault, Jeff Koons, Peter Blake, Yoko Ono, Don Letts, Jeff Wall, Vivienne Westwood, Ian McEwan, Philip Pullman and Zadie Smith – to name just a few. It has also played host to debut solo shows from some of today's highest profile artists including Damien Hirst, Luc Tuymans and Steve McQueen.

The ICA is never afraid of breaking the rules and doing something different, so be prepared to expect the unexpected – no-one who's serious about contemporary art can afford to ignore it.

🍴 FOOD & DRINK 🍴

The ICA Café Bar: Open Tue-Sun, 11am to 11pm, this excellent bar serves up imaginative sandwiches and salads, tasty mains and tempting puds at very reasonable prices.

21 LONDON TRANSPORT MUSEUM

Address: Covent Garden Piazza, WC2E 7BB (☎ 020-7379 6344.
🖳 ltmuseum.co.uk).
Opening hours: Daily, 10am to 6pm (11am Fridays). Closed 24-26th December.
Cost: £13.50 adults, £10 concessions (seniors/students/recipients of some benefits),
under-16s free. Tickets are valid for unlimited visits for one year.
Transport: Covent Garden tube.
Amenities: Two cafés, shop, library, wheelchair access.

The London Transport Museum (or LT Museum) preserves and explains the capital's rich and fascinating transport heritage and demonstrates how it was integral to London's growth as the world's most iconic city. It's situated in a Victorian iron and glass building, designed by William Rogers in 1871, which has been home to the museum since 1980 and underwent a £22m refurbishment in 2005-2007.

The first collection was assembled at the beginning of the 20th century by the London General Omnibus Company (LGOC) to preserve buses being retired from service. The LGOC was taken over by the London Electric Railway (LER)

and the collection expanded to include rail vehicles and continued to grow while responsibility for public transport passed through various bodies, until being assumed by Transport for London (TfL) in 2000. It now covers all aspects of the city's transportation.

The museum contains many examples of buses, trams, trolleybuses and rail vehicles from the 19th and 20th centuries, as well as exhibits related to the operation and marketing of passenger services, and the impact that the developing transport network has had on the city and its population.

Highlights include 'London – The First World City', exploring how transport allowed London to become the world's first truly cosmopolitan city; 'Victorian Transport', which details innovations that took place in Victorian London; 'World's First Underground', which tells the history of London's tube network; and 'London in the 1920s and 1930s' which explores the innovation of bus use across the city. The museum also relates how public transport helped London operate through two world wars and explains how modern transport systems work.

 ALLOW...

You should allow a half or whole day to explore all the attractions of the museum, as alongside all the vintage vehicles there's also a poster collection, library, two cafés and a shop.

MALL GALLERIES 22

Address: 7 Carlton House Terrace, The Mall, SW1Y 5BD (☎ 020-7930 6844, 🖥 mallgalleries.org.uk).
Opening hours: Daily, 10am to 5pm during exhibitions (unless otherwise stated), including Bank Holidays.
Cost: Free except for Federation of British Artists (FBA) exhibitions: £2.50 adults, £1.50 concessions and groups (min. 10 people).
Transport: Charing Cross tube or rail.
Amenities: Café, shop, wheelchair access.

The Mall Galleries (next door to the Institute of Contemporary Arts) are one of the coolest art venues in London, following refurbishment in 2007. It's a major contemporary art showcase, with three main galleries, a bookshop and a café, and is home to the Federation of British Artists (FBA). The FBA consists of eight of the UK's leading art societies (all hold their Annual Exhibition at the Mall Galleries) – including the Royal Society of British Artists, the Royal Society of Portrait Painters and the Royal Society of Marine Artists – with over 500 member artists. The Galleries serve as a national focal point for contemporary figurative art by living artists working in the UK.

 FOOD & DRINK

Mall Galleries Café: The chocolate cake is highly recommended.
The ICA Café Bar: Just next door if you fancy something more substantial.

In addition to the member societies, other societies and individual artists stage shows at the Galleries. They also host several of the UK's premier open art competitions, and more than 100 prizes are administered each year, including the £30,000 Threadneedle Prize, one of the UK's leading showcases for paintings and sculpture. In March 2012, the Galleries unveiled a radical re-development of

the former East Gallery, known as the 'Threadneedle Space'.

The Galleries' education department runs a schools' programme, plus a wide range of activities for adults, including talks and tours, workshops and artist demonstrations. Projects include a drawing school and summer courses run by the New English Art Club, as well as the Hesketh Hubbard Art Society, the largest life drawing society in London. The bookshop specialises in tickets for events and books relating to British figurative art, ranging from reference guides to tutorial DVDs.

23   ROYAL ACADEMY OF MUSIC MUSEUM

Address: Marylebone Road, NW1 5HT (☎ 020-7873 7373, 💻 ram.ac.uk/museum).
Opening hours: Mon-Fri, 11.30am to 5.30pm; Sat noon to 4pm. Closed Sundays and Bank Holidays.
Cost: Free.
Transport: Baker Street or Regent's Park tube.
Amenities: Restaurant, bar, wheelchair access.

This museum is a delight for anyone with an interest in music. The Royal Academy of Music is Britain's oldest degree-granting music school with a history dating back nearly 200 years. It was founded in 1822 by Lord Burghersh (1784-1859) and was granted its Royal Charter in 1830 by George IV. It moved to its current, custom-built premises in Marylebone Road in 1911.

👁 DON'T MISS!

The Academy hosts a musical masterclass most days, so time your visit right and you can listen to skilled performances by instrumentalists and vocalists for free. Check the 'What's On' section of the website for more information.

The Academy (as it's usually called) has been a college of the University of London since 1999 and is the country's leading conservatoire. It has trained thousands of accomplished musicians; its most famous alumni include Sir Elton John, Annie Lennox, Michael Nyman, Sir Simon Rattle and the late Sir John Dankworth and Sir Henry Wood (of Proms fame).

The museum is situated in the York Gate building, which was designed in 1822 by John Nash (1752-1835) as part of the main entrance to Regent's Park. It regularly hosts exhibitions and events, including recitals, most of which are free to attend. It also displays material from the Academy's world-renowned collection of instruments, manuscripts, paintings, busts, drawings, teaching aids and artefacts, batons, furnishings, memorabilia and other objects.

Highlights include Cremonese stringed instruments from 1650 to 1740, a collection of English pianos from 1790 to 1850 from the famous

Mobbs Collection, and original manuscripts by Purcell, Mendelssohn, Liszt, Brahms, Sullivan and Vaughan Williams, as well as collections named after individuals such as conductor Sir Henry Wood and the Foyle (Yehudi) Menuhin Archive. The Academy also has a restaurant and bar.

ROYAL COLLEGE OF ART   24

Address: Kensington Gore, SW7 2EU (☎ 020-7590 4444, 💻 rca.ac.uk).
Opening hours: Most exhibitions are open daily from 10am to 5.30pm (see website for details).
Cost: Free.
Transport: High Street Kensington or South Kensington tube.
Amenities: Café, bar, shop, wheelchair access.

The Royal College of Art (RCA) is the world's only wholly postgraduate university of art and design. It's right at the cutting edge of design trends and has produced some of the best-known names in architecture, automotive design, photography, industrial design, textiles, fashion, ceramics and jewellery design.

The RCA's galleries and lecture theatres are home to a lively programme of exhibitions, events and talks, most of which are free. The major event is the annual RCA summer show which takes place at the Kensington and Battersea campuses. It showcases the cream of work by postgraduate students – some 500 exhibitors from 40 countries in 2012 – and is recognised by those in the know as a great place to pick up art by tomorrow's David Hockney or Zandra Rhodes.

The RCA was founded in 1837 as the Government School of Design and was renamed the Royal College of Art in 1896; in 1967 it was granted a Royal Charter, endowing it with university status.

In the early 1900s the RCA was the birthplace of 'The New Sculpture' movement, when students included such luminaries as Henry Moore. The '30s and '40s saw the introduction of courses in graphic design and fashion, and in the '50s and '60s the RCA was at the centre of the explosion of pop art culture and fashion design. The '60s saw an industrial design course established, along with vehicle design (the Audi Quattro and Porsche 911 began life here). More recently it has produced a new type of student, including Gavin Turk and Tracey Emin, part of the 'Young British Artists' movement.

 FOOD & DRINK

Montparnasse Café: Just 10 minutes' walk from the RCA is a small slice of Paris in Thackery Street (W8 5ET), serving café au lait, croque monsieur and copies of *Le Monde*.

Today, the RCA is the world's most influential art college with an unrivalled creative environment.

25   ROYAL COLLEGE OF MUSIC MUSEUM

Address: Prince Consort Road, SW7 2BS (☎ 020-7591 4300, 🖥 rcm.ac.uk/visit/museum).
Opening hours: Tue-Fri, 11.30am to 4.30pm. Closed during Christmas and Easter holidays.
Cost: Free. Guided museum tours (maximum 25 people) £5 per head, £4 concessions.
Transport: South Kensington tube.
Amenities: Restaurant, bar, library, wheelchair access.

The Royal College of Music (RCM) is a conservatoire founded by royal charter in 1882, housed in a beautiful red brick Victorian building. It was created to establish a school of music to rank alongside the conservatoires of Berlin, Leipzig, Paris and Vienna. The building was designed by Sir Arthur Blomfield (1829-1899) in Flemish Mannerist style – using red brick dressed with buff-coloured stone – and opened in May 1894. It was largely financed by donations from Yorkshire industrialist Samson Fox, whose statue stands in the entrance hall.

The RCM's main venue is the Amaryllis Fleming concert hall, a 468-seat, barrel-vaulted room built in 1901. The Britten theatre, which seats 400, was opened by Queen Elizabeth II in 1986 and is used for opera, ballet, music and theatre. Tickets are available for events at both venues (☎ 020-7591 4314, 🖥 rcm.ac.uk/events for details).

The College has had a distinguished list of teachers and alumni, including most of the composers who brought about the 'English musical renaissance' of the 19th and 20th centuries, including Samuel Coleridge-Taylor, Gustav Holst, Ralph Vaughan Williams and John Ireland. More recently, Andrew Lloyd Webber and the guitarist John Williams were students here.

The museum houses a collection of over 1,000 instruments and accessories from the 15th century to the present day. Among them are some remarkable and unfamiliar instruments such as the contrabassophon, serpent and glass armonica, plus trombones owned by Elgar and Holst. The RCM also holds significant collections of research material, including autographs (musical scores in the composer's own handwriting) such as Haydn's *String Quartet Op. 64/1*, Mozart's *Piano Concerto K491* and Elgar's *Cello Concerto*.

👁 DON'T MISS!

One of the RCM's greatest treasures is its anonymous clavicytherium (c.1480), related to the harpsichord and believed to be the earliest surviving stringed keyboard instrument.

ROYAL INSTITUTE OF BRITISH ARCHITECTS   26

Address: 66 Portland Place, W1B 1AD (☎ 020-7580 5533, 🖳 architecture.com).
Opening hours: Exhibition Galleries: Mon-Sat, 10am to 5pm. Library: Tue-Wed and Fri, 10am to 5pm; Sat 10am to 1.30pm. Bookshop: Mon-Fri, 9.30am to 5.30pm; Sat 10am to 5pm. Café: Mon-Fri, 8am to 6pm. Restaurant: Mon-Fri, noon to 3pm.
Cost: Free.
Transport: Goodge Street and Oxford Circus tube.
Amenities: Restaurant, café, bar, shop, library, gardens, wheelchair access.

I t befits an organisation that represents architects to be housed in an intriguing, inventive building, and 66 Portland Place does the Royal Institute of British Architects (RIBA) proud. Grade II listed, it was designed by the architect George Grey Wornum, with sculptures by Edward Bainbridge Copnall and James Woodford.

 FOOD & DRINK

The RIBA Restaurant: Modern fare in stunning designer surroundings with a set menu starting from £19.50.
  The RIBA Café: Enjoy breakfast, lunch, morning coffee or afternoon tea on the stunning first floor landing café.
  The RIBA Bar: Imaginative salad bar plus sandwiches, light bites, coffee and cocktails.

Opened in 1934 by George V, the building's design resulted from a competition that was won by Wornum (it attracted 284 entries), and is a prime example of early '30s Art Deco architecture.

The sculpted figures on the front depict the spirit of man and woman as creative forces of architecture. Along the Weymouth Street elevation, above the third storey window line, are five relief figures, by Bainbridge Copnall, of a painter, sculptor, architect (Sir Christopher Wren), engineer and working man.

The massive cast bronze outer doors, each weighing 1.5 tons, are the work of Woodford. The deep relief design depicts the Thames and its buildings, including the Guildhall, Houses of Parliament, St Paul's and the Horse Guards. The three children on the right-hand door represent the architect's children.

Inside, the most striking aspect of the design is a central stairwell in Demara and black birdseye marble. On the landing of the first floor, six finely moulded plaster panels (by Woodford), depicting the main English architectural periods, are set in the ceiling. The wide gallery on the second floor is the best vantage point from which to appreciate the ingenuity of Wornum's design.

The RIBA building is also worth visiting for its galleries housing exhibitions covering various aspects of building design, and has a bookshop and an extensive library.

27 SERPENTINE & SACKLER GALLERIES

Address: Kensington Gardens, W2 3XA (☎ 020-7402 6075,
🖳 serpentinegallery.org).
Opening hours: Daily, 10am to 6pm. See website for information about exhibitions.
Cost: Free.
Transport: Lancaster Gate or South Kensington tube.
Amenities: Shop, wheelchair access.

annual programme of temporary structures by internationally acclaimed architects and designers, which has become an important site for architectural experimentation. The series is unique and showcases the work of an international architect (or design team) who hasn't completed a building in England at the time of the gallery's invitation. Each pavilion is sited on the gallery's lawn for three months and in recent years has featured designs by Rem Koolhaas, Peter Zumthor and, in 2012, the Chinese artist-activist Ai Weiwei.

E stablished by the Arts Council in 1970 and housed in a classical (but unprepossessing) 1934 tea pavilion, the Serpentine Gallery is one of London's most important contemporary art galleries. The gallery's world-renowned, temporary exhibition programme showcases work by the finest contemporary artists working across a wide variety of media. Notable artists who have exhibited here include Man Ray, Henry Moore, Andy Warhol, Bridget Riley, Anish Kapoor, Andreas Gursky, Christian Boltanski, Gabriel Orozco, Tomoko Takahashi, Philippe Parreno, Louise Bourgeois, Richard Prince, Wolfgang Tilmans, Gerhard Richter, Gustav Metzger, Damien Hirst and Jeff Koons. In summer 2012, the gallery presented a major exhibition of the work of artist Yoko Ono.

The Serpentine Gallery Pavilion commission (begun in 2000) is an

In 2013, the Serpentine Gallery will open a new space, the Serpentine Sackler Gallery (named after Dr Mortimer and Theresa Sackler), designed by the celebrated, award-winning architect Zaha Hadid. It will be an innovative arts venue for the 21st century housed in an early 19th-century, Grade II listed building, The Magazine (with a restaurant/café).

 FOOD & DRINK

Orangery Restaurant: Situated in the gardens of nearby Kensington Palace, the Orangery is highly regarded for its afternoon teas.
 Lido Café: Enjoy a cuppa or a glass of wine overlooking the Serpentine.

WESTMINSTER ABBEY MUSEUM

28

Address: 20 Dean's Yard, SW1P 3PA (☏ 020-7222 5152,
🖳 westminster-abbey.org)
Opening hours: Mon-Sat, 10.30am to 4.30pm. Closed Sundays. The Abbey closes
for special events, including state occasions, so check before visiting.
Cost: Entry to the museum is included in the admission fee to the Abbey; £16
adults, £13 students and over-60s, £6 11-18-year-olds, under-11s free.
Transport: St James's Park or Westminster tube.
Amenities: Café, kiosk, shop, wheelchair access.

The museum of Westminster Abbey is tucked away in a vaulted undercroft, one of the oldest parts of the building dating back almost to the church's foundation in 1065 by Edward the Confessor. It contains some of the strangest relics of Britain's past: a collection of funeral effigies of royal and other notable persons. The earliest of these, including figures of Edward III, Henry VII and Elizabeth I, were made from wood and designed to replace the deceased's body during funeral events.

From the 17th century onwards, they were made from wax and used as memorials rather than funeral stand-ins. Those on show include Charles II, William III, Mary II and Queen Anne, as well as Frances Stuart, a lady of Charles II's court, who's dressed in her finery and displayed with her pet parrot. Later wax effigies include Viscount Nelson – though he was actually buried at Paul's – and William Pitt the Elder (Earl Chatham).

The museum is, however, more than just a waxworks display and contains other interesting exhibits such as the funeral saddle and shield of Henry V, panels of medieval stained glass and replicas of regalia used during coronation rehearsals – the originals are kept in the Tower of London. Pride of place goes to the Westminster Retable, England's oldest painted panel altarpiece, which experts believe was painted in the 1270s and donated by Henry III. Though showing its age, you can still make out depictions of Christ's miracles and an image of St Peter, the Abbey's patron saint.

 DON'T MISS!

Poets' Corner in the South Transept is the final resting place of Robert Browning, Chaucer, Dickens, Dr Johnson and Lord Tennyson, among others, and there are also memorials to dozens of literary luminaries, from WH Auden to Oscar Wilde.

monument to Charles James Fox

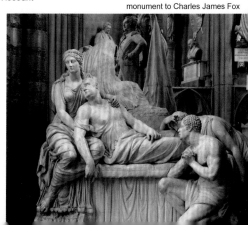

29   ALEXANDER FLEMING MUSEUM

Address: St Mary's Hospital, Praed Street, W2 1NY (☎ 020-3312 6528, 🖥 imperial.nhs.uk/aboutus/museumsandarchives).
Opening hours: Mon-Thu, 10am to 1pm. Closed 24th December to 2nd January and on Public Holidays.
Cost: £4 adults, £2 children, students, senior citizens and the unemployed.
Transport: Paddington tube/rail.
Amenities: Hospital restaurant/café and shop. No disabled access to museum.

While a museum dedicated to the founder of penicillin might not set the pulse racing, this is an engaging tribute to an important man. Alexander Fleming (1881-1955) discovered the antibiotic in 1928 in a basic and under-funded laboratory at St Mary's Hospital (founded in 1845). His breakthrough was the result of an accident when an experiment was contaminated, resulting in the discovery of the antibacterial powers of penicillin.

A reconstruction of Fleming's restored laboratory, displays and a video uncover the remarkable story of how a chance discovery led to a lifesaving drug. There are also exhibits about Fleming himself and his commitment to the further development of his discoveries.

During the First World War Fleming served in battlefield hospitals in France, where he discovered that antiseptics were killing more soldiers than infection. Ten years after returning to St Mary's, he made his great discovery, and his research was later taken up by Howard Florey and others, enabling the mass-production of penicillin during World War Two. Fleming was awarded the Nobel Prize in Physiology or Medicine in 1945.

30   BENJAMIN FRANKLIN HOUSE

Address: 36 Craven Street, WC2N 5NF (☎ 020-7839 2006, 🖥 benjaminfranklinhouse.org).
Opening hours: Daily, 10.30am to 5pm, except Tue. Tours, Wed-Sun at noon, 1pm, 2pm, 3.15pm and 4.15pm, plus guided tours on Mondays at the same times. Closed Tuesdays.
Cost: £7 adults, £5 seniors and students, free for under 16s. Tours with a guide £3.50.
Transport: Charing Cross tube/rail or Embankment tube.
Amenities: Shop, limited wheelchair access.

This architecturally important Grade I listed house was built around 1730 and retains many original features, but what makes it extra special is that it's the only remaining home of Benjamin Franklin. Franklin (1706-1790) was born in Boston, Massachusetts, but lived and worked in this house for 16 years until the eve of the American Revolution (the house was the first de facto US embassy). He was also a key founder of the United States of America and the only statesman to sign all four documents that created the new nation. His work as a philosopher, printer and more helped the progress of the Age of Enlightenment, and he's regarded as the father of electricity.

This inventive museum comprises several sections, including the Student Science Centre which allows the recreation of experiments from Franklin's time in London. Its most compelling attraction is the Historical Experience which takes a 'museum as theatre' approach. You're 'accompanied' by an actress who plays Polly Hewson, Franklin's landlady's daughter, who became like a daughter to him. This live performance, with lighting, sound and visual projections, brings the whole 18th-century experience to life.

Benjamin Franklin

BRITISH DENTAL ASSOCIATION MUSEUM   31

Address: 64 Wimpole Street, W1G 8YS (☎ 020-7563 4549, 🖥 bda.org/museum).
Opening hours: Tue and Thu, 1-4pm.
Cost: Free.
Transport: Oxford Circus or Bond Street tube.
Amenities: Wheelchair access.

The British Dental Association (BDA) Museum tells the absorbing – and often painful – history of dental care. From 19th-century dental floss to toothache cures, clockwork drills to toothpaste adverts, it displays over 30,000 items

relating to dentistry in the UK, dating from its time as a gruesome public spectacle to the complex procedures of today.

The BDA Museum began life in 1919, when Lilian Lindsay (the first woman to qualify as a dentist in the UK and the BDA's first female president in 1946), donated several old dental instruments that she had been storing in a box under her bed! The museum was developed primarily for the education of BDA members, but in 1967 it opened its doors to the general public. In autumn 2005 it was redesigned to make it more accessible. The collection includes dental instruments and equipment, furniture, photographs, archives, and decorative art. It's an absorbing museum that – hopefully – won't give you nightmares.

32   BRITISH OPTICAL ASSOCIATION MUSEUM

Address: The College of Optometrists, 41-42 Craven Street, WC2N 5NG
(☎ 020-7766 4353, 🖥 college-optometrists.org/en/knowledge-centre/museyeum).
Opening hours: Mon-Fri, 9.30am to 5pm. Closed weekends, Bank Holidays and
on other selected days. Visits are supervised and must be booked in advance by
phone.
Cost: The museum is free. Tours of the college's meeting rooms cost £5.
Transport: Charing Cross tube/rail.
Amenities: Wheelchair access.

Regarded as one of the best optical museum collections in the world, the MusEYEum (pun intended) at the College of Optometrists has over 16,000 exhibits relating to the human eye, dating back to the 17th century. Founded by the British Optical Association in 1901, it's the oldest museum of its kind and an eye-opener in more ways than one.

The collection includes all manner of eyewear from monocles to spectacles – some previously worn by famous people such as Dr Johnson and the comedian Ronnie Corbett – as well as equipment used by optical professions to treat diseases and correct vision, such as test charts, ophthalmoscopes, contact lenses and a rather fearsome array of model eyes. More aesthetically pleasing are the paintings with a visual theme, which include a portrait of Benjamin Franklin wearing a fur hat and spectacles, and fans with built-in spyglasses which allowed the holder to, er, keep an eye on their peers. If that isn't enough, the building is also allegedly haunted!

33   FARADAY MUSEUM AT THE ROYAL INSTITUTION

Address: 21 Albemarle Street, W1S 4BS (☎ 020-7409 2992, 🖥 rigb.org).
Opening hours: Mon-Fri, 9am to 6pm; the restaurant, bar and café remain open
until 10pm.
Cost: Free. eGuides can be hired for £3.
Transport: Green Park tube.
Amenities: Restaurant, bar, café, wheelchair access.

The Faraday Museum, which commemorates the scientific pioneer Michael Faraday (1791-1867), occupies two rooms in the basement of the old 18th-century Royal Institution building, and showcases his life's work.

Faraday was a pioneer in the fields of electricity and magnetism and a prolific experimenter, whose greatest discoveries include the principles behind the electric motor, generator and transformer.

Michael Faraday

Faraday joined the RI as a chemical assistant in 1813 and did most of his work here. The highlight of the exhibition is a reconstruction of his laboratory as it was in the 1850s; it contains original equipment, including his first electric generator, magneto-spark apparatus, a large electromagnet, a vacuum pump and jars of chemicals. There are also some of his personal effects.

The RI collections include the original apparatus and papers of many notable scientists who researched, lectured and lived in the building, including Sir Humphry Davy (who discovered sodium and potassium), John Tyndall (successor to Faraday), James Dewar (liquefaction) and George Porter (Nobel Prize for Chemistry 1967).

FITZROY HOUSE   34

Address: 37 Fitzroy Street, W1T 6DX (☎ 020-7255 2422, 🖥 fitzroyhouse.org).
Opening hours: Daily, by appointment, 11am to 5pm.
Cost: Free.
Transport: Warren Street, Great Portland Street or Goodge Street tube.
Amenities: Coffee/tea served, wheelchair access.

Set in the heart of Fitzrovia, Fitzroy House is a fine example of a Georgian townhouse. Built in 1791, it imitates the designs of Robert Adam, the architect who designed Fitzroy Square. The house is one of the last remaining structures on the block that retains its original exterior. Fitzrovia has been home to many famous people, including H G Wells, George Orwell, Charles Dickens, Virginia Woolf and George Bernard Shaw – who lived with his mother on the 1st floor of 37 Fitzroy Street from 1881-1882.

Today, Fitzroy House is better known as the previous home of controversial American writer and philosopher L (Lafayette) Ron Hubbard (1911-1986), who lived and worked there for three years in the '50s, and it's now a museum dedicated to his life and work. Visitors can step into this '50s time capsule to view its faithfully restored communications office equipment (including Adler typewriters and a Western Union Telefax), original manuscripts, rare books and artefacts.

35　GUARDS MUSEUM

Address: Wellington Barracks, Birdcage Walk, SW1E 6HQ (☎ 020-7414 3428/3271, chapel ☎ 020-7414 3299, 🖥 theguardsmuseum.com).
Opening hours: Daily, 10am to 4pm.
Cost: £5 adults, £2.50 senior citizens (65 and over), students and ex-military, £1 serving military personnel, children (16 and under) free.
Transport: St James's Park tube.
Amenities: Shop, wheelchair access.

The Guards Museum is a captivating collection that traces the history of the five regiments of Foot Guards – Grenadier, Coldstream, Scots, Irish and Welsh Guards – which, together with the two regiments of Household Cavalry, make up Her Majesty's Household Division.

The museum opened in 1988 and tells the story of the Guards' regiments from the 17th century to the present day. Displays include different Guards' uniforms chronicling the evolving dress over 350 years, paintings, weapons, models, sculptures and artefacts such as mess silver. The collection is intended as an educational aid to help young Guardsmen learn about their regimental heritage and to show a wider audience the multi-faceted nature of the Guards' operational lives, both in combat and on ceremonial duties.

The engrossing Guards Museum also has a delightful shop, known as 'The Guards Toy Soldier Centre'.

36　HANDEL HOUSE MUSEUM

Address: 25 Brook Street, W1K 4HB (☎ 020-7495 1685, 🖥 handelhouse.org).
Opening hours: Tue, Wed, Fri and Sat, 10am to 6pm; Thu 10am to 8pm; Sun noon to 6pm. Closed Mondays, including Bank Holidays.
Cost: £6 adults, £5 concessions, £2 children 5-16 (free at weekends), under-5s free.
Transport: Bond Street tube.
Amenities: Wheelchair access.

This finely restored Grade I listed Georgian building was home to noted baroque composer George Frederic Handel (1685-1759) from 1723 until his death. Handel was the first occupant of what was then a new house, and this is London's only museum to a composer. It's where Handel composed some of his greatest works, including *Messiah*, *Zadok the Priest* and *Music for the Royal Fireworks*.

The house celebrates the composer and his work with concerts, special events and regular exhibitions, all designed to 'bring Handel's world to life'. There's an impressive display of Handel-related items, including the Byrne Collection which includes books, letters, early editions of operas and oratorios, portraits and sculpture. As can be seen from some portraits, Handel was a man with a healthy appetite.

Concerts (☎ 020-7399 1953 or see website) are staged at the museum on Thursdays at 6.30pm (tickets £9, £5 for students).

Handel

HOUSEHOLD CAVALRY MUSEUM 37

Address: Horse Guards, Whitehall, SW1A 2AX (☎ 020 7930 3070, 🖳 householdcavalrymuseum.co.uk).
Opening hours: Daily, 10am to 6pm (March to September), 10am to 5pm (October to February). Closed Good Friday and 24-26th December.
Cost: £6 adults, £4 concessions and children aged 5-16, £15 families (max. 2 adults and 3 children).
Transport: Westminster or Embankment tube or Charing Cross tube/rail.
Amenities: Shop, wheelchair access.

The Household Cavalry Museum is a unique living museum – about real people doing a real job in a real place. Unlike other military museums, it offers a rare 'behind-the-scenes' look at the ceremonial and operational roles of the Household Cavalry Regiment (you can even see troopers working with horses in the original 18th-century stables through a large glazed partition). The experience is brought to life through personal stories, first-hand accounts of the troopers' rigorous training and rare objects.

Over the centuries the Household Cavalry has amassed an outstanding collection of unique treasures from ceremonial uniforms and gallantry awards, to musical instruments, and silverware by Fabergé. Modern additions include Jacky Charlton's football cap (he did his national service with the regiment)

and Sefton's bridle – the horse that was injured in the 1982 Hyde Park bombings.

Much of the collection has resulted from the close association between the Household Cavalry and royalty, whom the regiment has protected from rebels, rioters and assassins for over 300 years.

38   POLISH INSTITUTE & SIKORSKI MUSEUM

Address: 20 Prince's Gate, SW7 1PT (☎ 020-7589 9249, 🖳 pism.co.uk and sikorskimuseum.co.uk).
Opening hours: Tue-Fri, 2-4pm. First Sat of the month, 10.30am to 4pm. Closed February.
Cost: Free.
Transport: Knightsbridge or South Kensington tube.
Amenities: No wheelchair access.

The Polish Institute and Sikorski Museum was created after the Second World War to preserve the memory of Polish armed forces in the West and their contribution to the allied victory, an undertaking which was impossible at that time in Poland due to the Russian occupation. The Institute is named after General Wladyslaw Sikorski (1881-1943), military and political leader, and Prime Minister of the Polish Government in Exile during the war. General Sikorski died in a plane crash in 1943, and his widow Helena donated her husband's papers and memorabilia to the Institute, which was created on 2nd May 1945 and named in Sikorski's memory. The institute acted as a museum, archive and publishing house for much of Western Polonia, particularly with regard to war issues.

The Sikorski Museum is a small museum but what it lacks in size it makes up for in character. It contains thousands of photographs, documents and Second World War artefacts, plus rare exhibits relating to the Napoleonic era, 18th-century Polish armour (Winged Hussars) and regimental colours from 1918-1946.

39   ROYAL GEOGRAPHICAL SOCIETY

Address: Lowther Lodge, 1 Kensington Gore, SW7 2AR (☎ 020-7591 3000, 🖳 rgs.org/whatson).
Opening hours: Pavilion, Mon-Fri, 10am to 5pm and during exhibitions. Closed on Public Holidays and between Christmas and New Year.
Cost: Free, including exhibitions.
Transport: Kensington, Knightsbridge or South Kensington tube.
Amenities: Wheelchair access.

The Geographical Society of London was founded in 1830 to promote the advancement of geographical science. Like many learned societies at the time, it began life as a dining club. Under the patronage of William IV, it later became known as the Royal Geographical Society (RGS) and was granted a Royal Charter by Queen Victoria in 1859. It moved in 1913 to Lowther Lodge (Grade II* listed), an important example of

Victorian Queen Anne architecture with Gothic influences.

The Society's work includes publishing, supporting field research and expeditions, lectures, conferences and its collections. It has supported many famous explorers, including Charles Darwin, Sir Edmund Hillary, David Livingstone and Ernest Shackleton, and some pioneering expedition reports are among its treasures. Today the Society has 15,000 members and fellows and a collection of over 2m documents, maps, photographs, paintings, periodicals, artefacts and books, spanning 500 years of geography, travel and exploration.

It organises over 150 events across London each year, many open to the public, including exhibitions in the Pavilion and the Foyle Reading Room.

ROYAL MEWS   40

Address: Buckingham Palace, SW1W 1QH (☎ 020-7766 7302, 🖥 royalcollection. org.uk/visit/royalmews).
Opening hours: 30th March to 31st October, daily 10am to 5pm; 1st November to 20th December and 1st Feb to 29th March, Mon-Sat 10am to 4pm. Closed 22nd to 31st December and during state visits and royal events.
Cost: £8.25 adults, £7.50 concessions, £5.20 under 17s, under 5s free, £22 families (2 adults, 3 under 17s).
Transport: Green Park or Hyde Park Corner tube or Victoria tube/rail.
Amenities: Wheelchair access, shop.

Home to the Queen's horses, carriages and cars, the Royal Mews is one of the busiest parts of the Royal household. Located just behind Buckingham Palace, it houses the state carriages and cars, as well as the horses that play such an important role in the Royal Family's ceremonial and personal life. The main part of the Mews – the stables, clock tower and coach houses – was designed by John Nash in 1825 as part of George IV's upgrade of Buckingham Palace. There was room for 54 horses, although Queen Victoria had as many as 200 horses at the Mews, while Prince Albert also kept cows there!

Many eye-catching royal carriages are kept at the Mews, including the Gold State Coach. Richly gilded and weighing four tons, it was built in 1762 and has been used at every coronation since George IV. A more familiar sight is the 1902 State Landau, an elegant open-topped carriage which was made for Edward VII's coronation and conveys the Queen during state visits. More unusual modes of transport include Queen Victoria's State Sledge (but there are no royal reindeer!).

41 ROYAL OPERA HOUSE COLLECTIONS & TOURS

Address: Bow Street, Covent Garden, WC2E 9DD (☎ 020-7304 4000,
🖳 rohcollections.org.uk/exhibitions.aspx and roh.org.uk/whatson/tour.aspx).
Opening hours: Exhibitions, Mon-Fri, 10am to 3.30pm. For information about
'Backstage' (1¼ hrs) and 'Velvet, Gilt and Glamour' (¾ hr) tours, see website.
Cost: Backstage Tour £12 adults, £11, seniors/students, £8.50 under-16s; Velvet,
Gilt and Glamour Tour £9.50 (enquire about concessions).
Transport: Covent Garden tube.
Amenities: Two restaurants, two bars, shop, wheelchair access.

The Royal Opera House (ROH) has a fascinating history, with the first opera house being constructed in 1732. The current (3rd) theatre was designed by Edward Middleton Barry (1830-1880) and dates from 1858, although only the façade, foyer and auditorium (Grade I listed) are original, following extensive reconstruction in the '90s.

The ROH Collections celebrate the history of the ROH, with a constantly changing programme commemorating anniversaries and significant events, as well as the companies and the building itself. Each season, two main exhibitions fill the costume cases and the amphitheatre gallery for six months each, and can be freely viewed by visitors.

The ROH 'Velvet, Gilt and Glamour Tour' (4pm most days) commences at the highest part of the auditorium, where you can admire the rich red curtains of the stage, the stunning ceiling, the glittering gold of the proscenium arch, and the red and gold lights which replaced the old gas lamps. The 'Backstage Tour' visits the backstage and front of house areas and includes insight into the redevelopment of the ROH and a look at aspects of its current productions.

Margot Fonteyn & Rudolf Nureyev

SPENCER HOUSE

Address: 27 St James's Place, SW1A 1NR (☏ 020-7499 8620, 🖥 spencerhouse.co.uk).

Opening hours: Tours (1 hr) on Sundays (except January and August), 10.30am to 5.45pm, by timed ticket, which can only be purchased in person from 10.30am.

Cost: £12 adults, £10 concessions (students, seniors and under 16s). Children aged under ten aren't admitted.

Transport: Green Park tube.

Amenities: Garden, Wheelchair access.

According to the website, this is 'London's most magnificent private palace'. It's undoubtedly one of the capital's best examples of a Palladian mansion, conceived as a showcase of classical design, but it was also meant for pleasure, and the festive theme running through the decoration of the many state rooms provides a visual treat.

The house was built in 1756-66 for the Spencer family by the neo-classical architect John Vardy (he was replaced in 1758 by James 'Athenian' Stuart, who did the interiors). The first Earl Spencer – an ancestor of the late Diana, Princess of Wales – and his wife were prominent society figures, and the house hosted lavish entertainments.

Spencer House was one of London's first examples of the neo-classical style that was to sweep the country, and it's one of the last remaining of the many private palaces that once adorned central London. It's a splendid illustration of 18th-century aristocratic taste, lavishly furnished with period paintings (including some by Reynolds), *objets d'art* and furniture, with a number of exquisite state rooms open to the public.

CITY & EAST LONDON

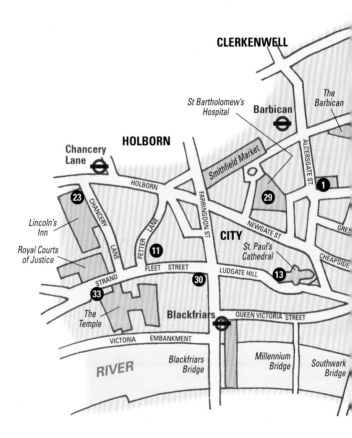

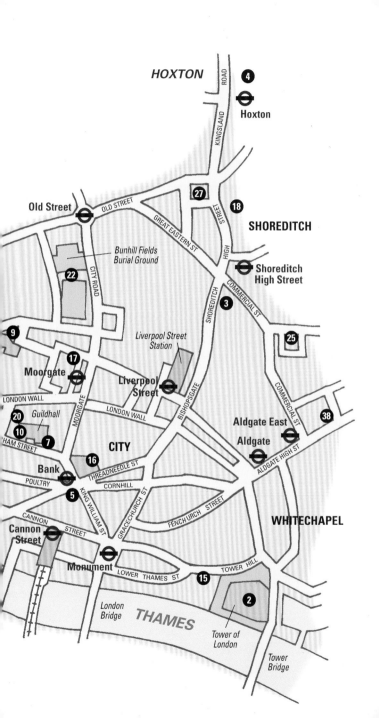

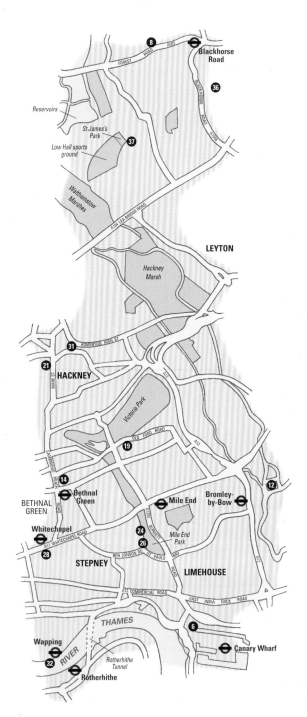

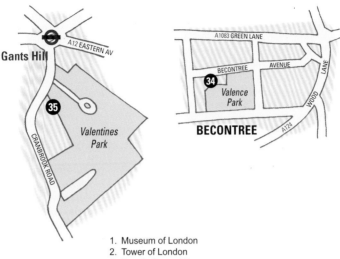

1. Museum of London
2. Tower of London
3. Dennis Severs' House
4. Geffrye Museum
5. Mansion House
6. Museum of London Docklands
7. Roman London's Amphitheatre & Guildhall Art Gallery
8. William Morris Gallery
9. Barbican Art Gallery
10. Clockmakers' Museum
11. Dr Johnson's House
12. House Mill Museum
13. St Paul's Cathedral Crypt
14. Victoria & Albert Museum of Childhood
15. All Hallows by The Tower & Crypt Museum
16. Bank of England Museum
17. British Red Cross Museum
18. Calvert 22 Foundation
19. Chisenhale Gallery
20. City of London Police Museum
21. Hackney Museum
22. Honourable Artillery Company Museum
23. Inns of Court & City Yeomanry Museum
24. Matt's Gallery
25. Museum of Immigration & Diversity
26. Ragged School Museum
27. Rivington Place Gallery
28. Royal London Hospital Museum
29. St Bartholomew's Hospital Museum
30. St Bride's Crypt
31. Sutton House
32. Thames River Police Museum
33. Twinings Museum
34. Valence House Museum
35. Valentines Mansion
36. Vestry House Museum
37. Walthamstow Pumphouse Museum
38. Whitechapel Gallery

1   MUSEUM OF LONDON

Address: 150 London Wall, EC2Y 5HN (☎ 020-7001 9844, 🖳 museumoflondon.
org.uk/london-wall).
Opening hours: Daily, 10am to 6pm. Closed 24-26th December.
Cost: Free, although a £3 donation is suggested. There's a fee for some special
events and temporary exhibitions.
Transport: Barbican or St Paul's tube.
Amenities: Two cafés, shop, wheelchair access.

The Museum of London is the largest urban history museum in the world and although it's primarily concerned with the social history of London, it also maintains its archaeological interests. The history begins before you even enter the museum – fragments of the original London Wall from Roman times are just outside – and once through the doors, your journey takes you along a timeline from Neanderthal man to city slicker. Even Londoners admit that they leave the museum with new knowledge of their city and visitors to the capital couldn't choose a better place to start.

The Museum of London is an amalgamation of two earlier museums: the Guildhall Museum, founded in 1826, and the London Museum, founded in 1912. The Guildhall Museum was largely archaeological, its first acquisition being a fragment of Roman mosaic, while the London Museum had wider interests, collecting modern objects, paintings and costumes, alongside archaeology.

Both collections came together after the Second World War and the new Museum of London opened in 1976. The architects were Philip Powell and Hidalgo Moya, who adopted an innovative approach to museum design, whereby the galleries were laid out so that there was only one route through the museum. The museum underwent a £20m redesign in 2010, breathing new life into the permanent galleries and increasing the space by a quarter, allowing a further 7,000 objects to be displayed.

London Before London Gallery

The permanent galleries each present a different chronological period in London life.

ALLOW...

You can spend at least a day, and preferably longer, at the Museum of London. On a short visit, you can take one of the regular free gallery tours (½ hr) which take place Sun-Fri on the hour between 11am and 4pm, and on Saturdays at noon, 3pm and 4pm. Ask for details at the information desk.

Level 1

On the entrance level, the galleries cover the time from prehistory to the 1660s. Highlights include the following:

London Before London: This gallery goes back 450,000 years to explore the Thames valley up until the Romans arrived, and tells how the river shaped the land and how a handful of inhabitants carved out an existence around it. Interesting exhibits include the remains of the Shepperton woman who lived over 5,000 years ago.

Roman London: From 50 to 410 AD, the Romans built Londinium into the largest city and most important port in Britannia. The gallery recreates Roman rooms and shows some of the objects they left behind – coins, ceramics and even a leather bikini. Many were unearthed during building work in the City of London, such as the marble sculptures from the Temple of Mithras.

Medieval London: Over a millennium of London life is captured here, from Saxons, Vikings and Norman invaders to the golden age of the Tudors under Elizabeth I. Displays take in key events such as the re-founding of Lundenburg in 886 by King Alfred and the Black Death which wiped out half the population in 1348.

Medieval London

Interesting objects include a gold and garnet brooch from the mid-600s found buried in a grave in Covent Garden and a toy knight made from pewter which was played with around 1300.

War, Plague & Fire: A tumultuous period from the 1550s to the 1660s is the focus of this gallery, which takes in the Civil War (1642-51), the Great Plague of 1665 and the Great Fire of 1666, which destroyed a third of the city. London was growing beyond its city walls and becoming

Great Fire of London

wealthy, and some of the museum's greatest treasures are from the Cheapside Hoard, a cache of some 500 gemstones and jewellery from Elizabethan and Jacobean times found buried under a floor in a building in Cheapside. Look out also for Oliver Cromwell's death mask and a reconstruction of Shakespeare's Rose Theatre.

Level 2

Walk up to the next level for the new Modern London galleries, which include:

Expanding City: This gallery looks at the development of London between 1666 and the 1850s as its influence in the world grew, attracting the first waves of immigrants and importing exotic goods from the burgeoning British Empire. A 240-year-old printing press illustrates the rise in communications and technology,

while a recreation of Georgian pleasure gardens shows how Londoners amused themselves, and an 18th-century prison cell reveals what happened to those who stepped out of line.

👁 DON'T MISS!

The Rhinebeck Panorama is an extraordinary bird's-eye view of London painted in the early 1800s, which was discovered in a barrel in the US city of Rhinebeck, New York (hence the name). It's preserved under a glass walkway in the Expanding City gallery on Level 2.

People's City: In the years between the 1850s and 1940s, London's rich got richer while its poor got poorer (twas ever thus). This gallery illustrates the divisions between the two and the wider conflicts of the time. Seek out Charles Booth's Poverty Map of London, which is reproduced as an interactive map so you can see how much districts such as Fulham and Greenwich have changed since the late 1880s. A much wealthier London is illustrated by an Art Deco lift from Selfridges' department store in 1928.

World City: From the '50s onwards, this gallery reveals a city characterised by youth and diversity, featuring modern icons such as a Vespa scooter, Apple Mac computer and fashion from Mary Quant to Alexander McQueen.

The City Gallery: This celebrates the City of London itself, through displays that showcase the area's unique character, a place where ancient traditions exist

Expanding city

Dress and Fashion

Nursery Garden

alongside cutting edge architecture. Its centrepiece is the magnificent Lord Mayor's Coach, commissioned in 1757 for the Lord Mayor's Show and still used annually.

A changing programme of free exhibitions showcase creative talent in London, and there are also major presentations: London's Lost Jewels: The Mystery of the Cheapside Hoard opens in 2013. Participation events include everything from cookery workshops to walks, and there are courses and groups relating to London's history and archaeology for adults of all ages and interests. Children are also well catered for.

At the centre of the museum, the Sackler Hall is a large, contemporary hub that provides a space for rest and refreshment, and a bank of computers which let you explore the museum's 1m-plus objects. You can also do this before you visit via the museum's website (museumoflondon.org. uk/collections-research/collections-online).

 FOOD & DRINK

Museum Café: There are two to choose from, or you can bring your own sandwiches and eat them in the lunch space near the entrance.

London Wall Bar & Kitchen: Next door to the museum is this Benugo-owned restaurant (a percentage of your bill goes to the museum), serving favourites such as pork chop with spiced salt & rosemary potatoes, seared tuna salad and chocolate fudge cake. Open from lunchtime to 11pm (020-7600 7340).

2 TOWER OF LONDON

Address: Tower Hill, EC3N 4AB (☎ 020-3166 6000, ⌨ hrp.org.uk/toweroflondon).
Opening hours: Tue-Sat, 9am to 5.30pm; Sun-Mon, 10am to 5.30pm (4.30pm November to February). Closed 24-26th December and 1st January.
Cost: £20.90 adults, £17.60 concessions, £10.95 under-16s, under-5s free, £55 families (up to 6 children). Tickets are slightly cheaper when purchased online (and circumvent queues!).
Transport: Tower Hill tube or by riverboat to Tower Pier.
Amenities: Two restaurants, café, kiosk, bar, five shops, limited wheelchair access.

Palace, fortress, armoury, treasury and prison, the Tower of London has performed many roles since it was built in 1078 by William the Conqueror. He intended it to be a symbol of his power to overawe the 'huge and brutal populace' of his newly-conquered London. Almost 1,000 years later the Tower is still an awesome sight, attracting some 2.5m people a year and the UK's most popular historic attraction.

A UNESCO World Heritage Site since 1988, the Tower of London is undeniably drenched in history, much of it of the dark and bloody variety. It's where Anne Boleyn and Katherine Howard lost their heads to Henry VIII – a memorial marks the spot of the executioner's block on Tower Green – and where Edward IV's two young sons were allegedly murdered by Richard III.

 ALLOW...

The website (⌨ hrp.org.uk/toweroflondon) recommends spending at least three hours at the Tower and makes suggestions of what to see if you have only an hour or two to spare. Allow for queues at busy times (buy tickets online) to see major attractions, such as the Crown Jewels.

For the first 500 years or so, the Tower was a royal residence and centre of administration. Its image as a place of imprisonment comes from Tudor times and later, and among the many well-known figures 'sent to the Tower' were Elizabeth I, Sir Walter Raleigh, Guy Fawkes and even East End gangsters Ronnie and Reggie Kray. Most escaped with their lives. Although executions were a regular event on Tower Hill, only seven prisoners were afforded the 'privilege' of being put to death on Tower Green. (During the First and Second World Wars, it again became a prison, and witnessed the executions of 12 men for espionage.)

Beefeater

 DON'T MISS!

St Thomas's Tower is home to the Medieval Palace and a recreation of Edward I's bedchamber, which reveals the high degree of luxury medieval monarchs enjoyed during their stays at the Tower.

The Tower refers to the White Tower, the keep at the heart of the castle, although it has become the catch-all name for the entire complex which includes over 20 towers! The White Tower, so called because Henry III ordered it whitewashed, has been described as 'the most complete 11th-century palace in Europe' and at 90ft (27m) tall, it dominated the London skyline. The rest of the castle grew up around it as a series of walls; towers and a moat were added by later monarchs – Richard I, Henry III and Edward I – in the 12th and 13th centuries. Its layout today is much as it was in the 1300s, not least because Victorian architects focused on restoring its medieval splendour at the cost of later additions.

The Tower has been a tourist attraction since at least the Elizabethan era, when people visited to see the Royal Menagerie and displays of armour, while the Crown Jewels have been on public display since 1669. Today's Tower is more notorious for its coach parties and high prices, but there's still plenty to captivate anyone with an interest in English history. Highlights include the following:

Beefeaters: Royal bodyguards since the early 16th century, the Yeoman of the Guard (their nickname comes from the fact that their lofty position allowed them to eat as much beef as they wanted from the king's table) are the curators of the Tower. All are former serving soldiers and their responsibilities include assisting visitors, caring for the ravens (see below) and ensuring that the Tower is secure – it's still locked each night in the 'Ceremony of the Keys' which dates back to the 14th century. Yeoman Warders are the Tower's tour guides and their hour-long tours, which leave every 30 minutes from the main entrance, don't stint on the grislier aspects of its history.

Crown Jewels: British monarchs have stored their wealth in the Tower since the late 11th century and the

Crown jewels

Royal Regiment of Fusiliers, and its museum (☎ 020-7488 5610, 🖥 fusiliermuseumlondon.org). The Royal Fusiliers regiment was formed at the Tower in 1685 by James II – the first time a company had been granted the title 'Royal' – and took its name from a new type of musket (the fusil). It has fought in almost every major campaign in the last 350 years, and in 1968 joined three other Fusilier regiments to form the Royal Regiment of Fusiliers. The museum tells the regiment's story through the experiences of individual soldiers, recorded in a rich archive of war diaries and personal letters, while its diverse collection includes 12 Victoria Cross medals and the bearskin of George V, a former Colonel-in-Chief.

Crown Jewels are now on dazzling display in the (heavily fortified) Jewel House in the Waterloo Block. They include the Sovereign's Sceptre with Cross which is adorned with the 530.2 carat Cullinan I diamond – the largest colourless cut diamond in the world – and the solid-gold St Edward's Crown which is used to crown monarchs at Westminster Abbey. Almost all the treasures date from 1661 onwards as the original Crown Jewels were destroyed by Oliver Cromwell and had to be remade for Charles II's coronation.

Fusilier Museum: The Tower is home to the headquarters of the

Ravens & Other Beasts: There's a legend that the Tower and kingdom will fall if the six resident ravens ever leave, which is unlikely as the birds have had their wings clipped. They are cared for by the Ravenmaster and fed daily on raw meat, and can be spotted patrolling their empire like VIPs. They are the remnants of a Royal Menagerie which once held captive exotic species such as lions, monkeys and (possibly)

a polar bear which, it's said, would go fishing in the Thames. Don't miss the excellent exhibition, Royal Beasts, in the Brick Tower, which tells the story of this cruel and unusual zoo.

White Tower: Worth seeing for its own intriguing history, the Tower also hosts exhibitions by the Royal Armouries. 'Fit for a King' presents 500 years of royal armour and includes several suits of armour made for Henry VIII – when he was young and fit and, later, old and fat – as well as elaborate armour worn by horses. There's also an exhibition called Power House which showcases major institutions at the Tower, including the Ordnance Office which controlled the supply of arms, the Royal Mint which minted coins until the 19th century, and the Constable of the Tower who ran the castle on the monarch's behalf.

You can escape the crowds and get a good sense of the castle's proportions by walking along its walls. Along the way there's a chance to explore some of the many other towers, such as the Bloody Tower, where the Princes were held, and the Beauchamp Tower with its prisoners' graffiti. You can also see the castle's defences, including replica siege engines used to repel invaders. The Chapel of St Peter ad Vincula provides somewhere for quiet contemplation, and is the last resting place of some of the queens and courtiers who met their end at the Tower.

With such a colourful history, it's a great place to bring children and there are plenty of interactive games (some can be played online). But be warned – there are no fewer than five shops selling everything from Crown 'jewels' to toy Beefeaters, so it's likely to be an expensive if memorable day out.

FOOD & DRINK

New Armouries Restaurant: Snacks, mains and children's choices inspired by famous London food markets (housed in a building once used to store military hardware).

Raven's Kiosk: Outdoor café selling drinks, sandwiches and bite-size bangers and mash. Mind you don't feed any to the ravens – they bite!

3 DENNIS SEVERS' HOUSE

> **Address:** 18 Folgate Street, Spitalfields, E1 6BX (☎ 020-7247 4013, 💻 dennissevershouse.co.uk).
>
> **Opening hours**: Sundays, noon to 4pm; Mondays following the first and third Sundays of the month, noon to 2pm. Evening candlelit tours on Mondays and some Wednesdays, 6-9pm (bookings necessary – see website). There are also evening tours and extended opening hours over Christmas.
>
> **Cost**: £7 Monday lunchtime, £10 Sunday, evening tours from £14.
>
> **Transport**: Liverpool Street tube/rail.
>
> **Amenities:** No wheelchair access (ground floor only).

This is one of London's most singular, intriguing attractions, in one of its most magical properties. Part exhibition, part installation, it's a work of fantasy, designed to create an atmosphere redolent of the 18th century and paint a picture of what life was like then.

It's the brainchild of an American artist, Dennis Severs, who purchased the house in the '70s, when the old Huguenot district of Spitalfields was rundown and little valued, unlike today when parts of it have been gentrified and it's home to artistic and literary luminaries such as Tracey Emin and Jeanette Winterson.

 ALLOW...

A visit to Dennis Severs' House takes around 45 minutes, according to the website. If you want to spend longer, the 'exclusive silent night' tour lasts about one and a half hours and includes time to sit and sip a glass of champagne in a room of your choice (unlikely to be the garret).

Severs began to live in the house as he imagined its original inhabitants would have done, and spent a lot of time in (and slept in) every room in order to 'harvest the atmosphere'. As a result, he gradually gave life to an invented family, whose imagined lives became a detailed 'still life drama' for visitors to experience. They're a family of Huguenot silk weavers – the Jervis family – invisible but very much present in Folgate Street.

Severs filled the house with period fittings and furniture, as well as authentic smells and sounds, to create a genuine atmosphere. Each of the house's ten rooms reflects a different era of the building's past – a snapshot of the life of the family who 'lived' here between 1724 and 1914. Dennis Severs died in 1999, but the house has been preserved and is open for tours.

Your exploration begins in the cellar, moves up to the kitchen and takes in the rest of the house, room by room. Along the way it reveals the lives of different generations of the Jervises:

the prosperous Georgian family in the well-appointed first floor rooms, the Victorian weavers surviving in the squalid garret. How you experience the journey very much depends on your imagination, for each room appears as if the occupant(s) have just left it, leaving such clues as a half-eaten plate of food, a discarded wig or a full chamber pot. Severs' motto for the house was 'You either see it or you don't' and your visit is a very personal experience.

You're 'instructed' to remain quiet during the tour – Severs was known to eject visitors who talked too much – and touching objects isn't encouraged; as such it's the antithesis of a modern hands-on museum and isn't ideal for younger children. Some find this attitude a little precious on the part of those running the house, while others find it healthy in our noisy era when people seem incapable of concentrating for more than 30 seconds.

The atmosphere of a bygone age is best maintained if you refrain from looking out of the windows – which allow the 21st century to intrude – and the night-time, candlelit (and most expensive) tours are the most atmospheric, especially those which take place around Christmas.

 FOOD & DRINK

The Water Poet: Boho pub serving gastro grub such as Razor clams in cider and grilled calves' liver, with a reputation for serving a fine Sunday lunch – just across the road from Dennis Severs' House.

Spitalfields Market: From Carluccio's to Giraffe, there's a wide choice of eateries at this trendy market place.

4 GEFFRYE MUSEUM

Address: Kingsland Road, Hackney, E2 8EA (☎ 020-7739 9893, 🖥 geffrye-museum.org.uk).
Opening hours: Tue-Sat, 10am to 5pm; Sundays and Bank Holiday Mondays, noon to 5pm. Closed Good Friday, 24-26th December and 1st January. Gardens closed 1st November to 31st March. A restored alms house is open on selected Saturdays, Tuesdays and Wednesdays (see website).
Cost: Museum and gardens free. Tour of the alms house, £2.50 adults (under-16s free).
Transport: Hoxton rail.
Amenities: Restaurant, shop, gardens, wheelchair access.

The Geffrye Museum of the Home and its tranquil gardens are something of a haven in the scruffy clutter of Hackney, with its heavy traffic, Turkish shops and Vietnamese eateries. This corner of the borough has not yet been gentrified and is the last place you'd expect to find a museum devoted to the history of British middle-class interior design.

From furniture and textiles to paintings and decorative arts, the Geffrye traces the changing style of domestic interiors from 1600 to the present day. The museum is named after Sir Robert Geffrye (1613 to 1703), former Lord Mayor of London and Master of the Ironmongers' Company. Under his bequest, 14 alms houses were built in 1715, mainly for the widows of ironmongers. A decision to relocate the residents to a more salubrious part of London in the early 20th century left the houses in danger of demolition. A petition to save the site was successful and in 1914 it reopened as a furniture museum.

 DON'T MISS!

It's well worth timing your visit for a day when the restored 18th-century alms house is open. It recreates two rooms from the 18th and 19th centuries, with the stark simplicity of the 1780s room in complete contrast to the genteel clutter on show 100 years later.

Today, the Geffrye Museum occupies both the alms houses – now Grade I listed – and a modern wing which provides space to display current design and temporary exhibitions, as well as a shop and restaurant.

The period rooms are the main draw. There are 11 in total – plus an alms house open on selected days – and all are based on real London houses and show remarkable attention to detail. They range from a late Jacobean hall, via Georgian parlours and Victorian drawing rooms, to a loft-style apartment from '90s London,

Drawing room 1830

20th centuries, and a walled herb garden with more than 170 kinds of herb. The gardens are designed to reflect the key features of middle-class town gardens over the centuries.

The museum's comprehensive website provides a brief virtual tour of each of the 11 rooms and five gardens, as well as allowing you to search the collection, so that you can do your homework before you visit.

🍴 FOOD & DRINK 🍴

Geffrye Museum Restaurant: Contemporary English food including a variety of vegetarian dishes, home-made soups, bagels and brownies, with a glorious view of the gardens.
   Song Que Café: Popular Vietnamese eatery in nearby (no.134) Kingsland Road, serving classic beef noodle soup, as well as bargain lunch options starting from just £5.90 (💻 songque.co.uk).

---

revealing as much about social change as our attitudes to décor. The earliest room presents the hall as the main living room of the Stuart house, where the family (and servants) congregated to eat, entertain, relax and do business. Half a century later, even the middle classes had moved into the privacy of the parlour.

The rooms also reveal how design ideas are being constantly recycled. The 1790 parlour is decorated with the first wallpaper which wouldn't look out of place in a modern living room. The neat horizontal lines of the '30s mansion block flat echo the simplicity of the Georgian parlour, and the plain wooden floors in the 1998 warehouse conversion hark back to more austere Stuart times. Music and readings from the relevant period add to the atmosphere.

In addition, there are regular exhibitions about subjects relating to the museum's displays, as well as seminars, workshops, drama and music. See website for the current programme of events.

The museum also has four period gardens, depicting garden design, layout and planting from the 17th to

A living room in 1965

5 MANSION HOUSE

Address: Walbrook, EC4N 8BH (☎ 020-7626 2500, 🖥 cityoflondon.gov.uk/about-the-city > Tours of Mansion House).

Opening hours: Guided tours (1hr) on a first-come first-served basis on certain Tuesdays at 2pm (check website for details). Also open (free) during the annual Open House London weekend (see 🖥 londonopenhouse.org).

Cost: Tours £6 adults, £4 concessions; group tours by arrangement.

Transport: Bank tube.

Amenities: Wheelchair access.

The Mansion House is a City gem – a rare surviving grand Georgian town palace which is well worth a visit. It's the official residence of the Lord Mayor of the City of London, and houses the Lord Mayor's private office, a department of the City of London Corporation, as well as providing a centre for business meetings, conferences, banquets and entertaining. (The Lord Mayor is elected for one year, the position being unpaid and apolitical, not to be confused with the Mayor of London, which is a paid, elected, political position with a four-year term.)

The Mansion House has magnificent interiors and elegant furniture, and is used for a number of the City's grandest official functions, including an annual dinner hosted by the Lord Mayor, at which the Chancellor of the Exchequer gives his 'Mansion House Speech' about the state of the British economy.

 ALLOW...

Guided tours take an hour and are led by trained City of London Guides. Tours leave from the A-board near the porch entrance to Mansion House in Walbrook (exit 8 from Bank tube station).

Until the mid-18th century, the Lord Mayor was based at his own

Egyptian Hall

Among the Mansion House's treasures, is a magnificent collection of gold and silver plate – one of the best in the world and still used on ceremonial occasions – as well as one of the finest art collections outside London's

lodgings or livery hall, but after the Great Fire of 1666 it was decided to erect a permanent mayoral 'home'. The Mansion House was eventually built between 1739 and 1752 by the architect George Dance the Elder on the site of a former livestock market. Its location, on a junction shared with the Royal Exchange and Bank of England, is at the very heart of Roman London.

The design is a classical Palladian style with ornate gold trim, Corinthian columns and a grand Egyptian Hall (seating 350) on the first floor. The hall isn't Egyptian in style, but is based on designs of Roman buildings in Egypt by the classical Roman architect Vitruvius, a style which was very much in vogue in the 18th century. Other important rooms include the Drawing Rooms which hold some of the Samuel Art Collection (see below) and the elegant Long Parlour. The second floor houses a ballroom and the private apartments of the Lord Mayor and his/her family, while the third and fourth floors contain meeting rooms and staff rooms.

The Mansion House also served as a City jail and was the venue for the Lord Mayor's court, which was held in its Justice Room. Prisoners were held in cells in the cellars, where famous defendants included the suffragette Emmeline Pankhurst who was an early campaigner for women's rights.

public art galleries. This includes the Harold Samuel Art Collection which comprises 84 Dutch and Flemish paintings by 17th-century masters such as Frans Hals, Nicoleas Maes, Jacob Ruisdael and Jan Steen. Bequeathed to the City in 1987, it's probably the best collection of Dutch art in Britain and adds further splendour to the Mansion House's interior.

DON'T MISS!

When visiting the Salon, take time to admire the magnificent lead crystal chandeliers, made by F&C Osler in 1875, which – according to the craftsmen who clean and maintain them – are unmatched in their quality and clarity. Amazingly, the Mansion Hall once shared a previous set of chandeliers with the Guildhall and they were moved back and forth for important occasions – a risky undertaking which resulted in some disastrous breakages.

HM The Queen with the Lord Mayor

6 MUSEUM OF LONDON DOCKLANDS

Address: West India Quay, Canary Wharf, E14 4AL (☎ 020-7001 9844,
🖥 museumindocklands.org.uk).
Opening hours: Daily, 10am to 6pm. Closed 24-26th December.
Cost: Free.
Transport: Canary Wharf tube or West India Quay DLR.
Amenities: Restaurant/bar, café, shop, wheelchair access.

Located on the Isle of Dogs (a former island in East London, now bounded on three sides by one of the largest meanders in the River Thames), this used to be called the Museum in Docklands. This was appropriate, as the museum is housed in a Grade I listed Georgian 'low' sugar warehouse, built in 1802, and the Isle of Dogs was at the heart of London's docks, home to the West India Docks, East India Docks and Millwall Dock. The three dock systems were unified in 1909 when the Port of London Authority took control of them.

👁 DON'T MISS!

A collection of stunning paintings by war artist William Ware (1915-97) illustrates how heavily the docks were targeted by the German Luftwaffe during the Blitz in 1940. See them in the Docklands at War 1939-1945 gallery on the second floor.

At the heart of the Museum of London Docklands collection is the museum and archives of the Port Authority. And while it's somewhat overshadowed by its better-known big brother, the Museum of London (one of the world's largest urban history museums), the Docklands branch is well worth visiting.

Its collections cover the period from the first port of London in Roman times to the closure of the docks in the '70s and the area's subsequent redevelopment. It shows how the Thames became an international gateway, bringing invaders, merchants and immigrants to one of the world's longest serving ports. It delivers a real sense of how crucial the Thames has been to the growth of London, and explores the social and economic significance of the port of London, once the world's busiest port.

It's a large museum, with 12 permanent galleries, including a children's gallery, and is modern and contemporary in its approach, using all the latest techniques, including videos presented by Tony Robinson (the excitable host of Channel 4's archaeological TV programme *Time Team*).

There are lots of historical objects, models and pictures, with impressive displays and exhibits, including a scale model of Old London Bridge, showing its development from medieval to Tudor times (in the Thames Highway gallery), and a walk-through of one of Wapping's 19th-century streets, which portrays an area described in Victorian times as 'both foul and picturesque' (Sailortown). And it doesn't pull its punches by avoiding difficult subjects. The West India Docks were built from the proceeds of the sugar industry and were a base for the international slave trade, and there's a permanent gallery on the subject called London, Sugar & Slavery.

Elsewhere, there are fascinating objects such as the jawbones of whales caught by Thames-based whalers in the 16th century, a gibbet cage which was used to hang pirates in the 1700s and a consul shelter where wardens could hide from bombs during the Blitz. A cast iron column from one of the docks, melted out of shape, shows the intensity of the fires caused by Hitler's bombs.

The museum regularly hosts talks, temporary exhibitions and events related to the river and docks; for example, 2012 saw the introduction of Many East Ends, an exploration of the surrounding area. There's also a shop and restaurant, and the museum's close proximity to Canary Wharf means there's no shortage of alternative places to eat.

 ALLOW...

You need at least half a day to fully explore this museum, longer if you want to check out the surrounding quays and wharfs. To get a feel for the history of the Thames and its docks, it's best to travel to the museum by boat. Thames Clippers (🖥 thamesclippers.com) operate regular services from the London Eye/Embankment taking around 30 minutes.

7 ROMAN LONDON'S AMPHITHEATRE & GUILDHALL ART GALLERY

Address: Guildhall Yard (off Gresham Street), EC2V 5AE (☎ 020-7332 3700, ⌨ cityoflondon.gov.uk and enter 'Guildhall Gallery' into the search box).
Opening hours: Mon-Sat, 10am to 5pm, Sundays noon to 4pm. Closed 24-26th December and 1st January, and when civic functions are taking place (see website).
Cost: Free. There are fees for some exhibitions, e.g. £5 adults, £3 concessions, under-16s free.
Transport: Bank, Mansion House, Moorgate or St Paul's tube.
Amenities: Wheelchair access.

In 1988, the Museum of London made one of its most significant archaeological discoveries of recent years when it unearthed London's only Roman amphitheatre in Guildhall Yard. The City of London was keen to integrate the remains into its plans for a new art gallery, so excavations and building work took place at the same time, over six years.

The 'doors' to the amphitheatre re-opened in 2002, for the first time in nearly 2000 years. The surviving remains, which include a stretch of the stone entrance tunnel, east gate and arena walls, are protected in a controlled environment well below the modern pavement and within the Guildhall Art Gallery. It's an original and striking presentation which allows you to 'walk' among visible Roman remains. It also gives a good idea of the amphitheatre's scale, with the aid of digital technology, atmospheric lighting and sound effects. Outside, in the Guildhall Yard, a curved line of dark stone bricks marks the edge of the old amphitheatre, which was around 100m wide and would have held up to 7,000 people. As London's total population at the time was around 20,000, it was clearly a massively important venue!

The amphitheatre was originally built in 70 AD, from wood, and

Roman Amphitheatre

destroyed by fire during an air raid in 1941, which also saw the loss of more than 150 artworks. Undeterred, the City carried on staging annual exhibitions, including the Lord Mayor's Art Award and the City of London Art Exhibition, until it was decided in 1985 to redevelop the site.

The new gallery was designed by Richard Gilbert Scott, who had earlier worked on the Guildhall restoration. It opened in 1999 and displays around 250 of the collection's 4,000-plus works of art. The collection dates back to the 17th century but many works are from the Victorian era, and include paintings by Constable, Millais, Dante Gabriel Rossetti, Solomon, Poynter and Landseer, among others.

More recently, the City has concentrated on buying paintings that depict London subjects, such as the Great Fire in 1666 and the opening of Tower Bridge in 1894, as well as street scenes capturing City life.

renovated in the 2nd century, with proper walls and tiled entrances. It was used for various public displays including gladiatorial contests, executions and religious ceremonies. St Augustine, writing about a gladiatorial contest there, described it as 'seething with savage enthusiasm'. When the Romans left Britain in the 4th century, the amphitheatre lay neglected for centuries, and the area was only reoccupied in the mid-11th century. In the early 12th century, the first Guildhall (London's old administrative centre) was built a few yards to the north.

When you finish walking in the Romans' footsteps, take time to explore the Guildhall Art Gallery. The first gallery on the site was built in 1885 as a showcase for works collected by the City of London Corporation but was

---

 ALLOW...

A couple of hours should be enough to take in both sites. Free tours of the collection highlights and amphitheatre take place every Friday at 12.15, 1.15, 2.15 and 3.15pm, given by qualified City of London Guides and lasting approximately 45 minutes.

8 WILLIAM MORRIS GALLERY

Address: Lloyd Park, Forest Road, Walthamstow, E17 4PP (☎ 020-8496 4390, 🖳 wmgallery.org.uk).
Opening hours: Wed-Sun, 10am to 5pm. Closed over Christmas and New Year.
Cost: Free.
Transport: Walthamstow Central tube.
Amenities: Café, shop, wheelchair access.

William Morris

It's a superb example of Georgian domestic architecture dating from around 1744, once known as Water House, a nod to the ornamental moat at the back of the house where young Morris would fish and ice skate. A map from 1758 shows the building with its original east and west wings. Today, only the original west wing remains; the east wing was demolished in the early 1900s and a new extension has been built in its place to restore the building's symmetry. One of the finest exterior features is the Corinthian-style porch.

This is the only public gallery devoted to William Morris (1834-1896) – artist, designer, writer, socialist, conservationist, and father of the Arts and Crafts movement. Reopened in 2012 following a £5m redevelopment, its internationally important collection illustrates the life, achievements and influence of Morris and his contemporaries.

The gallery is housed in a substantial (Grade II* listed) Georgian dwelling which was the Morris family home from 1848 to 1856. William lived here with his widowed mother and eight siblings as a teenager and young man. The house and grounds were purchased in 1856 by the publisher Edward Lloyd (1815-1890), whose family donated it to the people of Walthamstow. Lloyd Park first opened to the public in 1900.

> **👁 DON'T MISS!**
>
> The *Kelmscott Chaucer* is William Morris's edition of the works of Geoffrey Chaucer, designed and printed using his private printing press. It's the most ambitious of his book projects and recalls much of the original medieval splendour. See it in the Ideal Book gallery.

The William Morris Gallery was opened in 1950 by Prime Minister Clement Atlee to display a diverse collection, including printed, woven and embroidered fabrics, rugs, carpets, wallpapers, furniture, stained glass and painted tiles, all designed by Morris and his artist colleagues, who included Dante Gabriel Rossetti, Edward Burne-Jones and William De Morgan.

The refurbished museum consists of nine galleries, each with a theme, taking visitors on a chronological journey through Morris's life. Meet the Man

introduces him, while Starting Out looks at his early influences, which included the Pre-Raphaelite artists and Victorian art patron John Ruskin, and presents some of his early drawings. Morris and Co explores the work of the firm of Morris, Marshall, Faulkner & Company, established in 1861, which includes stained glass for churches and wallpaper designed for Queen Victoria. The Workshop is inspired by Merton Abbey where the creative work took place – younger visitors can try their hand at skills such as assembling a stained glass window – while The Shop recreates Morris's fashionable Oxford Street store.

Ideal Book looks at Morris's love of early literature, while Fighting for a Cause examines his political battles – he was a radical socialist in later life – and Arts and Crafts presents designs from the movement he helped to create. The final gallery focuses on Sir Frank Brangwyn, an apprentice of Morris who was one of the founders of the gallery and who donated part of his large art collection in the '30s to the people of Walthamstow.

The museum also holds temporary exhibitions – in 2012 it hosted *The Walthamstow Tapestry* by Turner Prize winner Grayson Perry – and special events, most of which are free. There's also a charming tea room and a very tempting shop!

Morris Snakeshead

 FOOD & DRINK

William Morris Gallery Tea Room: Enjoy afternoon tea, a *panini* sandwich or a glass of wine, accompanied by delightful views over Lloyd Park. All profits go towards the upkeep of the gallery.

  Hoe Street: There are plenty of local eateries and delis along this lively road leading from Walthamstow Central Station to the gallery.

9 BARBICAN ART GALLERY

Address: Level 3, Barbican Centre, Silk Street, EC2Y 8DS (☎ 020-7638 8891, ⌨ barbican.org.uk/art).

Opening hours: Mon-Tue and Fri-Sun, 11am to 8pm; Wed 11am to 6pm; Thu 11am to 10pm. Closed over Christmas. The Curve open daily, 11am to 8pm (Thursdays until 10pm).

Cost: £12 adults, £8 concessions, £7 under-18s, under-13s free. Tickets are discounted by at least £1 when purchased online. Entrance to The Curve is free.

Transport: Barbican tube.

Amenities: Two restaurants, three cafés, number of bars, gardens, wheelchair access.

The Barbican Art Gallery is tucked away inside the monolithic Barbican Centre, Europe's largest arts and conference venue, owned, funded and managed by the City of London Corporation. The centre is a major venue for music concerts – the London Symphony Orchestra and the BBC Symphony Orchestra are based in the Barbican Hall – and also houses two theatres, three cinema screens and one of the largest public libraries in London.

👁 DON'T MISS!

Art is free in The Curve, a semi-circular gallery on the centre's ground floor, which displays new commissions and installations created specifically for the space.

The Art Gallery is on the third floor and presents a changing programme of exhibitions, focusing on fine art, photography and design from the 20th and 21st centuries, showcasing everyone from acclaimed architects to Turner prize-winning artists. Major exhibitions in 2012/13 included a retrospective on photography from the '60s and '70s entitled 'Everything Was Moving'. Accompanying each exhibition is a programme of talks and events.

The Barbican Arts Centre (Grade II listed) is a prominent example of British Brutalist concrete architecture. Although it divides opinion – it was once voted 'London's ugliest building'– it's worth visiting in its own right. There are green oases among all the concrete: the conservatory is a hidden tropical paradise, home to finches, exotic fish and over 2,000 species of plants and trees, while outside, the main focal point is the lake and its neighbouring terrace and gardens, impressive public spaces with waterside seating and city views.

Organised tours (1½ hrs, £8, £6 concessions) of the architectural heritage of the Barbican take place four times a week (see website for details) and include a well-deserved coffee at the end.

The Barbican Centre also has a bookshop and a number of bars and restaurants – including the excellent Searcys.

CLOCKMAKERS' MUSEUM 10

Address: Guildhall Library, Aldermanbury, EC2V 7HH (☎ 020-7332 1868, 🖥 clockmakers.org).
Opening hours: Mon-Sat, 9.30am to 4.45pm. Closed Sundays, Bank Holidays and Saturdays before a Bank Holiday Monday.
Cost: Free.
Transport: Bank, Moorgate or St Paul's tube.
Amenities: Shop, library, wheelchair access.

The Clockmaker's Museum – situated in the 15th-century Guildhall – is the oldest collection specifically of clocks, watches and sundials in the world, and one of the finest. It's displayed in a single room containing some 600 English and European watches, 30 clocks and 15 marine timekeepers. The majority of items date from between 1600 and 1850, and you explore them to the backdrop of numerous ticks and chimes.

The Worshipful Company of Clockmakers was established by Royal Charter granted by Charles I in 1631 and is the oldest surviving horological institution in the world. Until the 19th century, England and London led the world in the manufacture of the highest quality timepieces, and most freemen and liverymen of the Company are still involved in horology, whether clock or watchmaking, designing, trading, restoring or using horology for scientific purposes.

The museum's treasures include clocks and watches by early Masters such as Thomas Tompion, known as 'Father of English Clockmaking' (he built some 5,500 watches and 650 clocks during his career). But perhaps the most important group is that of the marine chronometers or timekeepers, which enabled accurate sea navigation and were a major factor in Britain's dominance of world trade and its naval power.

Among the most celebrated marine chronometers are those made by John Harrison (1693-1776) – dubbed 'the man who found longitude'. He made it his mission to perfect an accurate marine chronometer and submitted four clocks to the Board of Longitude. He eventually won the Admiralty's £20,000 prize with his fourth submission, known as H4.

👁 DON'T MISS!

John Harrison's fifth marine chronometer – H5 – has pride of place in the museum. He was required to produce it for the Board of Longitude to prove his success with H4 was not a fluke! His other four timepieces are in the National Maritime Museum in Greenwich.

Ramsey 'Nativity' Watch

11 DR JOHNSON'S HOUSE

> **Address:** 17 Gough Square, EC4A 3DE (☎ 020-7353 3745,
> 🖥 drjohnsonshouse.org).
> **Opening hours**: May to September, Mon-Sat, 11am to 5.30pm; October to April,
> Mon-Sat, 11am to 5pm. Closed Sundays and Bank Holidays.
> **Cost**: £4.50 adults, £3.50 senior citizens and students, £1.50 children aged 5-17
> (under-5s free), £10 families.
> **Transport**: Chancery Lane, Holborn or Temple tube.
> **Amenities**: Shop, no wheelchair access.

Samuel Johnson (1709-1784) was a biographer, editor, essayist, lexicographer, literary critic, moralist and poet; some claim he was the most distinguished man of letters in English history. He was also the subject of perhaps the world's most famous biography, by James Boswell. So it's a shame and a surprise that this property is little visited.

The house was built around 1700 and is one of the few surviving residential properties of its vintage in the City of London. It was Johnson's home and workplace between 1748 and 1759, and it was here that he compiled the first English dictionary. Johnson moved to London in 1737 with his friend David Garrick, the actor, to work as a journalist. He was commissioned to write the first comprehensive *Dictionary of the English Language* in 1746, which was published in 1755.

This elegant property has been restored to its original condition, with panelled rooms, period furniture, prints and portraits. Exhibits about Johnson's life and work give an interesting insight into the man, and place his work in context. The house's location adds to the atmosphere, set amid a maze of courtyards and passages redolent of old London.

Johnson was a fascinating, contradictory character. Tall and robust, yet prone to ill health, he was prey to a range of tics which suggests that he probably suffered from Tourette's syndrome. However, he was very learned and eloquent, and his circle of friends included Charles Burney and Joshua Reynolds, who were entertained at Gough Square. Johnson was also a compassionate man who supported a number of poor friends in his house, even when struggling to look after himself.

> **👁 DON'T MISS!**
>
> Look out for drawing of Dr Johnson's great friend, Hester Lynch Piozzi (formerly Mrs Thrale), and an oil painting by James Northcote of a black man who may well be Francis Barber, Johnson's devoted manservant.

HOUSE MILL MUSEUM 12

Address: Three Mill Lane, Bromley-by-Bow, E3 3DU (☎ 020-8980 4626,
🖥 housemill.org.uk).
Opening hours: May to October, Sundays 11am to 4pm; also first Sundays in March, April and December. Guided tours (¾ hr).
Cost: £3 adults, £1.50 concessions, children free.
Transport: Bromley-by-Bow tube.
Amenities: Café, no wheelchair access.

The House Mill is a Grade I listed tidal mill set in a beautiful riverside location in London's East End. Built in 1776 by Daniel Bisson, it's believed to be the largest tidal mill still in existence in the world. Built across the river, the mill trapped sea and river water at high tide; the out-flowing water then turned four large water wheels which in turn drove 12 pairs of millstones. The mechanism still survives, along with other historic machinery.

 FOOD & DRINK

Miller's House Café: The former's miller's home houses a pleasant café serving sandwiches, baguettes, bagels, drinks, cakes and light snacks, which you can also eat in the tranquil riverside garden.

According to the Domesday Book there were similar mills in this area as long ago as the 11th century. In medieval times the site was known as Three Mills and provided flour for the bakers of Stratford-atte-Bow (modern-day Bow) who supplied bread to the City of London. In 1728, Three Mills was purchased by Peter Lefevre, a Huguenot, who entered into partnership with Daniel Bisson. In addition to flour-making, the mills prepared grain for a (gin) distillery based in Clerkenwell.

House Mill ceased operation in 1941 after the area was bombed during the Second World War and it was threatened with demolition in the mid-'70s but was saved by the intervention of the governors of a local museum. Restoration began in 1989 and the former Miller's House next door was rebuilt as a visitor centre and café.

The mill is now owned by the River Lea Tidal Mill Trust, which plans to reinstate the water wheels and other machinery in order to demonstrate grinding. With the addition of modern turbines, the wheels will also be used to generate power.

13 ST PAUL'S CATHEDRAL CRYPT

Address: St Paul's Churchyard, EC4M 8AD (☎ 020-7246 8350, 🖥 stpauls.co.uk).
Opening hours: Open for sightseers daily, 8.30am to 4pm. For services, see website.
Cost: £15 adults, £14 concessions (students & seniors), £6 under-18s, under-7s free, £36 families. Fee include a multimedia guide and 90-minute guided tour. Save £2 when buying tickets online. Free for worshippers.
Transport: St Paul's tube.
Amenities: Restaurant, café, shop, wheelchair access.

St Paul's dominates London in more ways than one. At 365ft (111m) high and set atop the City's highest hill, St Paul's dome was, until 1962, the tallest structure in London. Sir Christopher Wren's masterpiece is the fifth church to stand here – the first was built in 604 AD – and took 35 years to complete between 1675 and 1710.

Tours of St Paul's Cathedral take in its magnificent interior, the galleries that wind around its dome, its chapels and the crypt (the largest in Europe), which was the last resting place of some of the nation's greatest heroes, poets and scientists including Sir Christopher Wren, the Duke of Wellington and Lord Nelson, whose black marble sarcophagus has centre stage directly beneath the dome.

The former Treasury in the crypt now hosts Oculus, a 270° film experience that tells the 1,400-year history of the church; it takes viewers on a virtual tour of the building, and flies you through Wren's Great Model, the room-sized model he built for Charles II.

St Paul's has a number of extensive collections, including a Library housing some 21,500 volumes, an Architectural Archive and an Object Collection composed of over 3,000 significant items associated with the life and work of St Paul's. Many objects are in regular use, including fonts, altars, monuments and paintings (you can explore the collection online).

The St Paul's Cathedral Arts Project is an on-going programme which seeks to explore the relationship between art and faith. Projects have included installations by Antony Gormley, Yoko Ono and Martin Firrell.

The cathedral also has a bookshop, café and restaurant.

👁 DON'T MISS!

Rising 280ft (85m) above London, the Golden Gallery encircles the highest point of St Paul's dome, providing panoramic views across the City and River Thames. It's well worth the climb – 528 steps – but if you cannot manage it, Oculus (see left) can take you there.

VICTORIA & ALBERT MUSEUM OF CHILDHOOD 14

Address: Cambridge Heath Road, E2 9PA (☎ 020-8983 5200, ⌨ vam.ac.uk/moc).
Opening hours: Daily, 10am to 5.45pm. Closed 24-26th December and 1st January.
Cost: Free.
Transport: Bethnal Green tube.
Amenities: Café, shop, wheelchair access.

Somewhat overshadowed by its parent museum in Kensington, this free attraction is well worth the journey east, and nostalgic adults often enjoy it as much as children do. The museum is housed in an iron-framed building that resembles a Victorian train station. Grade II listed, it has lots of natural light to help show off its many, varied exhibits from the V&A's collection of childhood-related objects. Dating from the 17th century to the present day, they include toys, clothes, games, art, furniture and photographs. There's also a regular programme of temporary exhibitions, as well as activities and workshops.

The permanent displays are arranged in three main galleries: Moving Toys, Creativity and Childhood. Moving Toys has wonderfully old-fashioned toys, such as spinning tops, rocking horses and Jack in the Boxes, as well as unusual playthings from other countries, such as a battery-operated Chinese lion and a rather disturbing tilting dentist from the wild woods of West Virginia!

Creativity is about the ability to challenge, question and explore, and features toys related to the development of imagination. This gallery is home to dolls and teddy bears, puppet theatres and Lego sets, TV themed toys and objects made by children, including an African helicopter built from recycled tin cans.

Childhood tells the social story of childhood, and examines children's clothing over the past 250 years, including toys designed for role play and leisure activities from card games to buckets and spades.

The excellent website allows you to take a virtual tour of the museum.

👁 DON'T MISS!

Many adults are drawn to the Homes exhibit, where there are some rare and beautiful dolls' houses dating from the 17th century, many of which are veritable works of art.

15 ALL HALLOWS BY THE TOWER & CRYPT MUSEUM

Address: Byward Street, EC2R 5BJ (☎ 020-7481 2928, 🖳 ahbtt.org.uk).
Opening hours: Usually Mon-Fri, 8am to 5pm; Sat 10am to 4pm, Sun 10am to 3pm (except during services).
Cost: Free. Small fee for groups.
Transport: Tower Hill tube.
Amenities: Café (Kitchen@Tower), brass rubbing, wheelchair access.

All Hallows-by-the-Tower is an ancient, Grade I listed church overlooking the Tower of London that is positively dripping with history. London's oldest church, it was established in 675 by the Saxon Abbey at Barking and built on the site of a Roman building. It was expanded and rebuilt several times between the 11th and 15th centuries, and its location by the Tower meant that people condemned to execution were sometimes laid to rest here, if only temporarily.

All Hallows survived the Great Fire of 1666 (which started just a few hundred yards away) but suffered extensive bomb damage during the Second World War. However, many parts of the old church survive, including the 15th-century outer walls and the 7th-century Saxon doorway from the original church. There are also three beautiful 15th- and 16th-century wooden statues of saints and a lovely baptismal font cover carved in 1682 by Grinling Gibbons.

The Crypt Museum tells the history of the church and displays sections of a Roman pavement and artefacts discovered during excavations. Free guided tours (2 to 4pm) of the church are provided on most days between April and October.

16 BANK OF ENGLAND MUSEUM

Address: Threadneedle Street, EC2R 8AH (☎ 020-7601 5545, 🖳 bankofengland. co.uk/education/museum/index.htm).
Opening hours: Mon-Fri, 10am to 5pm. Closed weekends and Bank Holidays.
Cost: Free.
Transport: Bank tube.
Amenities: Wheelchair access.

Housed in a replica of the 18th-century Bank building designed by Sir John Soane (the current building is 20th century), the museum tells the story of the Bank of England from its foundation in 1694 to its current role as the UK's central bank. It should appeal to anyone with an interest in social history, politics and (strangely) classic children's literature.

Displays include pikes and muskets once used to defend the Bank as well as

Roman and modern gold bars; you can test the weight of the gold bars which are reassuringly heavy at 28lb (12.7kg). There are collections of banknotes and coins dating back to the 17th century, a wide range of books and documents, paintings, cartoons and photographs, a small but significant silver collection, plus statues, furniture, and other artefacts.

There's also a permanent display about Kenneth Grahame (author of *The Wind in the Willows*), who worked at the Bank for 30 years. In 1903 he thwarted an attempted armed robbery by locking the assailant in the Bank's waiting room, despite being shot at three times.

Bank of England

BRITISH RED CROSS MUSEUM 17

Address: 44 Moorfields, EC2Y 9AL (☎ 020-7877 7058, 🖥 redcross.org.uk/about-us/who-we-are/museum-and-archives).
Opening hours: Open to researchers by appointment, Mon-Fri, 10am to 1pm and 2-4pm. At least 24 hours' notice is required to view the collection.
Cost: Free.
Transport: Moorgate tube.
Amenities: Wheelchair access.

The British Red Cross Museum charts the history of the humanitarian organisation from its foundation in 1870 to the current day. It was created to provide aid to both warring armies during the Franco-Prussian War (1870-71) and has been active in numerous wars and conflicts since, including both world wars.

The museum's collection is rich and diverse, including photographs chronicling its work since the First World War, some 1,000 promotional posters, and paintings by Second World War artist Doris Zinkeisen. Archives record the history and activities of the organisation, including the papers of its first chairman, Colonel Robert Loyd-Lindsay (later Lord Wantage).

In addition, there are badges and medals, fundraising materials spanning all its campaigns, uniforms and stretchers, and early medical and first-aid equipment. One of its most moving objects is the Changi quilt, made by women interred in Japanese prison camps after the invasion of Singapore in 1942 to alleviate boredom, but also to send the message that they were still alive.

18 CALVERT 22 FOUNDATION

Address: 22 Calvert Avenue, E2 7JP (☎ 020-7613 2141, 🖥 calvert22.org).
Opening hours: Wed-Sun, noon to 6pm (9pm on Thu).
Cost: Free.
Transport: Old Street or Liverpool Street tube.
Amenities: Café, wheelchair access.

Calvert 22 is the UK's only non-profit gallery dedicated to presenting contemporary art and culture from Russia, the Commonwealth of Independent States (CIS) and Eastern European countries. Named after its address in a Shoreditch street, Calvert 22 was founded in 2009 by Russian businesswoman Nonna Materkova, who left her native St Petersburg for London in the late '90s. Her vision provides space for emergent and more established contemporary artists in a programme of exhibitions, talks and events, and provides a resource for anyone wishing to study the culture of the countries which comprised the former 'Eastern bloc'.

The gallery has presented shows by leading artists such as Alexander Brodsky, described as the 'most important Russian architect alive today', and Olga Chernysheva, who captures everyday life in post-Communist Russia in photography, video and watercolour. Other exhibitions have focused on artists from former Silk Road republics such as Kazakhstan, Tajikistan and Uzbekistan, and presented highlights from the Innovation Prize, Russia's version of the Turner Prize.

There's also a pleasant café.

19 CHISENHALE GALLERY

Address: 64 Chisenhale Road, E3 5QZ (☎ 020-8981 4518, 🖥 chisenhale.org.uk).
Opening hours: Wed-Sun, 1-6pm (9pm first Thursday of the month during exhibitions).
Cost: Free.
Transport: Mile End tube.
Amenities: Wheelchair access.

For over 25 years, Chisenhale Gallery has been one of London's most innovative organisations for contemporary visual art, with a reputation for producing important solo commissions with artists at a formative point in their career.

It's a non-profit organisation with an integrated artistic, education and outreach programme, which is artist led with a core focus on commissioning ground-breaking new work, developing audiences and legacy building. The gallery enables emerging or under-represented artists to make significant steps and pursue important new directions in their practice.

The events programme hosts a diverse range of artists, curators and writers, and comprises exhibition-related talks and film screenings. These include 'Interim', a programme of major one-off live events and performances that take place in the main gallery between exhibitions; and '21st Century', a monthly programme of live events, film screenings, talks and research projects taking place concurrent to the gallery programme in the adjoining studio space.

CITY OF LONDON POLICE MUSEUM 20

Address: Wood Street Police Station, 7 Wood St, EC2P 2NQ (☏ 020-7601 2352, 🖵 citypolicemuseum.org.uk).
Opening hours: Tue-Wed, 11am to 4pm; Fridays, 2-6pm. Visitors should confirm opening times, which are liable to change, while groups of over ten people are requested to make a booking.
Cost: Free.
Transport: St Paul's tube.
Amenities: Wheelchair access (but please notify museum in advance).

medals won by City policemen in the 1908 Olympics. It also recounts grisly tales of the City's criminal past (murders, robberies, assassinations and gun battles), including a small collection related to the Jack the Ripper murders of 1888, with photographs of the victims and information about the investigation, and another covering the Houndsditch Murders of 1910 which led to the infamous Siege of Sidney Street.

The City of London Police (COLP) is responsible for law enforcement within the City of London – the rest of Greater London is policed by the Metropolitan Police Service – and has its headquarters at Wood Street Police Station, where there's a small but interesting museum dedicated to the history of crime and policing in the Square Mile.

The City has been 'policed' since Roman times – Wood Street is built on the site of a Roman fortress – but the COLP wasn't formed until 1839. The museum reveals its history, including uniforms, early walkie-talkies, London's first police call box, and even gold

21 HACKNEY MUSEUM

Address: Ground Floor, Technology and Learning Centre, 1 Reading Lane, E8 1GQ
(☎ 020-8356 3500, 🖥 hackney.gov.uk/cm-museum.htm).
Opening hours: Tue-Wed and Fri, 9.30am to 5.30pm; Thu 9.30am to 8pm; Sat
10am to 5pm. Closed Sundays, Mondays and Bank Holidays.
Cost: Free.
Transport: Hackney Central rail.
Amenities: Shop, wheelchair access.

Hackney Museum is a local museum with a world view. The area has always attracted new settlers and the museum reflects the diversity of its community through themed displays and temporary exhibitions. It also runs projects about events affecting local people – in 2012 the London Olympics was a major theme.

Opened in 2002, the museum covers over 1,000 years of borough history, from a Saxon boat carved from a single tree to a toy car made from old shoes and metal scraps by an African boy refugee. Of particular interest is a rare gold coin brought to London by a Jewish family escaping persecution in Nazi Germany; it was part of a hoard unearthed in a Hackney garden in 2007 and later returned to its owners' descendants.

Meanwhile, art lovers will enjoy the Chalmers collection of paintings and decorative objects, bequeathed to the council by Alexander Chalmers in 1927.

As you explore the museum, you can listen to interviews capturing the experiences of real people – and there are also plenty of interactives to keep younger visitors amused.

22 HONOURABLE ARTILLERY COMPANY MUSEUM

Address: Armoury House, City Road, EC1Y 2BQ (☎ 020-7382 1541,
🖥 armymuseums.org.uk and search under the 'Museum Search' tab).
Opening hours: By appointment only.
Cost: Free, but a donation is appreciated.
Transport: Moorgate or Old Street tube.
Amenities: Wheelchair access.

The Honourable Artillery Company is the oldest regiment in the British Army, with a royal charter dating back to 1537, and it still maintains an active regiment as part of the Territorial Army. It has taken part in many historic conflicts, including the opposition of the

Spanish Armada in 1588, the English Civil War (1642-1651) and, more recently, Afghanistan.

First opened in 1987, the museum was refurbished and re-opened in 2011, although the public must visit by appointment or attend an event at

Armoury House, which has a wealth of elegant rooms as well as the largest garden in the City of London.

The museum displays collections of uniforms, weapons and medals, which include those won in competition – the company has a long tradition of distinction in shooting – and those earned in combat. They include two Victoria Crosses won by members of the 1st Battalion for their actions at Gavrelle, France, in 1917.

INNS OF COURT & CITY YEOMANRY MUSEUM   23

Address: 10 Stone Buildings, Lincoln's Inn, WC2A 3TG (☎ 020-7405 8112, 🖥 iccy.org.uk/museum.htm).
Opening hours: Mon-Fri, 10am to 4pm by appointment only.
Cost: Free.
Transport: Chancery Lane tube.
Amenities: Shop, gardens, wheelchair access (limited).

The Inns of Court and City Yeomanry is a squadron in the Territorial Army which was formed in the '60s from three historic volunteer forces: the Inns of Court Regiment, the City of London Yeomanry and the Essex Yeomanry.

The Inns of Court Regiment has an unusual history, being originally comprised of lawyers who gathered to defend London against possible Spanish invasion in 1584. The regiment maintained its links with the legal profession through later conflicts – during the Civil War, lawyers fought for the Royalists while their clerks took the side of the Roundheads – and this led George III to nickname them 'The Devil's Own'. He wasn't a great fan of lawyers, even those pledged to defend his realm!

The regiment's collection is housed (appropriately) in a Georgian house (dating from 1774) in Lincoln's Inn and includes uniforms, weapons, medals and memorabilia, as well as an excellent archive. One of its greatest treasures is its set of drums – possibly the oldest complete set in the British Army – which beat the time for troops of lawyers during the Napoleonic Wars.

24 MATT'S GALLERY

Address: 42-44 Copperfield Road, E3 4RR (☎ 020-8983 1771, 🖳 mattsgallery.org).
Opening hours: Wed-Sun, noon to 6pm.
Cost: Free.
Transport: Mile End tube.
Amenities: Shop, wheelchair access.

It has to be this way, Lindsay Seers

M att's Gallery is a contemporary art space established by Robin Klassnik (the gallery is named after Klassnik's dog) in Hackney in 1979, moving to its current premises in 1993. It's a not-for-profit gallery, funded by the Arts Council and other major trusts and foundations, which exists to support artists with the time and space to take risks, test their limits and develop their ideas and techniques. Equal emphasis is placed on the gestation of the work and the final exhibition, providing the best conditions for experiencing art and challenging audiences

Artists are generally at the young or emerging end of the career spectrum and exhibitions vary widely in scope, but are usually interesting. In 2012 the gallery presented 'Revolver', featuring works by ten artists made between 1983 and 2012, displayed in discrete spaces in the gallery in a three-part series of short exhibitions of up to four artists.

25 MUSEUM OF IMMIGRATION & DIVERSITY

Address: 19 Princelet Street, E1 6QH (☎ 020-7247 5352,
🖳 19princeletstreet.org.uk).
Opening hours: Group visits (1-2 hrs) by appointment. There are also open days (see website for details).
Cost: No set fee, but most groups (maximum of 30-40 people) are expected to make a donation of at least £5 per person or £100 per group.
Transport: Shoreditch High Street tube.
Amenities: Wheelchair access (ground floor only).

T he Museum of Immigration and Diversity is a unique museum – Europe's only cultural institution devoted to the movement of people in search of a better life – in one of East London's prettiest streets. It's housed in an unrestored (Grade II* listed) house built in 1719 which was originally home to a Huguenot silk merchant, Peter Abraham Ogier, who fled religious persecution in France. When the Huguenots moved on in the 19th century, they were replaced by Irish immigrants escaping the potato famine. Then, between 1870 and 1914, thousands of Jewish settlers arrived from Eastern Europe, fleeing anti-Semitism and Tsarist pogroms, and part of the house became a synagogue.

The moment you step through the door of 19 Princelet Street you realise that you're entering a rare and remarkable building, made all the more poignant by its fragile state and air of decay. There's a touching exhibition entitled 'Suitcases and Sanctuary', exploring the history of the immigrants who shaped Spitalfields, seen through the eyes of children.

RAGGED SCHOOL MUSEUM 26

Address: 46-50 Copperfield Road, Mile End, E3 4RR (☎ 020-8980 6405, 🖳 raggedschoolmuseum.org.uk).
Opening hours: Wed-Thu, 10am to 5pm. Also open from 2-5pm on the first Sunday of each month.
Cost: Free.
Transport: Mile End tube.
Amenities: Shop, wheelchair access (ground floor only).

This little-known museum is housed in a group of warehouses which together once formed the largest 'ragged' school in London. It was founded by Thomas Barnardo (of Barnardo's fame), who worked as a 'missionary' among the poor of London's East End and opened his first 'ragged' school in 1867 to provide free basic education to poor children.

The Ragged School Museum opened in 1990 to tell the story of the schools and the broader social history of the East End. At its heart is a recreation of a Victorian classroom, with authentic desks, slate writing boards and even dunce hats, where children can experience life in Victorian times, with lessons led by a costumed actor. There's also a reconstruction of a domestic East End kitchen as it would have been in 1900.

Both schoolroom and kitchen are hands-on, interactive displays, and paint a vivid picture of life for the Victorian poor. There are also several display galleries, telling the story of the surrounding area over the last 200 years.

30 ST BRIDE'S CRYPT

Address: Fleet Street, EC4Y 8AU (☎ 020-7427 0133, 🖥 stbrides.com).
Opening hours: Mon-Fri, 8am to 6pm; Sat-Sun variable opening times (check in advance). Guided tours on some Tuesday afternoons from 3-4.30pm (check website for dates).
Cost: Free. Tours £6 per person.
Transport: St Paul's or Blackfriars tube.
Amenities: No wheelchair access to crypt.

St Bride's is one of London's oldest church sites, probably dating back to the Middle Saxon conversion in the 7th century. The current church is the eighth on the site and was built by Sir Christopher Wren from 1672 to replace the 11th-century Norman church that was lost in the Great Fire of London. Set back from Fleet Street, the church is a striking sight, Grade I listed and with Wren's distinctive tiered spire which is said to have inspired the shape of modern wedding cakes.

Bomb damage during the Second World War destroyed much of Wren's church, but also opened up the crypt and revealed substantial Roman remains as well as over 200 (named) skeletons buried between 1740 and 1852. The church's long and interesting history is now documented in the large crypt museum which displays a Roman

pavement and evidence of a building from the 2nd century AD, making it the location of some of London's earliest known Roman remains. The museum also tells the story of the seven previous churches which stood on the site and some of the people who worshipped here.

31 SUTTON HOUSE

Address: 2 & 4 Homerton High Street, Hackney, E9 6JQ (☎ 020-8986 2264, 🖥 nationaltrust.org.uk/main/w-suttonhouse).
Opening hours: Opening times vary according to the season (see website for details).
Cost: £3 adults, £1 children, £6.90 families. Free for National Trust members.
Transport: Hackney Central rail.
Amenities: Café, shop, wheelchair access.

It's well worth making the effort to see this Grade II* listed Tudor mansion, which is stranded among housing estates in London's East

End. Built in 1535 by Sir Ralph Sadleir, Principal Secretary of State to Henry VIII, it retains much of the atmosphere of a Tudor home (although the façade was altered in the Georgian period), including original carved fireplaces, oak-panelled rooms, Tudor windows and a lovely, tranquil courtyard. Now owned by the National Trust, Sutton House is the oldest domestic building in Hackney.

The house fell on hard times in the second half of the 20th century, when squatters moved in. Following their eviction, it was restored and renovated. Amazingly, many of the original Tudor features survived this period, and some of the squatters' graffiti and murals have been left, and provide an interesting contrast with the rest of the house. An exhibition details the history of the house and its various inhabitants, and includes the sights and sounds of a Tudor kitchen.

THAMES RIVER POLICE MUSEUM 32

Address: Wapping Police Station, Wapping High Street, Wapping, E1W 2NE (🖥 thamespolicemuseum.org.uk, ✉ curator@thamespolicemuseum.org.uk).
Opening hours: Visits are by pre-arranged tour only. Apply in writing (or email) to the Thames Police Museum to the above address.
Cost: Free.
Transport: Wapping rail.
Amenities: No wheelchair access.

This museum is located in the headquarters of the Metropolitan Police's Marine Policing Unit, and provides a unique insight into the history of the world's first officially organised police force, which preceded the Metropolitan Police by 31 years. It's a proper 'old time' museum, nicely low-tech, which traces the story of the Thames River Police from its formation in 1798 to the present day.

The Thames Police was established as a result of the losses suffered by importers while cargoes were unloaded on the unprotected river, which were calculated at the time to be at least £500,000 a year. The initial force was around 50 officers, whose task was to police the 33,000 people who worked in the river trades (a third of whom were known criminals!). The force quickly justified itself, and by the later 19th century steam launches were being used (replacing rowing galleys and sailing boats), while by 1910 most

patrols were power driven. In the early 21st century, other challenges face the force, notably terrorism – it's all documented here.

33 TWININGS MUSEUM

Address: 216 Strand, WC2R 1AP (☎ 020-7583 1359, 🖳 shop.twinings.co.uk/shop/strand).
Opening hours: Mon-Fri, 8.30am to 7.30pm; Sat 10am to 5pm, Sun 10am to 4pm.
Cost: Free.
Transport: Temple tube.
Amenities: Café, shop, wheelchair access.

O ccupying a narrow shop opposite the Royal Courts of Justice, Twinings is thought to be the oldest company in London to have traded continuously on the same site with the same family since its foundation. It was founded by Thomas Twining (1675-1741) who bought an old coffee house in 1706. He daringly introduced tea – then an exotic drink enjoyed by the wealthy – and in 1717 opened the Golden Lyon to sell tea and coffee. In 1787, his grandson Richard Twining built the handsome doorway, which incorporates two Chinese figures to acknowledge the fact that tea-drinking began in China.

At the back of the long narrow shop is the small museum, which tells the story of the Twining family and displays tea-related paraphernalia collected over 300 years. Among the exhibits are a copy of Queen Victoria's Royal Warrant from 1837, old advertisements and a selection of tea caddies. There's also a non-descript wooden box labelled TIP, which is an acronym for 'to insure promptness'; patrons of coffee/tea houses would drop a penny into the box to encourage quick service – the origin of the term 'tip'.

34 VALENCE HOUSE MUSEUM

Address: Becontree Avenue, Dagenham, RM8 3HT (☎ 020-8227 2034, 🖳 lbbd.gov.uk/valence).
Opening hours: Mon-Sat, 10am to 4pm. Closed Sundays and Public Holidays.
Cost: Free.
Transport: Chadwell Heath rail or Becontree tube and 62 bus.
Amenities: Café, park, wheelchair access.

T his attractive local history museum is located in a 15th-century (Grade II* listed) manor house. The timber-framed building, still partially surrounded by a moat, is situated in Valence Park, although the area takes its name from Agnes de Valence and her brother Aylmer, Earl of Pembroke, who occupied the land in the early 1300s. The estate was bought by London County Council in 1921 and became the museum for Barking and Dagenham in 1974.

The museum building underwent major restoration in 2007-2010, and has been voted by *The Guardian* newspaper as one of the 50 best free attractions in London. The Valence House gallery traces the history of the house and the people who have called it home. There are also permanent exhibitions on history and life in the area, including the rise and fall of Barking Abbey, industrial innovation and sporting heritage. You can explore beautiful oak-panelled rooms, view a recently-discovered 400-year-old wall painting and, if you're 'lucky', catch a glimpse of one of the resident ghosts.

Valence House Museum

VALENTINES MANSION   35

Address: Emerson Road, Ilford, IG1 4XA (☎ 020-8708 8100, 🖳 valentinesmansion. com and valentines.org.uk).
Opening hours: Tue-Wed, 10am to 5pm; Sundays 11am to 4pm.
Cost: Free. Guided tours £3 per person (see website for details).
Transport: Gants Hill tube.
Amenities: Café, shop, gardens, wheelchair access.

Valentines Mansion (Grade II* listed) is a splendid William III country house built in 1696-7 for Lady Elizabeth Tillotson, widow of the Archbishop of Canterbury. It has changed hands many times since, and externally the house is an 18th-century structure, although some features inside are earlier, including much of the panelling and joinery.

The estate was acquired in 1912 by Ilford council and was used variously as a home for wartime refugees, a hospital and a council department. The house stood empty for 15 years until 2009 when a grant of several million pounds from the Heritage Lottery Fund enabled it and the grounds to be restored to their former glory.

Today, Valentines features a recreated Victorian kitchen and Georgian rooms, with glorious views over the surrounding parkland. The Grade II listed gardens include an exceptional formal 18th-century garden, historic herb/kitchen garden and Victorian rose garden. Additional attractions include contemporary art exhibitions, family activities and a farmer's market on the fourth Sunday of the month, while the grounds host county cricket matches and the Redbridge Town Show.

36 VESTRY HOUSE MUSEUM

Address: Vestry Road, Walthamstow, E17 9NH (☎ 020-8496 4391,
⌨ walthamforest.gov.uk/pages/services/vhm.aspx).
Opening hours: Wed-Sun, 10am to 5pm.
Cost: Free.
Transport: Walthamstow Central tube/rail.
Amenities: Shop, garden, wheelchair access (ground floor only).

Vestry House Museum is an unexpected gem, hidden away in a rural corner of this busy East London suburb, and housing a miscellany of local treasures. It was built in 1730 as a workhouse, as a plaque above the entrance still attests: 'If any would not work, neither should he eat.' It later became a police station, then a private house, and opened as a museum in 1931.

Grade II listed, the house displays reconstructions of a Victorian parlour from 1890, and a prison cell tableau based on the case of a drunk and disorderly labourer arrested in 1861. Its star exhibit is the Bremer car, built by local engineer Frederick Bremer in 1892 and a candidate for the oldest British petrol-driven car. Galleries include Domestic Life, which shows 19th-century household utensils and the Costume gallery displaying antique clothing in a magnificent wood panelled room (although the 16th-century panelling is from another house).

Vestry House is very much a local museum and there are regular themed exhibitions and family events. This Grade II listed former sewage pumping station built in 1885 is now home to a unique museum telling the story of industry, technology and transport in the Lea Valley.

37 WALTHAMSTOW PUMPHOUSE MUSEUM

Address: 10 South Access Road, Walthamstow, E17 8AX (☎ 020-8521 1766,
⌨ walthamstowpumphousemuseum.org.uk).
Opening hours: Usually Wed, Thu and Sun. Confirm dates and times with museum:
☎ 07930-662252, ✉ l.collier418@btinternet.com).
Cost: £3 adults, £1 seniors, under 16s free when accompanied by an adult.
Transport: Walthamstow Central tube or Walthamstow Queens Road rail.
Amenities: Café, shop, wheelchair access.

The Pumphouse has been redundant since the '70s, but in 2012 a major project began to restore the pump house bays, along with its two rare Marshall 'C' steam engines. It will also display pioneering achievements in road, rail, air and sea transport in the local area, from the Stratford railway works to the Thames Ironworks and Shipping Company which transported Cleopatra's needle from Egypt to London in 1877.

As well as the Pumphouse, transport buffs can view a collection of vintage cars and buses, an early Victoria Line tube train carriage and a replica of the AVRO plane, built by Edwin Alliott Verdon Roe (1877-1958), which won a competition for the first all-British aircraft to be flown by a British pilot at Alexandra Palace in 1907.

Work on a new museum gallery is expected to be completed by 2014; in the meantime, the Pumphouse hosts regular rallies and other events.

WHITECHAPEL GALLERY 38

Address: 77-82 Whitechapel High Street, E1 7QX (☎ 020-7522 7888, 🖥 whitechapelgallery.org).
Opening hours: Tue-Sun, 11am to 6pm (Thursdays until 9pm). Closed Mondays.
Cost: Usually free, but donations are welcome.
Transport: Aldgate East tube.
Amenities: Dining room, shop, wheelchair access.

Whitechapel is associated in many minds with grisly crimes rather than art – it was the setting for Jack the Ripper's murders – but it's also the home of one of Britain's most forward-thinking and influential art galleries.

The gallery is located in a striking building with a distinctive façade designed by Charles Harrison Townsend and was founded in 1901 to 'bring great art to the people of the East End of London'. It exhibits the work of contemporary artists and is noted for its temporary exhibitions. It exhibited Picasso's *Guernica* in 1938 as part of a touring exhibition organised by the English artist and collector Roland Penrose to protest against the Spanish Civil War, and was later a pioneer of the Pop Art movement. The gallery also premiered international painters such as Frida Kahlo, Jackson Pollock and Mark Rothko, and showcased British artists, including Lucian Freud, Gilbert and George, and David Hockney.

In addition to its exhibitions (see website) the recently expanded gallery has historic archives, educational resources, art courses, a bookshop and an excellent dining room (run by Angela Hartnett).

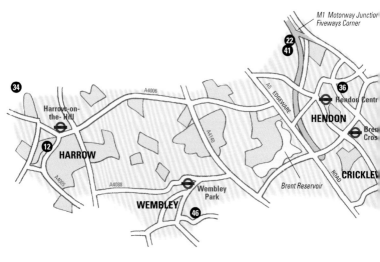

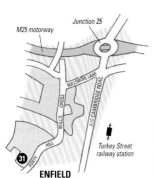

1. British Library
2. Estorick Collection
3. Sir John Soane's Museum
4. Wellcome Collection
5. Burgh House & Hampstead Museum
6. Cartoon Museum
7. Charles Dickens Museum
8. Fenton House
9. Foundling Museum
10. Freud Museum
11. Grant Museum of Zoology
12. Harrow School Museum
13. Hunterian Museum
14. Jewish Museum
15. John Wesley's Methodist Museum
16. Keats House
17. Kenwood House & The Iveagh Bequest
18. Magic Circle Museum
19. Museum of The Order of St John
20. Petrie Museum of Egyptian Archaeology
21. Pollock's Toy Museum
22. Royal Air Force Museum
23. Royal College of Physicians Museum
24. Sherlock Holmes Museum

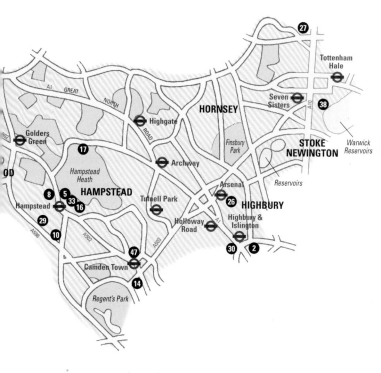

1 BRITISH LIBRARY

Address: 96 Euston Road, NW1 2DB (☎ 020-7412 7332, 🖥 bl.uk).
Opening hours: Mon-Fri, 9.30am to 6pm (8pm Tue); Sat 9.30am to 5pm; Sun and most Public Holidays, 11am to 5pm.
Cost: Free.
Transport: King's Cross St Pancras tube/rail.
Amenities: Restaurant, three cafés, shop, wheelchair access.

The British Library is the national library of the UK and the world's largest library in terms of the total number of items it holds. It's also a major research library with a collection of over 150 million items from many countries, including books, manuscripts, journals, newspapers, magazines, sound and music recordings, videos, play-scripts, patents, databases, maps, stamps, prints and drawings. The Library's collections include around 14m books, along with substantial holdings of manuscripts and historical items dating back as far as 2000 BC.

The Library has three permanent galleries: The Sir John Ritblat Gallery, The Philatelic Exhibition and Conservation Uncovered, described below.

The Sir John Ritblat Gallery: Sub-titled Treasures of the British Library, this gallery is named after a major donor who provided £1m for the library's display cabinets, and is a permanent display of some of the world's rarest and most precious manuscripts and books. It contains over 200 beautiful and fascinating items, including sacred texts, historic documents, landmarks of printing, masterpieces of illumination, major advances in science and map-making, and great works of literature and music.

Discover some of the world's most exciting and significant books and documents, from the *Lindisfarne Gospels* (698 AD), with their wonderful illustrations, to the *Gutenberg Bible* (1455), the first book printed in Europe. From the genius of Leonardo da Vinci's sketchbooks to the earliest versions of some of the greatest works of English literature, including Shakespeare's *First Folio* (1623), Jane Austen's *History of England* (1791) and Lewis Carroll's *Alice in Wonderland* (1865).

Also on display is the *Diamond Sutra*, the world's earliest dated printed book, made with carved wood blocks in 868 AD, the only surviving copy of the epic poem *Beowulf*, thought to date from the 10th or 11th century, and the

Earl of Essex's death warrant (1601), signed by Elizabeth I.

Isaac Newton, William Blake

The Philatelic Exhibition: A permanent exhibition area for the Library's Philatelic Collections, where you can see some of the world's rarest and most significant stamps. The Exhibition (on the upper ground floor) includes some 80,000 items and offers a unique opportunity to see many of the great rarities in an exhibition entitled *The British Library Philatelic Rarities.*

Conservation Uncovered: This exhibition in the Conservation Centre details the methods and skills used to preserve the Library's collections, including book and sound conservation.

The Library also stages frequent thematic exhibitions exploring such subject areas as maps, sacred texts and the history of the English language. More recent exhibitions have included Writing Britain, which examined how the landscapes of Britain permeate great literary works; Mughal India: Art, Culture and Empire; and *On the Road*

(Jack Kerouac's manuscript scroll), one of the defining books of the Beat Generation.

At the heart of the British Library is a tall glass tower – the King's Library Tower – which houses 65,000 books collected by George III (reigned 1760-1820). It's considered one of the most significant collections of the Enlightenment, containing books printed mainly in Britain, Europe and North America from the mid-15th to the early 19th centuries.

The library also has a shop and a number of excellent places to eat.

Royal Manuscripts

2   ESTORICK COLLECTION

Address: 39A Canonbury Square, N1 2AN (☎ 020-7704 9522,
🖳 estorickcollection.com).
Opening hours: Wed-Sat, 11am to 6pm; Thu 11am to 8pm; Sun noon to 5pm.
Closed Mondays, Tuesdays, Easter Sunday and over Christmas and the New Year
(see website for dates).
Cost: £5 adults, £3.50 concessions, schoolchildren and students free.
Transport: Highbury & Islington tube/rail.
Amenities: Café, shop, garden, wheelchair access.

Little-known outside the local area, this is a hidden London gem – housed in a handsome 19th-century house – not just Britain's only gallery devoted to modern Italian art, but one of the world's best collections of early 20th-century Italian art, particularly the Futurism movement.

The collection's title comes from the exotically-named Eric Estorick (1913-1993), an American sociologist, writer and art collector, who later became a full-time art dealer. He was very successful and his clients included a number of Hollywood stars, among them Lauren Bacall, Burt Lancaster and Billy Wilder. Eric and his wife Salome's art collection was put on display at a number of museums, including the Tate, and they received offers to purchase it from the Italian government and from museums in the United States and Israel, all of which they rejected.

Not long before his death, Estorick set up the Eric and Salome Estorick Foundation, to which he left his Italian collection, and 39A Canonbury Square was purchased to house it. The house, previously the home and office of architect Sir Basil Spence, the British architect, is Grade II listed and a fine example of Georgian architecture.

Futurism was founded in 1909 by the poet Filippo Tommaso (FT) Marinetti and was Italy's most significant contribution to 20th-century European culture. It sought to move beyond Italy's old, conservative cultural heritage and develop a new aesthetic, based on modern ideas and drawing inspiration from machines, speed and technology. Marinetti was soon joined by the painters Umberto Boccioni, Carlo Carrà, Giacomo Balla and Gino Severini and the composer Luigi Russolo, all of whom were eager to extend Marinetti's ideas to the visual arts.

During his honeymoon in Switzerland in 1947, Estorick discovered Umberto Boccioni's book, *Futurist Painting and Sculpture* (1914), and this marked the beginning of his passion for Italian art. Before returning to England the newlyweds visited the studio of the erstwhile Futurist Mario

The Boulevard, Gino Severini

Sironi in Milan, where Estorick bought 'hundreds and hundreds of drawings and as many paintings as I could get into my Packard Convertible Roadster', and his collection grew from there throughout the '50s.

 DON'T MISS!

As well as paintings, the collection includes sculpture and figurative art, including work by Medardo Rosso, who, on the death of Rodin, was called 'the greatest living sculptor' by the French writer and critic Apollinaire. There are also sculptures by Giacomo Manzu and Marino Marini, hailed as bringing about the rebirth of Italian sculpture in the 20th century.

Other major artists whose work features in the collection include Amedeo Modigliani – noted for his graceful, elongated portraits and figure studies – who is represented by a fine series of drawings and an oil portrait of Dr François Brabander, and Giorgio de Chirico, the founder of Metaphysical Art. His enigmatic, dream-like imagery, which was to exert a profound influence on the Surrealists, is also represented in the collection with his important early work, *The Revolt of the Sage*. In addition, there's a large number of paintings and drawings by Mario Sironi and Massimo Campigli.

The Estorick collection has six galleries and an art library (open by

Modern Idol, Umberto Boccioni

appointment) containing over 2,000 books, periodicals and catalogues focusing on 20th-century Italian art, plus copies of every Futurist manifesto. There's also a bookshop and a café (see box).

The gallery regularly stages temporary exhibitions (see website for details) and well-regarded talks and educational events. The permanent collection is internationally acclaimed, particularly for its Futurist works.

 FOOD & DRINK

Estorick Caffè: The museum's licensed Italian café (free access – a favourite with locals) in the beautiful landscaped garden is a great spot for an al fresco lunch.

3   SIR JOHN SOANE'S MUSEUM

Address: 13 Lincoln's Inn Fields, Holborn, WC2A 3BP (☎ 020-7440 4263, 🖳 soane.org).

Opening hours: Tue-Sat, 10am to 5pm. Closed 24-26th December and 30th December to 1st January. An atmospheric candlelit evening (6-9pm) is held on the first Tuesday of each month. There's also a tour on Saturdays at 11am, with tickets on sale from 10.30am. Bookings aren't possible for candlelit evenings or tours, so expect queues.

Cost: Free. Saturday tours £10.

Transport: Holborn tube.

Amenities: Shop, wheelchair access.

Sir John Soane (1753-1837) was a bricklayer's son who became one of Britain's greatest, most innovative architects, noted for his designs of the Bank of England (see page 124 for the **Bank of England Museum**) and the **Dulwich Picture Gallery** (see page 261). The museum is housed in his former home which he designed both to live in and to house his antiquities and works of art. Soane believed in the 'poetry of architecture' and the house is an embodiment of his experiments and ideas about how light and space should work.

👁 DON'T MISS!

The crowning glories of the Soane collection are the three Canalettos (*Riva degli Schiavoni*, *The Rialto Bridge from the North* and *Piazza S. Marco*) and two series of Hogarth paintings, *A Rake's Progress* and *An Election*. Canaletto's *Riva* was described by the late J G Links, the world's leading expert on the artist, as among the finest half-dozen Canalettos in existence, while the Hogarths represent two of the three surviving series of 'modern moral subjects' painted by Hogarth (the other one is in the National Gallery).

used top-lighting – sometimes with coloured glass – and lots of mirrors to produce an atmospherically lit environment. The effect is especially striking when the building is lit by candlelight.

Soane was a great collector and he amassed a huge assortment of interesting objects and artworks, so many that he had to be creative to house it all, including having panels hung with paintings lining the walls that can be pulled out like leaves or which unfold from the walls. At one stage, Soane and his family lived in just two small rooms, so great was the collection. It's now a happy sort of ordered chaos and deserves to be better known.

The building has a distinctive, striking front, with a projecting first-floor loggia, Coade Stone statues and Gothic pedestals. Internally, Soane

Riva degli Schiavoni, Canaletto

Exhibits include Roman cremation urns, a human skeleton, the Egyptian alabaster sarcophagus of Seti I, the marble tomb of Soane's favourite dog, and pieces from the classical, medieval, Renaissance and Oriental periods, including furniture, timepieces, stained glass, paintings, sculpture, jewellery, 30,000 architectural drawings, 6,857 historical volumes and 252 historical architectural models. There's also a library.

The museum was established in Soane's own lifetime by a private Act of Parliament in 1833, which took effect on Soane's death in 1837. The Act required that the house be kept 'as nearly as possible' as it was when he died, and that's largely been the case. Soane fell out with his two sons, hence his decision to bequeath his property as a museum.

Soane's first house in Lincoln's Inn Fields (no. 12 next door to the museum, built in 1792) was recently acquired by the museum and restored, revealing hitherto unseen interiors, such as the geometric staircase painted to resemble the walls of a Roman catacomb. It opened in July 2012 and provides the museum with modern facilities, including a stunning new gallery space (designed by Caruso St John) to hold temporary exhibitions, a shop and a cloakroom. The museum also now boasts a purpose built Conservation Studio to preserve Soane's collection, as well as a lift to improve access to this house of treasures.

ALLOW...

The museum allows an hour for a group visit but you can easily spend two or three hours taking in the wonders on view. The website helpfully suggests a number of themed trails, with downloaded guides, such as – London in the Soane – objects with a special link to the capital – and Caring for Soane's Collection, which looks at the work of conservationists in the house.

4 WELLCOME COLLECTION

Address: 183 Euston Road, NW1 2BE (☏ 020-7611 2222,
🖥 wellcomecollection.org).
Opening hours: Tue-Wed and Fri-Sat, 10am to 6pm; Thu 10am to 10pm; Sun 11am
to 6pm; Public Holidays, noon to 6pm. Closed Christmas and New Year (see website
for dates).
Cost: Free.
Transport: Euston Square tube and Euston rail.
Amenities: Café, shop, library, wheelchair access.

This is one of London's most original and interesting, albeit lesser-known, museums, housed in an impressive, sleek building. It's an unusual collection of medical artefacts and works of art (the foyer includes a 1950 work by Pablo Picasso and another by Anthony Gormley, while a figure by Marc Quinn is displayed in a glass case next to the entrance), which 'explore ideas about the connections between medicine, life and art in the past, present and future'. The website dubs it a 'free destination for the incurably curious' and is a useful mirror for the collection, being detailed, interactive (including audio and video presentations), visually interesting, current (including a blog) and full of nuggets of obscure information.

The Collection is named after Sir Henry Wellcome (1853-1936), an American-British pharmaceutical entrepreneur, philanthropist, pharmacist and collector, whose will created the Wellcome Trust, the world's largest independent charitable foundation funding research into human and animal health. It spends over £600m annually – largely on biomedical research and the medical humanities – and the Wellcome Collection is part of the Trust.

The museum charts the development of medicine through the ages and across many cultures, and explores the impact of medicine on our lives, through a mixture of galleries, events and a library. Sir Henry Wellcome was a keen collector of medical artefacts and amassed over a million items. The Wellcome Collection displays a modest number of these, including some extremely varied items such as used guillotine blades, Napoleon's toothbrush,

Sir Henry Wellcome

ivory carvings of pregnant women, shrunken heads, royal hair, ancient sex aids, a Chinese torture chair and a Picasso drawing.

Peruvian mummy

👁 DON'T MISS!

Some of the more bizarre objects in the Medicine Man exhibition include a 19th-century chastity belt made from iron and velvet, a set of Chinese porcelain fruit concealing 'erotic' models of people in sexual positions, and a turtle-shaped leather container made by Sioux Indians designed to contain a baby girl's umbilical cord which was attached to the cradle as an amulet to protect against disease.

themes include skin decoration; sleep and dreaming; the relationship between madness and art; the history of human drug use and our attitudes to it; personal experiences of aging and dementia; and the hidden past of 26 skeletons found in sites around London.

There's also a café (see box), bookshop, conference facilities and a members' club.

The Wellcome Library contains over 2m items, including 750,000 books and a large collection of manuscripts, some 6,000 in Sanskrit alone. The library is open to the public, but you must register on your first visit and become a member to use it fully (see website for details). Wellcome Images is one of the Library's major visual collections and also forms part of the Wellcome Collection. It's one of the world's richest and most unique image collections, with themes ranging from medical and social history to contemporary healthcare and science. The collection also contains historical images from the Wellcome Library collections, Tibetan Buddhist paintings, ancient Sanskrit manuscripts written on palm leaves, beautifully illuminated Persian books and much more.

The Wellcome Collection has three spaces: upstairs is an exhibition drawn from Sir Henry's finds entitled Medicine Man, while next door is Medicine Now with some striking art on medical themes, including a postcard wall where visitors are encouraged to contribute drawings. Downstairs there's a series of temporary exhibits which are often challenging and provocative – recent

🍴 FOOD & DRINK 🍷

Museum café: Whether you're after a quick cup of coffee and a pastry, afternoon tea or a light meal with a glass of wine, the excellent Peyton & Byrne café fits the bill.

torture chair

5 BURGH HOUSE & HAMPSTEAD MUSEUM

Address: New End Square, NW3 1LT (☎ 020-7431 0144, 🖳 burghhouse.org.uk).
Opening hours: House and museum: Wed-Fri and Sun, noon to 5pm; Sat, ground floor and art gallery only, noon to 5pm.
Cost: Free.
Transport: Hampstead tube.
Amenities: Café, garden, no step-free access.

Burgh House (Grade I listed) – built in 1704 in the time of Queen Anne – is a handsome building and one of the oldest houses in Hampstead, with its original panelled rooms and staircase. It's named after the Reverend Allatson Burgh, a notably unpopular cleric, who purchased it in 1822. Among its many tenants was Rudyard Kipling's daughter, Elsie Bambridge, in the '30s.

Nowadays the house is home to Hampstead Museum. It wouldn't claim to be one of the capital's great collections, but it's varied and interesting, and, like so many of London's local displays, often passes under the radar – of both local residents and visitors. The museum traces Hampstead's long history, from prehistoric times to the present day,

and holds over 3,000 objects. Most exhibits relate to social history, fine art, and notable former Hampstead residents, of which there have been many. Look out for the so-called 'High Hill Penguin', commissioned by the publishing house in 1960 and signed by famous local authors at Hampstead's High Hill Bookshop.

 FOOD & DRINK

Buttery Café: The Burgh House café has a pretty garden, which is full of nooks and crannies. It's a civilised place to enjoy a coffee or glass of wine and justifiably popular with Hampstead locals.

Highlights of the fine art collection include work by the internationally known CRW Nevinson, Fred Uhlman, Donald Towner and Duncan Grant. Local artists including Sidney Arrobus, Mari I'Anson, Betty Greenhalf and Gillian Lawson are also well represented. It additionally holds the Patrick Allingham Bequest, which consists of the largest archive and collection of Helen Allingham material in the world. There's also a display dedicated to painter John Constable, who spent time in Hampstead, and to the poet John Keats, who lived in the area for a short time (see **Keats House** on page 163).

CARTOON MUSEUM

Address: 35 Little Russell Street, WC1A 2HH (☎ 020-7580 8155,
💻 cartoonmuseum.org).
Opening hours: Mon-Sat, 10.30am to 5.30pm, including Bank Holidays; Sun, noon to 5.30pm.
Cost: £5.50 adults, £4 concessions, £3 students, under 18s free. Children aged 12 and under must be accompanied by an adult.
Transport: Holborn or Tottenham Court Road tube.
Amenities: Shop, library, wheelchair access (ground floor only).

The unique Cartoon Museum (opened in 2006) is dedicated to preserving the best of British cartoons, caricatures, comics and animation, from the 18th century to the present day. The collection contains over 2,300 original cartoons, caricatures and comic pages, while the Heneage Library holds over 6,000 books and 6,000 comics.

The museum is housed over two floors of a former dairy. On the ground floor cartoons are displayed chronologically, starting with the early 18th century, when high-society types back from the Grand Tour introduced the Italian practice of caricature to polite society. From Hogarth, the displays move on to British cartooning's 'golden age' (1770-1830), while Modern Times covers political wartime cartoons and social commentary produced between 1914 and 1961. The 'new satire' section features works published from 1961 onwards and includes Ralph Steadman, Steve Bell, Dave Brown, Matt and others. In the downstairs displays, the artists' names are immediately recognisable, while upstairs – where comic strip art from the *Beano*, *Dandy* and *2000AD* is displayed – it's more about characters such as Dan Dare, Judge Dredd and Rupert the Bear.

Steve Bell

The Young Artists' Gallery includes work with a less 'authorised' feel, designed to appeal to younger audiences, while a workshop space hosts regular children's classes in the arts of animation and claymation.

Exhibitions have focused on Ronald Searle, Pont, Fougasse, Rowland Emett, *Beano* and *Dandy*, Mike Williams, Mel Calman, cartoons from private London clubs, *Viz*, *Alice in Sunderland* (Bryan Talbot) and Robert Dighton, as well as well-known political 'targets' such as Tony Blair and Margaret Thatcher.

DON'T MISS!

Gerald Scarfe's famous Chairman Mao armchair, a 3D caricature of the Chinese leader presented as an easy chair, upholstered in red leather (of course!) and strangely reminiscent of Jabba the Hut.

7 CHARLES DICKENS MUSEUM

Address: 48 Doughty Street, WC1N 2LX (☎ 020-7405 2127,
🖳 dickensmuseum.com)
Opening hours: Daily, 10am to 5pm.
Cost: £8 adults, £6 concessions, £4 children (aged 6 to 16), free for under-6s.
Admission to the café, garden and gift shop is free.
Transport: Chancery Lane, Holborn or Russell Square tube.
Amenities: Café, shop, wheelchair access.

Charles Dickens's novels have done much to inform people's view of London, and the term 'Dickensian' is still used to describe certain parts of the city. Therefore it's surprising that not only is this museum not on the first page of the average 'to visit' list, but probably isn't on it at all.

The museum is spread over four floors of a typical Georgian terraced house, and the rooms have a traditional Victorian appearance. Dickens lived here for over two years, from March 1837 (a year after his marriage) until December 1839, and it's the only surviving house he occupied in London. He and his wife Catherine shared the house with the eldest three of their ten children, and their two eldest daughters were born here.

👁 DON'T MISS!

The most famous exhibit is probably the portrait of Dickens known as *Dickens Dream* by RW Buss, an original illustrator of *The Pickwick Papers*. This unfinished picture shows Dickens in his study at Gads Hill Place in Kent, surrounded by characters from his books.

It was a productive time for the author: he completed *The Pickwick Papers*, wrote *Oliver Twist* and *Nicholas Nickleby*, and worked on *Barnaby Rudge* at Doughty Street. so it's appropriate that it houses the world's most important Dickens' collection totalling over 100,000 items, including manuscripts, rare editions, paintings, personal items and a research library. The photographic collection contains over 5,000 photographs, 2,000 magic lantern slides, 1,000 35mm slides and a large number of colour transparencies. There are also over 500 portraits of Dickens, many interesting views of 19th-century London, illustrations from his novels, and cartoons and caricatures.

FENTON HOUSE

8

Address: Hampstead Grove, NW3 6SP (☎ 01494-755 563, 💻 nationaltrust.org.uk/fenton-house).

Opening hours: March to October, Wed-Sun, 11am to 5pm (check website for exact dates).

Cost: £6.50 adults, £3 children, £16 families, £2 garden only, £10 garden season ticket. Free for National Trust members.

Transport: Hampstead tube.

Amenities: Garden, wheelchair access (ground floor only).

Affluent, leafy Hampstead is full of sizeable, attractive properties and this is one of the earliest, largest and most architecturally important: a charming 17th-century merchant's house built around 1686 that has been virtually unaltered during 300 years of continuous occupation. It was bought in 1793 by the Fentons (hence the name), who made some Regency alterations that gave the house its current appearance. *Country Life* magazine described it as 'London's most enchanting country house' and it's now owned by the National Trust.

👁 DON'T MISS!

Fenton House's balcony overlooks one of the highest points in London and offers a panoramic view over the city, comparable with the famous view from Parliament Hill.

Fenton House is home to a collection of early keyboard instruments put together by the many-named Major George Henry Benton Fletcher (1866-1944). He had a varied career as a soldier, social worker and archaeologist – who dug with the famous Flinders Petrie – see the **Petrie Museum** on pages 167. The major's musical instruments are the subject of special talks and recitals for visitors (see website for dates).

The house also boasts collections of paintings (notably some fine portraits – artists represented in the collection including Jan Brueghel, Albrecht Dürer, John Russell, Francis Sartorius and GF Watts), porcelain (there are world-class collections of English, European and Oriental porcelain), 17th-century needlework pictures and Georgian furniture (of the decorative and delicate sort).

The enchanting garden is laid out on the side of a hill and divided into upper and lower levels. It's an almost rural haven, noted for its sunken walled section, with a glasshouse, vegetable beds, culinary herb border and flower beds. There's also a 300-year-old orchard of agreeably gnarled apple trees, producing over 30 different varieties of apple. You can sample them on the annual Apple Day each September.

9 FOUNDLING MUSEUM

Address: 40 Brunswick Square, WC1N 1AZ (☎ 020-7841 3600,
🖳 foundlingmuseum.org.uk).
Opening hours: Tue-Sat, 10am to 5pm; Sun 11am to 5pm. Closed Mondays and on
some Bank Holidays (see website for details).
Cost: £7.50 adults, £5 concessions, under-16s free.
Transport: Russell Square tube.
Amenities: Café, shop, wheelchair access.

The Foundling Museum's location
in a leafy Bloomsbury cul-de-sac
may have kept it off the main tourist
radar. This is a pity as, according to
the British broadsheet newspaper *The
DailyTelegraph*, it's 'one of London's
most intriguing collections'. It tells
the story of the Foundling Hospital,
London's first home for abandoned
children, which involves three major
figures in British history: philanthropist
Sir Thomas Coram (1668-1751),
artist William Hogarth (1697-1764)
and composer George Frederic
Handel (1685-1759). Coram founded
the Hospital, said to be the world's
first incorporated charity, after being
appalled by the number of abandoned,
homeless children living on London's
streets. Hogarth and Handel were
major benefactors.

The museum's collection charts
the history of the Foundling Hospital
between its foundation in 1739 and
closure in 1954. It's a fascinating
blend of art, period interiors and social
history, housed in a restored building
adjacent to the Hospital's
original home, which was
demolished in 1928.

The museum has two
principal collections. The
Foundling Collection
relates to the hospital
itself and the story of
the 27,000 children who
passed through its doors
during its 215-year history.
Especially poignant is the
collection of tokens mothers left with
their babies – coins, buttons, bits of
jewellery – allowing the hospital to
match a mother with her child should
she ever come back to claim it, though
sadly, this didn't happen very often. It
also includes the Gerald Coke Handel
Collection, the largest privately-held
collection of Handel material.

The museum – which was Britain's
first public art gallery – also exhibits
paintings and sculptures by Hogarth,
Thomas Gainsborough, Joshua
Reynolds and others.

 FOOD & DRINK

Foundling Museum Café: Run by
Zafferano, the museum's café serves
up imaginative sandwiches, salads
and pies; it was voted one of London's
top ten museum and gallery cafés by
Time Out.

FREUD MUSEUM

Address: 20 Maresfield Gardens, NW3 5SX (☎ 020-7435 2002, 🖵 freud.org.uk).
Opening hours: Wed-Sun, noon to 5pm.
Cost: £6 adults, £4.50 senior citizens, £3 concessions (students, children 12-16, unemployed and disabled), under-12s free.
Transport: Finchley Road tube.
Amenities: Tea/coffee, garden, shop, wheelchair access (ground floor only).

The Freud Museum is an interesting, atmospheric museum, housed in the home of Sigmund Freud and his family after they fled the Nazi annexation of Austria in 1938. Built in 1920 in Queen Anne style, it's a striking and handsome red-brick house, which remained the Freud family home until 1982, when Anna Freud, Sigmund's youngest daughter (he had six children), died. Sigmund Freud himself didn't have the chance to live in the house for very long as he died a few weeks after the Second World War broke out in September 1939.

The Freuds were fortunate to be able to bring their furniture and household effects to London, including lovely Biedermeier chests, tables and cupboards, and a collection of 18th- and 19th-century Austrian painted country furniture. Their possessions include a drawing of Freud by Salvador Dali – the Surrealists were strongly influenced by his writings.

The museum's centrepiece is Freud's study, preserved as it was during his lifetime: the study in London is furnished exactly as it had been in Vienna, using Freud's notes which showed the position of everything so that it could be faithfully recreated. It's a showcase for Freud's impressive collection of antiquities (Egyptian, Greek, Roman and Oriental), totalling some 2,000 items. The house also contains many items from the life and works of Anna Freud, who continued her father's psychoanalytic work.

The museum hosts a series of courses, films and lectures about subjects relevant to Freud and to psychoanalysis in general. The house also has a beautiful garden and a interesting shop.

👁 DON'T MISS!

Freud's patients reclined on his psychoanalytic couch which now has pride of place in his study, covered with a richly coloured Iranian rug with chenille cushions piled on top. It was reputedly a gift from a grateful patient.

11 GRANT MUSEUM OF ZOOLOGY

Address: Rockefeller Building, University College London, 21 University Street, WC1E 6DE (☎ 020-3108 2052, 🖥 ucl.ac.uk/museums/zoology).
Opening hours: Mon-Sat, 1pm to 5pm. Closed on Public Holidays and for a few days around Easter and Christmas (see website).
Cost: Free.
Transport: Warren Street or Euston Square tube.
Amenities: Wheelchair access.

In an increasingly slick, high-tech world, the Grant Museum has a healthy air of the Victorian collector about it; it's how museums used to be, with the emphasis on exhibits in cases rather than interactive displays, soundscapes and other such recent innovations. The Grant is London's only remaining university zoological museum, with some 67,000 specimens covering the entire animal kingdom. It was founded in 1828 as a teaching collection, named after Robert Grant (1793-1874) – the first Professor of Zoology and Comparative Anatomy in England. His collection remains the basis of the museum, along with exhibits donated by Thomas Henry Huxley.

The somewhat macabre collection includes a plethora of skeletons, mounted animals and specimens preserved in fluid, many of which are now extinct or endangered. The dodo is a major draw, although the museum doesn't have a complete dodo skeleton (none exist anywhere), just a selection of bones from Mauritius where the birds lived until becoming extinct around 1700. There is, however, a complete skeleton of the quagga, a type of zebra from South Africa with fewer stripes than a 'standard' zebra, which was hunted to extinction by the 1870s, and a complete set of bones of the thylacine, a large marsupial carnivore which once inhabited Australia and New Guinea.

The Grant Museum is also home to a large number of insects, the most abundant group of animals in the world, with around 1m species. Other exhibits, including a stuffed gorilla, the skeleton of a 5m-long anaconda and a collection of bisected animals' heads all add to the pleasant sensation of having landed in a mad scientist's lair.

👁 DON'T MISS!

One of the weirdest items on display is a jar crammed full of preserved moles – 18 in total – which may once have been intended for a dissection class.

HARROW SCHOOL MUSEUM

12

Address: 5 High Street, HA1 3HP (☎ 020-8872 8205 for tours,
🖥 harrowschool.org.uk).
Opening hours: Old Speech Room Gallery – weekday afternoons (except Wed)
and on occasional Sundays (2.30-5pm) during term-time. Museum of Harrow Life –
open most Sundays during term time from 2.30-4.30pm (see website). Guided group
tours by appointment and also 'open' tours (no booking required).
Cost: Gallery and museums free. Open tours £5 per person (£4 concessions).
Transport: Harrow-on-the-Hill tube.
Amenities: Wheelchair access.

Harrow School is an English independent school for boys founded in 1572 by John Lyon (d 1592) under a Royal Charter granted by Elizabeth I. The construction of the first school building began in 1608, and was completed in 1615. The original buildings remain, although the school is now much larger and covers an area of some 400 acres (160ha), including golf course, woodland and its own working farm.

The school's long line of famous alumni includes eight former Prime Ministers (Churchill, Baldwin, Peel and Palmerston among them), numerous foreign statesmen, a number of royals and many leading figures in the arts and sciences, including Byron, Sheridan, Anthony Trollope, archaeologist Sir Arthur Evans, physicist Lord Rayleigh and inventor Henry Fox Talbot. More recent Old Harrovians include singer James Blunt, racing pundit John McCririck and screenwriter Richard Curtis.

The Old Speech Room was built in 1819-1821 to encourage public speaking. It was opened as a museum and gallery in 1976 to house the school's collections, which include Egyptian and Greek antiquities, English/European watercolours, modern British paintings, Japanese prints, books and natural history artefacts. The museum hosts themed exhibitions from its collections. The nearby Museum of Harrow Life displays items from the school's past and present, including a boy's room from the 1890s (when Churchill was a pupil) and the famous Harrow Football with its peculiar flattened shape.

Public tours of Harrow School take place on a regular basis, usually on Saturdays at 2pm (no advanced booking is necessary – see website for details), and group tours can also be arranged. Visitors are shown buildings that are representative of the school and its history, including the two museums.

 ALLOW...

The public tour starts from Bill Yard and takes around 90 minutes. Allow a similar amount of time when visiting the museums independently.

13 HUNTERIAN MUSEUM

Address: Royal College of Surgeons, 35-43 Lincoln's Inn Fields, Holborn, WC2A 3PE (☏ 020-7869 6560, 🖥 rcseng.ac.uk/museums).
Opening hours: Tue-Sat, 10am to 5pm. Free, curator-led guided tours (max 25 people) on Wednesdays at 1pm (phone to reserve a place).
Cost: Free.
Transport: Holborn tube.
Amenities: Shop, wheelchair access.

This museum might not be suitable for those of a squeamish disposition, but nevertheless it's fascinating. As might be expected from its location in the building of the Royal College of Surgeons, this is very much a medical exhibit, undoubtedly one of the world's greatest museum collections of comparative anatomy, pathology, osteology and natural history.

The museum is named after the noted Scottish surgeon John Hunter (1728-1793), whose collection of around 15,000 items was purchased by the government in 1799 and given to the Company (later the Royal College) of Surgeons. (His brother William Hunter's collection forms the basis for Glasgow's Hunterian Museum.)

Today's museum has around 3,500 items from John Hunter's original collection, plus another 2,500 or so objects acquired after 1799, including an odontological (dentistry) collection and natural history collections. They are rather grisly for some tastes – notably the large selection of preserved human and animal remains, with rows of jars of organs – but they're varied and fascinating, and show just how far medicine has (thankfully!) progressed in the last few centuries. The museum also holds exhibitions and talks.

Among the many items on display are a mummified hand, old wax models of dissections, diseased bones, Winston Churchill's dentures, plus photographs of pioneering plastic surgery and videos of modern operations.

Last, but by no means least, there's a display of body parts of notables (obtained by Hunter following post mortems performed at the request of and with the permission of their families), including the then Bishop of Durham's rectum.

👁 DON'T MISS!

One of the largest exhibits at the Hunterian is the skeleton of the 'Irish Giant', Charles Byrne, who grew to 7ft 7in (2.3m) tall. A minor celebrity, he died from drink aged just 22, and his corpse was purchased by John Hunter for £500.

JEWISH MUSEUM 14

Address: Raymond Burton House, 129-131 Albert Street, NW1 7NB (☎ 020-7284 7384, 🖥 jewishmuseum.org.uk).
Opening hours: Sun-Thu, 10am to 5pm; Fri 10am to 2pm; Sat closed.
Cost: £7.50 adults, £6.50 concessions, £3.50 children 5-16, under-5s free, £18 families (2 adults and up to 4 children). Admission is free to the Welcome Gallery, museum shop and the kosher café (10am to 5pm, Sun-Thu).
Transport: Camden Town tube.
Amenities: Café, shop, wheelchair access.

This internationally acclaimed collection allows visitors to explore Jewish culture, heritage and identity. It provides a vivid snapshot of Jewish life and 'places the Jewish story into the wider context of British history'. There's a huge variety of exhibits and the displays are well conceived and created, a blend of traditional items in cases and interactive, high-tech exhibits. The museum also touches on wider issues of minority groups and immigration, which is appropriate in London, one of the world's most cosmopolitan cities.

The permanent display is divided into four collections. The Welcome Gallery is a digital exhibit showing how British Jewish people live today, in the context of their everyday lives, while Judaism – A Living Faith presents the museum's outstanding collection of splendid Jewish ceremonial art, one of the world's finest Judaic collections. At its centre is an interactive Torah display, and the gallery explores Jewish religious practice at home and in the synagogue.

History – A British Story traces Britain's Jewish history, from the earliest known settlement in 1066 to today. Highlights include an evocation of a Jewish East End street, an interactive map exploring the history of Jewish settlement around the UK, and displays relating to refugees from Nazism.

🍴 FOOD & DRINK 🍸

Jewish Museum Café: A great place to sample traditional Jewish specialities, such as smoked salmon and cream cheese bagels, hummus and falafel wraps. All the food and drink is – not surprisingly – kosher.

The most poignant exhibition is the Holocaust Gallery which tells the story of Leon Greenman, who survived incarceration in six concentration camps; his wife and son died in Auschwitz, while Leon lived until 2008. There's also a film about other Holocaust survivors who settled in Britain.

The museum also has a lively programme of temporary exhibitions, events and talks (see website for details).

15 JOHN WESLEY'S METHODIST MUSEUM

Address: 49 City Road, EC1Y 1AU (☎ 020-7253 2262, 🖥 wesleyschapel.org.uk).
Opening hours: Mon-Sat, 10am to 4pm; Sun 12.30pm to 1.45pm. Closed Thursdays from 12.45-1.30pm (for services), between Christmas and New Year, and Bank Holidays (except Good Friday). See website for service times.
Cost: Free.
Transport: Old Street tube.
Amenities: Shop, wheelchair access (ground floor only to John Wesley's House).

Step back into 18th-century London with a visit to one of the city's finest surviving small Georgian houses. John Wesley's (1703-1791) house was built in 1779, and the founder of Methodism lived here for the last 12 years of his life, mainly in winter (summers were spent travelling and preaching around the country). It contains many of Wesley's belongings, including his study chair, bureau and bookcase, and a teapot made for him by Josiah Wedgewood, although unfortunately Wesley disapproved of tea! Just off Wesley's bedroom is a small prayer room, now a shrine to Methodists worldwide.

Wesley was already an ordained minister in the Church of England when he underwent an evangelical conversion at a bible reading in London in 1738. In his subsequent preaching he encouraged a life of prayer, bible study and charity work. Eventually Methodism became a separate denomination from the Church of England and today there are up to 70m Methodists worldwide.

The site is a complex of Georgian and Victorian buildings located in a superb Georgian courtyard near the financial district of London. It includes not only Wesley's house, but also his tomb, Chapel and the Museum of Methodism. Wesley's Chapel (Grade I listed) remained in continuous use until structural problems forced it to close in the early '70s, although it was repaired and reopened on 1st November 1978, its 200th anniversary.

The **Museum of Methodism** in the chapel's crypt traces its history from Wesley to the present day, and includes original letters penned by John and Charles Wesley, John's pulpit, items associated with Methodism's missionary work, plus a small gift shop.

 DON'T MISS!

John Wesley pioneered the use of Electro Convulsive Therapy (ECT) and his study displays the machine he used to generate electricity to treat depression and other disorders.

KEATS HOUSE 16

Address: Keats Grove, Hampstead, NW3 2RR (☎ 020-7332 3868, 🖥 cityoflondon.gov.uk/keatshousehampstead).
Opening hours: Winter (November to February), Fri-Sun, 1-5pm; Tue-Thu, pre-booked groups only. Summer (March to October), Tue-Sun, 1-5pm. Closed Mondays and Good Friday. See website for Christmas & New Year dates.
Cost: £5 adults, £3 concessions (pensioners, students and the unemployed), free for under 18s. See website for groups. Access to the garden is free.
Transport: Hampstead Heath rail or Hampstead tube.
Amenities: Garden, wheelchair access (ground floor only).

This Grade I listed building is a shrine to one of the leading poets of the English Romantic movement (along with Lord Byron and Percy Bysshe Shelley), in a part of London long favoured by literary and creative types. John Keats (1795-1821) lived here for a mere 17 months, from 1818, before travelling to Italy, where he died of tuberculosis aged just 25.

👁 DON'T MISS!

The garden at Keats House has been described as one of the most romantic in London and is planted to reflect its Regency heritage. It's here that Keats is said to have written *Ode to a Nightingale* while sitting under a plum tree.

The house was built between 1814 and 1816 and was originally two separate properties. John Keats lodged in one of them with his friend Charles Brown from December 1818 to September 1820, which although only a short period was one of his most productive. In 1838, the actress and one-time favourite of George IV, Eliza Jane Chester, purchased the houses and knocked them through to create one dwelling.

Keats House contains a large variety of Keats-related material, including books, paintings and household items. There are letters by Keats, books in which he wrote poetry, the engagement ring that he gave to his sweetheart Fanny Brawne (he died before they could be married), busts and portraits of Keats, and locks of his brown hair. Various rooms in the house have been faithfully recreated as they would have been when occupied by Keats, Brown, the Brawnes and Eliza Chester.

The museum holds regular literary and poetry events – related to Keats' work and to poetry in general – as well as talks and exhibitions about various aspects of life in Regency London, such as architecture, fashion and garden design. See website for details.

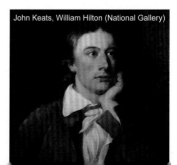
John Keats, William Hilton (National Gallery)

17 KENWOOD HOUSE & THE IVEAGH BEQUEST

Address: Hampstead Lane, NW3 7JR (☎ 020-8348 1286 or 0870-333 1181,
🖳 english-heritage.org.uk/daysout/properties/kenwood-house).

Opening hours: Estate, 7am to dusk; café 9am to 5pm. At the time of writing the
house was closed until autumn 2013 for major renovations, although the estate
grounds, gardens, gift shop and Brewhouse café remain **open**. See website for
more information.

Cost: Entry to the grounds is free; check website for prices to see the refurbished
house. Free for English Heritage members.

Transport: Archway or Golders Green tube, then 210 bus.

Amenities: Café, shop, park, gardens, wheelchair access.

Tucked away in beautiful landscaped parkland on Hampstead Heath, Kenwood House (Grade II* listed) is one of the most magnificent estates in London, now managed by English Heritage. This elegant villa was built in the 17th century (c.1616) and owned for over 200 years by the family of William Murray, the 1st Earl of Mansfield (1705-1793). It was remodelled by Robert Adam (1728-1792) between 1764 and 1773, who transformed the original brick house into a majestic neoclassical villa. Adam's richly decorated library, with its beautiful friezes and grand colonnades, is a masterpiece and considered one of the most important rooms in the country. In 1793-6, George Saunders (1762-1839) added two wings on the north side and the offices, kitchen buildings and a brewery.

Brewing magnate Edward Cecil Guinness, first Earl of Iveagh (1847-1927), bought Kenwood House and the remaining 74-acre estate in 1925 and on his death, bequeathed the house, land and part of his collection of paintings to the nation. The Iveagh Bequest includes important paintings by great masters, including Rembrandt, Vermeer, Turner, Reynolds and Gainsborough, recently joined by Constable's oil sketch *Hampstead Heath*.

The house is also home to the Suffolk collection of rare Jacobean portraits (moved here from **The Rangers House** – see page 271).

The parkland surrounding Kenwood was influenced by the great English landscape gardener Humphrey Repton (1752-1818), and was designed to be seen from a planned circuit walk that provides a series of evocative views, contrasts and 'surprises'. The gardens near the house contain sculptures by Reg Butler, Barbara Hepworth and Henry Moore, among others.

 FOOD & DRINK

The Brewhouse: Formerly the estate's brewery, this delightful café serves sandwiches, salads, pastries, soups and stews, plus veggie and children's options. In summer there's a stand outside serving ice cream and Pimm's.

MAGIC CIRCLE MUSEUM   18

Address: 12 Stephenson Way, NW1 2HD (☎ 020-7367 2222,
🖥 themagiccircle.co.uk).
Opening hours: Vary – see website for information about current events. Tours (two hours) are held by appointment.
Cost: Varies – contact the museum for information.
Transport: Euston rail or Euston Square tube.
Amenities: Wheelchair access.

apparatus of the past. At the top of the building, reached by a lift or the spectacular helical staircase, is a fully-equipped theatre, where magic shows are presented.

 ALLOW...

The Magical Circle Experience is a two-hour tour starting at 11.30am on Mondays, while Meet the Magic Circle is an evening event lasting around three hours.

Widely acclaimed as the finest magic headquarters in the world, The Magic Circle was founded in 1905 after a meeting of 23 amateur and professional magicians at Pinoli's restaurant in London. Meetings were held in a room at St George's Hall in Langham Place, where magicians David Devant – the greatest magician of his era and the first president of the Circle – and Nevil Maskelyne regularly performed.

The Magic Circle later moved to its current home in Stephenson Way, dubbed 'The Centre for the Magic Arts', designed and refurbished at a cost of £2.1m. The building includes the Clubroom and the Devant Room, with showcases displaying unique

The most priceless treasures, memorabilia and magical posters are displayed in the museum on the lower ground floor, which also houses lending and reference libraries containing the largest collection of magic books in Europe. Museum exhibits include magic tricks, props, posters, programmes, toys, photographs and artefacts related to magic and illusionists. Items of interest include props used by TV magicians Tommy Cooper and David Nixon, and a sound recording of Harry Houdini from an Edison cylinder.

The Magical Circle Experience is a tour of the building and museum, while there are regular Meet the Magic Circle evenings – usually twice a month on Tuesdays – performed by some of the Circle's top magicians, plus various other public events throughout the year. Would-be Harry Potters can join the Young Magicians Club (see
🖥 youngmagiciansclub.co.uk).

19 MUSEUM OF THE ORDER OF ST JOHN

Address: St John's Gate, St John's Lane, EC1M 4DA (☎ 020-7324 4005,
🖳 museumstjohn.org.uk and sja.org.uk).
Opening hours: Mon-Sat, 10am to 5pm. Closed Sun and Bank Holidays. Tours
of the gatehouse and crypt, 11am and 2.30pm on Tue, Fri and Sat. Large groups
should book in advance.
Cost: Free. Suggested 'donation' of £5 for tours (£4 concessions).
Transport: Farringdon tube.
Amenities: Wheelchair access (some areas inaccessible).

The story spans over 900 years: beginning with the Crusades and continuing through revolutions, war and peace, it shows how warrior monks set out from Clerkenwell to fight for the faith and tend the sick. The Order originally consisted of a group of Knights who took vows of poverty, chastity, obedience and the care of the sick. Later it took on a military role and took control of Crusader castles. When Palestine was recaptured by Muslim forces in 1291, the Order moved to Cyprus and then to Rhodes. In 1522, the Knights moved to Malta and stayed there until 1798, when the island was lost to Napoleon.

The Museum of the Order of St John tells the unique and fascinating story of the Order of the Hospital of St John of Jerusalem, founded after the first Crusade captured Jerusalem in 1099, and its more recent incarnation as the St John Ambulance (since 1877).

The museum occupies two sites in Clerkenwell: St John's Gate (1504), the entrance to the former Priory of the Knights of St John, and the Priory Church of St John, Clerkenwell, with its surviving 12th-century crypt. The diverse collections explore all aspects of the Order's history and include rare illuminated manuscripts (such as the Rhodes Missal of 1504), armour, weapons, paintings, coins, furnishings, ceramics, silverware and textiles, plus historic first-aid equipment and memorabilia from the St John Ambulance's role in the two world wars and beyond.

Since the 16th century the Clerkenwell buildings have been variously offices, a coffee house and a tavern (Dickens was a customer). The museum was founded more than a century ago and extensively refurbished in 2010.

 ALLOW...

An official tour of the crypt and museum takes around 80 minutes so allow around two hours if you're planning to explore by yourself.

PETRIE MUSEUM OF EGYPTIAN ARCHAEOLOGY

20

Address: Malet Place, WC1E 6BT (☎ 020-7679 2884, 🖳 ucl.ac.uk/museums/ petrie).
Opening hours: Tue-Sat, 1-5pm. Closed on Bank Holidays and over Easter and Christmas.
Cost: Free.
Transport: Euston Square, Goodge Street or Warren Street tube or Euston rail.
Amenities: Wheelchair access.

Long overshadowed by the British Museum's tourist-thronged Egyptian galleries, the Petrie Museum is an unsung wonder. It boasts around 80,000 objects and is one of the world's great collections of Egyptian (and Sudanese) archaeology. It covers life in the Nile Valley from prehistory through the time of the pharaohs, and the Ptolemaic, Roman, Coptic and Islamic periods.

While the British Museum's Egyptian collection is strong on the 'big stuff', the Petrie focuses on the minutiae, and provides a vivid picture of what everyday life was like through Egypt's many eras and cultures. There's a wealth of personal objects in the collection – including combs, hair curlers, mirrors and razors – which reveal how ordinary Egyptians lived.

The Petrie is a university museum, named after the noted archaeologist William Flinders Petrie (1853-1942), who worked on dozens of sites. He amassed a large collection, which he sold to University College London in 1913. The museum is now run by the Institute of Archaeology (part of UCL).

The collection is full of 'firsts', including one of the earliest pieces of linen from Egypt (dating from around 5,000 BC); the earliest 'cylinder seal' found in Egypt (around 3,500 BC); two lions from the temple of Min at Koptos from the first group of monumental sculpture (around 3,000

BC); a fragment from the first kinglist or calendar (around 2,900 BC); the earliest example of glazing; the oldest wills on papyrus paper; the only veterinary papyrus from ancient Egypt; and the largest architectural drawing, showing a shrine (1,300 BC). The collection is also strong on Roman-period mummy portraits from the 1st and 2nd centuries AD.

👁 DON'T MISS!

The Petrie has some incredible costume exhibits, including Roman socks, a suit of armour found in the palace at Memphis and a dancer's dress dating from the Pyramid Age around 2400 BC.

21   POLLOCK'S TOY MUSEUM

Address: 1 Scala Street, W1T 2HL (☎ 020-7636 3452, 🖵 pollockstoymuseum.com)
Opening hours: Mon-Sat, 10am to 5pm. Closed Sundays and Bank Holidays.
Cost: £6 adults, £5 concessions, £3 children aged 3 to 15, under 3s free.
Transport: Goodge Street tube.
Amenities: Shop, no wheelchair access.

This is a fascinating collection of toy theatres, teddy bears, wax and china dolls, board games, optical toys, folk toys, nursery furniture, mechanical toys and doll's houses. The museum takes its name from Benjamin Pollock (1856-1937), the last of the Victorian Toy Theatre printers. Pollock, a simple, modest man, became a legend in his own lifetime but chose to remain in his birthplace of Hoxton (Hackney), where he devoted his life to his pokey little shop, and kept it going for 60 years.

The Toy Museum was established by Marguerite Fawdry (1912-1995), who in 1954 wanted some wire slides for her son's toy theatre, and found the business closed after the owner went bankrupt. Following enquiries, she contacted a weary accountant who suggested she buy the whole lot. And so Fawdry bought up Benjamin Pollock's entire stock – and a museum was born.

The Toy Museum was established in 1956 in a single attic room at 44 Monmouth Street, near Covent Garden, and as it grew other rooms were annexed. By 1969 the business had outgrown its premises and moved to Scala Street, where it occupies two connected 18th-century residential houses with original period fire places, windows and doors, and rooms connected by narrow winding staircases.

The whole place exudes a slightly dusty and chaotic atmosphere and evokes those special times of childhood, with every corner filled with magical delights. But be warned, there's a toy shop on the way out so you're unlikely to leave empty-handed.

👁 DON'T MISS!

One room is packed full of dolls, all sitting on chairs or in cradles and seemingly staring at you. It's either cute or extremely creepy, depending on your point of view!

ROYAL AIR FORCE MUSEUM

22

Address: Grahame Park Way, Colindale, NW9 5LL (☎ 020-8205 2266,
🖥 rafmuseum.org.uk).
Opening hours: Daily 10am to 6pm. Some exhibits are open for fewer hours or
close at lunchtime (see website for information about individual halls). Closed 25-
26th December and 1st January.
Cost: Free, except for the 4D theatre, which costs £4.
Transport: Colindale tube or Mill Hill Broadway rail.
Amenities: Restaurant, café, shop, wheelchair access.

 DON'T MISS!

Ride with the Red Arrows or take
part in a First World War dogfight –
these are just two of the many rides
available in the museum's Black Hawk
flight simulator – good value at £3 a
time.

There are a number of permanent exhibitions, including one entitled Our Finest Hour, which uses film, audio and special lighting to recreate the atmosphere of the Battle of Britain. The Aeronauts Interactive Centre has over 40 'hands on' experiments to help visitors to understand how an aircraft flies.

The museum also has a huge collection of photographs, mostly black and white, while the library has tens of thousands of printed works from the 18th century to the present time. A film and sound collection boasts some 7m feet of film, dating from the pioneering days of flight (the earliest reel is from 1910) to the present day (see website for an extensive archive of exhibitions).

The museum is vast and it's difficult to take in everything on one visit. With this in mind, the website has a useful facility that helps you plan your visit and make the best use of your time.

S omewhat hidden away in an unfashionable north London suburb, on the old site of Hendon's London Aerodrome, the Royal Air Force (RAF) Museum is one of the world's best flight exhibits. It's Britain's only national museum devoted wholly to aviation (it's split between this site and RAF Cosford in the Midlands), with over 100 aircraft from around the world, from very early designs to current jets and military aircraft. The museum is housed in five huge buildings and covers aviation history from early balloon flights to the latest jet fighters. An upper floor allows visitors to overlook the hangars, while platforms allow you to get close to the aircraft.

23 ROYAL COLLEGE OF PHYSICIANS MUSEUM

Address: 11 St Andrews Place, NW1 4LE (☎ 020-3075 1543, 🖥 rcplondon.ac.uk/museum-and-garden).

Opening hours: Mon-Fri, 9am to 5pm, excluding Public Holidays and days when the college is closed for special events (see website). Guided tours for groups of six or more. Garden tours from March to November, first Wednesday of the month.

Cost: Free. Guided tours £5 per person.

Transport: Great Portland Street, Regent's Park or Warren Street tube.

Amenities: Garden, wheelchair access (some limitations).

The Royal College of Physicians of London was founded in 1518 as the College of Physicians (it acquired its 'Royal' prefix in 1674) by charter of Henry VIII. The main functions of the College were to grant licences to those qualified to practise – apothecaries as well as physicians – and punish unqualified practitioners and those engaging in malpractice.

The College moved to its present home in Regent's Park in 1964. Designed by Sir Denys Lasdun (1914-2001) and Grade I listed, it's an ultra-modern interpretation of classical architecture, in keeping with its Nash-designed neighbours.

The collections cover both the history of the college and that of the profession, and help to place the development of medicine and healthcare in its widest context. Much of it was donated by former members such as William Harvey (1578-1657), who bestowed his own library and collections to the College in 1656. The silver collection, some of which is still used during ceremonies, includes the earliest known piece of English hallmarked silver, while the art collection boasts over

5,000 paintings, prints, drawings and sculptures.

The medical exhibits are among the most interesting. They include the Symons collection of medical instruments, a 17th-century surgeon's chest and a set of rare Italian anatomical tables made from human nerves and blood vessels! Visitors can recover from the gore by strolling around the medicinal garden, planted with over 1,300 therapeutic plants.

 DON'T MISS!

The Hoffbrand collection of some 180 apothecary jars – in attractive blue and white Delftware – gives a clue to some of the strange ingredients that were used to treat ailments. Oil of swallows was apparently used as a cure for poor vision and drunkenness, while dried foxes' lungs were prescribed as a treatment for human respiratory disorders.

SHERLOCK HOLMES MUSEUM

Address: 221B Baker Street, NW1 6XE (☏ 020-7224 3688,
🖥 sherlock-holmes.co.uk).
Opening hours: Daily (except Christmas Day), 9.30am to 6pm.
Cost: £6 adults, £4 children (under-16s).
Transport: Baker Street or Marylebone tube.
Amenities: Shop, no wheelchair access.

This is an interesting concept: a museum dedicated to a fictional character and housed at an address that shouldn't exist – and does so only because of special dispensation. Although the building lies between numbers 237 and 241, towards the north end of Baker Street, it bears the number 221B, granted by the City of Westminster in 1990. This is to make it correspond with the stories written by Sir Arthur Conan Doyle whose famous detective Sherlock Holmes shared accommodation with Dr John Watson at 221B between 1881 and 1904, as tenants of Mrs Hudson. (The address didn't exist at the time the stories were published either; street numbers in Baker Street only went up to 100.)

The Grade II listed Georgian townhouse that hosts the museum was built in 1815, and was in fact a boarding house between 1860 and 1936. It's been faithfully recreated as it was in Victorian times, as described by Conan Doyle. Most notable is the famous first floor study overlooking Baker Street where Holmes' possessions – his deerstalker, magnifying glass, calabash pipe, notebook and various disguises – are on display. On the third floor is a re-enactment of scenes from Sherlock Holmes stories, with the main characters played out by wax models. There are sometimes 'real-life' characters who add to the air of authenticity, playing the parts of a policeman, maid and Mrs Hudson, who are on hand to help visitors with their enquiries.

 ALLOW...

An hour should be enough to fully investigate this museum, but prepare to be diverted by the shop, which sells everything from a syringe pen to a Holmes pipe tamper – and deerstalkers of course!

As well as a magnet for devotees of the Holmes stories, the house presents a great photographic opportunity for Victoriana fans.

25 UNIVERSITY COLLEGE LONDON ART MUSEUM

Address: South Cloisters, Gower Street, WC1E 6BT (☎ 020-7679 2540,
🖳 ucl.ac.uk/museums/uclart).
Opening hours: Mon-Fri, 1-5pm (for holiday closures see website).
Cost: Free.
Transport: Euston Square tube.
Amenities: Wheelchair access.

The University College London (UCL) is a public research university and the oldest (1826) and largest constituent college of the University of London. UCL's outstanding collections include the **Petrie Museum** (see page 167) and the **Grant Museum** (see page 158), in addition to the UCL Art Museum. Other UCL collections (see 🖳 ucl.ac.uk/museums/collections) can be viewed by appointment.

The little-known UCL Art Museum contains over 10,000 objects, many of international importance, including paintings, drawings, prints and sculpture, dating from 1490 to the present day. The UCL Art Collections – renamed the UCL Art Museum in 2011 – date from 1847 when a collection of sculpture models and drawings by the Neo-classical artist John Flaxman (1755-1826) was obtained. Extensive gifts of prints and drawings were later donated, including a bequest by George Grote (1794-1871) who inherited his family's collection of bound albums containing early German, Flemish, Dutch and Italian drawings.

The Vaughan Bequest of 1900 included drawings by Turner and De Wint, Rembrandt etchings, and early proofs and states (a type of proof) of Turner's *Liber Studiorum* and Constable's *English Landscape Scenery*.

The Sherborn Bequest of 1937 added many rare and important prints to the collection, including an early edition of Dürer's *Apocalypse* woodcuts and early states and proofs from Van Dyck's *Iconographia*.

The collection also contains prize-winning student work from the nearby Slade School of Art, dating from 1890 to the present day, including works by many important 20th-century British artists such as Stanley Spencer, Augustus John and Paula Rego.

👁 DON'T MISS!

The Flaxman Gallery, which underwent refurbishment in 2012, has as its centrepiece a full-size plaster cast of *St Michael Overcoming Satan*, which Flaxman based on Raphael's painting of *St Michael Vanquishing Satan* (1518) in the Louvre.

ARSENAL FOOTBALL CLUB MUSEUM 26

Address: Emirates Stadium, Northern Triangle Building, 75 Drayton Park, N5 1BU
(☎ 020-7619 5003, 🖳 arsenal.com/history/the-arsenal-museum).
Opening hours: Daily, 10am to 6pm (Sun 5pm); match days closes 30 minutes before kick-off.
Cost: £7 adults, £4 children (under 16). Admission is also included in a stadium tour (see 🖳 arsenal.com/emirates/emirates-stadium-tours).
Transport: Arsenal or Holloway Road tube.
Amenities: Shop, wheelchair access.

The Arsenal Football Club Museum is dedicated to the history of the club, from its beginnings in 1886 when it was founded by a group of munitions workers in Woolwich, south London. The exhibits are wide-ranging and encompass a range of exhibits and memorabilia, from effigies of famous players to the ball used in the club's 1936 FA Cup victory. Other exhibits include the golden boot won by Charlie George for scoring the winning goal in the 1971 cup final (and his shirt), Michael Thomas' boots from Arsenal's 1988-89 title-deciding match against Liverpool and Alan Smith's shirt from the 1994 UEFA Cup Winners' Cup Final. There's also a special trophy commemorating Arsenal's 2003-04 Premier League season, when they won the title having not lost a single match, plus medals, shirts and caps belonging to former players.

The facility also features the Legends Theatre and more than a dozen fully interactive sections based on Arsenal's history, such as The Invincibles, The Arsenal Spirit and Highbury Stadium.

27 BRUCE CASTLE MUSEUM

Address: Lordship Lane, N17 8NU (☎ 020-8808 8772, 🖳 haringey.gov.uk/brucecastlemuseum).
Opening hours: Wed-Sun, 1-5pm. Closed 25-26th December, New Year's Day and Good Friday. The gardens are open daily from 8am to dusk.
Cost: Free.
Transport: Seven Sisters or Wood Green tube.
Amenities: Gardens, wheelchair access.

Bruce Castle (Grade I listed) is a 16th-century manor house set in 20 acres (8ha) of parkland. The house and its detached tower are among the earliest examples of a brick building in England – parts may date back to Tudor times – although it was substantially remodelled in the 16th and 17th centuries. Its principal façade has ashlar quoining and tall paned windows, and is terminated by symmetrical matching bays.

Its name reflect a connection with the Bruis (or Bruce) family of Scotland, who were landowners in Tottenham until their English lands were seized by Edward I in 1306, after Robert the Bruce became King of Scotland.

The family of Sir Rowland Hill (1795-1879) – who reformed the British postal system and introduced the Penny Post – ran a progressive boys' school at Bruce Castle from 1827 to 1891. The building and the land were purchased in 1891 by Tottenham Urban District Council, and Bruce Castle opened as a museum in 1906 housing local history collections, along with an exhibition about postal history.

28 BRUNEI GALLERY

Address: School of Oriental and African Studies (SOAS), University of London, Thornhaugh Street, Russell Square, WC1H 0XG (☎ 020-7637 2388, 🖳 soas.ac.uk/gallery).
Opening hours: Tue-Sat, 10.30am to 5pm (Thu 8pm). Closed Sun-Mon and Bank Holidays.
Cost: Free.
Transport: Russell Square or Goodge Street tube.
Amenities: Shop, library, garden, wheelchair access.

The Brunei Gallery at the School of Oriental and African Studies (SOAS) hosts a programme of changing contemporary and historical exhibitions from Asia, Africa and the Middle East. It incorporates exhibition spaces on three floors, a bookshop, a lecture theatre, and conference and teaching facilities, plus a Japanese-style roof garden.

As well excellent temporary exhibitions – themes in 2012 included the British in Palestine and Thailand's sacred tattoo culture – there's a permanent display of Objects of Instruction: Treasures of the School of Oriental and African Studies in the Foyle Special Collections Gallery, aimed at publicising the school's remarkably rich but little-known collections. It houses a wide range of interesting and beautiful objects from across Asia and Africa, including illustrated Islamic manuscripts; Chinese and Japanese paintings and prints; Middle Eastern and East Asian ceramics; decorative Buddhist manuscripts and sculptures from Southeast Asia; contemporary African paintings and textiles; and important archaeological collections.

The school also stages a wide range of public events, from conferences to lectures and workshops.

CAMDEN ARTS CENTRE 29

Address: Arkwright Road, NW3 6DG (☎ 020-7472 5500, ▯ camdenartscentre.org).
Opening hours: Tue-Sun, 10am to 6pm (Wed until 9pm). Closed Mondays.
Cost: Free.
Transport: Finchley Road tube.
Amenities: Café, shop, garden, wheelchair access.

Camden Arts Centre – housed in a splendid Victorian Gothic building (Grade II listed) – is one of London's best contemporary art spaces and the largest arts venue in north London. Built in 1897 as the Hampstead Public Library, the building became the Hampstead Arts Centre in 1965 and was taken over by the local council in 1967 and renamed the Camden Arts Centre.

The beautiful and sensitively designed building (refurbished in 2004) combines the original Victorian Gothic features with a contemporary urban design to enhance the space and light. The new galleries attract artists of the highest calibre and are able to display a broad range of work, including installations, film and video, light sensitive drawings and sculpture. Exhibitions feature a mix of emerging artists, international artists showing for the first time in London, significant historic figures who inspire contemporary practice, and artist selected group shows relevant to current debate.

There are projects and courses aimed at adults and children. In addition, the Centre has a bookshop, a café and a glorious garden.

Installation, Noëmi Lakmaier

30 CENTRE FOR RECENT DRAWING

> **Address:** 2-4 Highbury Station Road, N1 1SB (☎ 20-3239 6936, 🖳 c4rd.org.uk).
> **Opening hours:** Thu-Sat, 1pm-6pm (but check website for exhibitions).
> **Cost:** Free.
> **Transport:** Highbury & Islington tube.
> **Amenities:** Wheelchair access.

The Centre for Recent Drawing (C4RD) is London's museum space for drawing and exists to examine, exhibit and encourage the production of drawing by artists, cartoonists, designers, illustrators, students and anyone who chooses to pick up a pen. It isn't a contemporary art gallery – C4RD prefers the word 'recent' as it's less commercial – and doesn't exist to promote particular artists' work. It's a non-profit volunteer-run independent organisation dependent on private donation.

Since 2004, C4RD has provided a public exhibition space and is now in the unique position of having a whole building dedicated to drawing. The Centre shows a constant rotating series of exhibitions demonstrating a broad variety of drawing practice – see website for information. It also houses residencies for those for whom drawing is a core part of their practice (the website also hosts online residencies).

C4RD welcomes all those with an interest in drawing, both from within and outside the arts, and presents the many possibilities that drawing can encompass.

31 FORTY HALL MUSEUM

> **Address:** Forty Hill, Enfield, EN2 9HA (☎ 020-8363 8196, 🖳 fortyhallestate.co.uk).
> **Opening hours:** Tue-Fri, 11am to 5pm, Sat-Sun (and most Bank Holidays), noon to 5pm. From November to March closes one hour earlier (at 4pm) from Tue-Fri and also on Boxing Day and New Year's Day.
> **Cost:** Free (charges apply for tours and special events).
> **Transport:** Turkey Street rail is a 20-minute walk or take 191 bus from Enfield Town, Enfield Chase or Southbury rail.
> **Amenities:** Café, gardens, wheelchair access.

Forty Hall (Grade I listed) and estate is Enfield 's 'Jewel in the Crown' and one of England's finest historic houses, built by former Lord Mayor of London, Sir Nicholas Rainton (1569-1646) in 1632. Situated at the edge of London, Forty Hall is important in understanding the growth of the city in the 17th century, and the life and times of the merchant classes who established London as a major international trading centre.

The estate was purchased by the borough of Enfield in 1951 and since 1955 has been open to the public and houses the borough's museum collection. The hall contains period furniture and furnishings, along with collections of 17th- and 18th-century watercolours and drawings. The wide-ranging museum collections focus on local and social history of the pre-1965 London boroughs of Edmonton, Southgate and Enfield (now the London Borough of Enfield), with the emphasis on everyday household ceramics and glass from the 19th and 20th centuries.

Following restoration in 2011-12, the Hall now feature an innovative events' programme focusing on art, ecology and heritage.

FREEMASONS' HALL & MUSEUM   32

Address: 60 Great Queen Street, WC2B 5AZ (☎ 020-7395 9257, 🖳 freemasonry. london.museum).
Opening hours: Mon-Fri, 10am to 5pm. Closed on Public Holidays and Christmas and New Year. Free guided tours (up to five a day, at 11am, noon, 2pm, 3pm and 4pm) of the Grand Temple and ceremonial areas.
Cost: Free.
Transport: Holborn or Covent Garden tube.
Amenities: Shop, library, wheelchair access.

The Freemasons' Hall has been the centre of English Freemasonry for 230 years. The present Art Deco building is the third Masonic Hall on the site; it was built as a memorial to those who died in the First World War and completed in 1933. Grade II* listed, it covers two acres and forms an irregular hollow pentagram with the Grand Temple at its heart.

The principal ceremonial rooms are on the first floor where three vestibules form a ceremonial approach to the Grand Temple, and are of increasing richness in their design. The second vestibule has displays about Freemasonry and further information about the history of the site and the building.

The museum contains an extensive collection of Masonic objects, including pottery and porcelain, furniture and clocks, jewels and regalia. Items belonging to famous Freemasons, including Winston Churchill and Edward VII, are displayed alongside samples from the extensive collection of prints, photographs and ephemera. The collection explores the different ranks, offices and branches of freemasonry and also explains some of the symbolism used, the charities established, as well as Freemasonry abroad and during wartime.

33 GOLDFINGER'S HOUSE

Address: 2 Willow Road, NW3 1TH (☎ 020-7435 6166, 🖳 nationaltrust.org.uk/2-willow-road).
Opening hours: Open March to October, Wed-Sun, 11am to 5pm (dates vary, see website). Entry is by guided tour (40 mins) at 11am, noon, 1pm and 2pm, on a first-come first-served basis. Non-guided viewing is also possible from 3pm to 5pm.
Cost: £6 adults, £3 children, £15 families. Free for National Trust members.
Transport: Hampstead tube.
Amenities: Wheelchair access (ground floor only).

This is a ground-breaking modernist home, designed in 1939 by the splendidly-named, Budapest-born architect Ernő Goldfinger. It's part of a terrace of three houses (the other two are privately owned) and is now managed by the National Trust. The building was constructed from concrete faced with red brick, the design leaving the spacious interior uncluttered by supporting structures. It has an elegant, space-saving spiral staircase at its heart, designed by the Danish engineer Ove Arup, while large windows give a sense of light and space, and allow panoramic views over Hampstead Heath. Carefully designed colour schemes impart different moods in various areas of the house, while ledges and recesses house works of art and interesting 'found' objects. Built-in cupboards preserve the house's purity of line.

Goldfinger also designed much of the furniture, which still has a contemporary air, and the property also houses his fine collection of modern art and personal possessions. The art collection is significant, including works by Marcel Duchamp, Max Ernst, Henry Moore and Bridget Riley.

34 HARROW MUSEUM BUILDINGS

Address: Headstone Manor, Pinner View, HA2 6PX (☎ 020-8861 2626, 🖳 harrow.gov.uk/info/200070/museums_and_galleries/934/harrow_museum/1).
Opening hours: Mon and Wed-Fri, noon to 5pm; weekends and Bank Holidays, 10.30am to 5pm (closes at 4pm, November to March). Manor house tours at 3pm (1 hr) during summer weekends only.
Cost: Free. Tours of Headstone Manor £3 (children free).
Transport: Headstone Lane rail or North Harrow tube.
Amenities: Café, shop, tours not wheelchair accessible.

Four remarkable buildings – Headstone Manor, the Tithe Barn, the Small Barn and the Granary – make up the absorbing local authority museum of the borough of Harrow. Situated in the beautiful manor grounds, the museum has been described as 'one of the most interesting domestic complexes in the whole country', containing examples of master craftsmen's workmanship dating from the 14th, 17th and 18th centuries.

The land on which Headstone Manor stands is recorded as having been owned in 825 AD by Wulfred, Archbishop of Canterbury. The moated Headstone Manor (Grade I listed) was built around 1310 and is the earliest-surviving timber-framed building in the area. Only two of the Manor's farm buildings survive, including the impressive Tithe Barn (Grade II* listed) built in 1506. The museum collection is comprised of objects and artefacts with strong links to the Harrow area, including items from the Kodak factory and the Whitefriar's glass factory which reflect its industrial past. But the buildings are the real stars.

ISLINGTON MUSEUM 35

Address: 245 St John Street, EC1V 4NB (☎ 020-7527 2837, 🖥 islington.gov.uk/islingtonmuseum).
Opening hours: Mon-Tue, Thu-Sat, 10am-5pm. Closed Wednesdays and Sundays.
Cost: Free.
Transport: Angel or Farringdon tube.
Amenities: Wheelchair access.

Islington Museum is a public museum dedicated to the history of the London Borough of Islington, which opened in May 2008, funded by a £1million grant from the Heritage Lottery Fund (replacing a previous museum at Islington Town Hall).

The museum houses a gallery covering nine themes on local and social history: childhood, food and drink,

fashion, leisure, healthcare, radicals, caring, home and wartime. Among the items on display are a bust of Lenin, who lived and worked in Clerkenwell in the early 1900s, and some of the book covers defaced by Joe Orton and Kenneth Halliwell (who were jailed in 1962 for stealing books from the library and 'modifying' the cover art – now a valued part of the museum's collection!).

The museum has a regular programme of temporary exhibitions, including visiting displays and items from its own collections. It also hosts talks, walks and children's events, and has an education room for visits by schools and other groups.

36 JEWISH MILITARY MUSEUM

Address: Shield House, Harmony Way, off Victoria Road, NW4 2BZ (☎ 020-8201 5656, 🖳 thejmm.org.uk).
Opening hours: Mon-Thu, 10am to 4pm. Sunday, groups by appointment. Visitors must telephone and book in advance.
Cost: Free.
Transport: Golders Green tube, then 183 or 240 bus to Bell Lane (Sentinel Square).
Amenities: Wheelchair access.

The Jewish Military Museum offers a fascinating mix of history and memorabilia, relating to the thousands of British Jews who fought and often lost their lives serving their country at war. Filled with stories, documentation and pictorial history, as well as rare military artefacts (some 4,000), the museum presents a journey through time, telling stories of the British Jews who served in the army, navy, air force and chaplaincy (rabbis), plus firemen, nurses and other volunteers.

The collection include letters written by a Jewish soldier in the trenches before being killed at the Somme in 1917, and a commemoration of Hannah Senesh, a young Jewish woman who, trained by the British, was parachuted into Yugoslavia in 1944 to help rescue Hungarian Jews, only to be captured, tortured and executed. It also includes exhibits from many battles and wars in which British Jews have served, including the Battles of Trafalgar and Waterloo, the Crimean and Boer Wars, the First and Second World Wars, the Falklands War, and modern campaigns such as Iraq and Afghanistan.

37 LONDON CANAL MUSEUM

Address: 12-13 New Wharf Road, N1 9RT (☎ 020-7713 0836, 🖳 canalmuseum.org.uk).
Opening hours: Tue-Sun, 10am to 4.30pm (7.30pm on the first Thursday of the month). Closed Mondays, except for Bank Holidays.
Cost: £4 adults, £3 concessions, £2 children, £10 families.
Transport: King's Cross tube.
Amenities: Wheelchair access.

The London Canal Museum (opened in 1992) tells the absorbing story of the capital's canals from their early days as vital trade routes – long before motorised vehicles and motorways – through years of decline and abandonment, to their resurrection as corridors of leisure for boaters, walkers and cyclists.

The museum is housed in a former Victorian ice warehouse once owned by ice-cream magnate Carlo Gatti. It features two floors of exhibits, including half a narrow boat, the *Coronis*, which allows you to experience the cramped conditions in which boatmen and their families lived (from the 1840s until the 1950s), plus recordings, displays and photographs of a way of life now long gone. The museum also tells the story of the Regent's Canal, built to link the Paddington Arm of the Grand Junction Canal (1801) with the Thames at Limehouse.

Visitors can take a short trip on a narrow boat through Islington Tunnel to the Regent's Canal (see website) and there are also guided towpath walks.

MARKFIELD BEAM ENGINE & MUSEUM   38

Address: Markfield Road, N15 4RB (☎ 01707-873628, 🖥 mbeam.org).
Opening hours: October to March, 2nd Sunday of the month, 11am to 4pm; April to September, 2nd and 4th Sunday of the month, 11am to 5pm. See website for 'steaming' dates.
Cost: Free.
Transport: Tottenham Hale tube/rail or South Tottenham rail.
Amenities: Café, park, wheelchair access.

Markfield Beam Engine and Museum is a 'Site of Industrial Heritage Interest' located in Markfield Park which borders the River Lea. The Tottenham and Wood Green sewage treatment works and pumping station was opened here in 1864, while the Markfield Beam Engine was built between 1886 and 1888 and commissioned on 12th July 1888. It's a 100 horsepower beam pumping engine housed in a Victorian engine house (both Grade II listed), which saw continuous service until late 1905, when it was relegated to standby duty for storm water pumping. It ceased operation in 1964 but was recently restored to full working order and can be seen operating under steam power on 'steaming' days.

The beam engine is a free-standing engine of the compound rotative type and drives two pumps, each of which could move 2m gallons of water a day. It's believed to be the last engine produced by Wood Bros of Sowerby Bridge, Yorkshire, and is the only surviving eight-column engine in its original location. The museum's heritage building has also been renovated and there's a café.

39 MARX MEMORIAL LIBRARY

Address: 37A Clerkenwell Green, EC1R 0DU (☎ 020-7253 1485,
📧 marx-memorial-library.org).
Opening hours: Mon-Thu, 1-2pm or by appointment.
Cost: Free.
Transport: Farringdon tube.
Amenities: Shop, wheelchair access.

The Marx Memorial Library preserves a treasure chest of books, periodicals and manuscripts relating to Marxism, Socialism and the working class movement, including the full run of the *Daily Worker* and *Morning Star* newspapers, the International Brigade Archive and an extensive photographic library. It also houses The Printers Collection: the archives of the printing and papermaking unions of the UK and Ireland.

Karl Heinrich Marx (1818-1883) was the German philosopher, sociologist, economic historian, journalist and revolutionary socialist who developed the socio-political theory of Marxism and published various books, including *The Communist Manifesto* (1848) and *Capital* (1867-1894). Marx spent more than half his life in London, from 1849 until his death on 14th March 1883, and the Library was set up as a permanent memorial on the 50th anniversary of his death. As well as providing access to its archives, it also stages public lectures and study classes.

It's located in a Grade II listed building dating back to the 1730s and long used by radicals and socialists. Lenin had an office there in the early 1900s, now open to visitors.

40 MCC MUSEUM

Address: Lord's Cricket Ground, St John's Wood, NW8 8QN (☎ 020-7616 8656,
📧 lords.org/history/mcc-museum).
Opening hours: April to October, Mon-Fri, 10am to 5pm; November to March, Mon-Thu, 11.30am to 5pm, Fri 11.30am to 4pm. Closed on match days. See website for information about tours (2 hrs).
Cost: £7.50 adults, £5 concessions.
Transport: St John's Wood tube.
Amenities: Tavern/restaurant, shop, wheelchair access.

The Marylebone Cricket Club – usually referred to by its initials MCC – was founded in 1787, and is the world's most famous cricket club. It's also responsible for the game's Code of Laws, which was adopted throughout the game in 1788, and the MCC remains the sport's governing body to this day.

The MCC Museum is the world's oldest sporting museum, housing a wide range of exhibits, although it's best-known as the home of 'The Ashes', a terracotta urn reputed to contain the ashes of a burnt cricket bail. After Australia beat England on an English ground (the Oval) for the first time in 1882, a satirical obituary in *The Sporting Times* declared that 'English cricket had died and the ashes taken to Australia'. The English media dubbed the next tour to Australia (1882-83) 'the quest to regain The Ashes'. The museum's collection also includes kit used by some of cricket's greatest players – such as Victor Trumper, Don Bradman and W G Grace.

MUSEUM OF DOMESTIC DESIGN & ARCHITECTURE

41

Address: 9 Boulevard Drive, London NW9 5HF (☎ 020-8411 5244, 🖳 moda.mdx.ac.uk/home).
Opening hours: Tue-Sat, 10am-5pm; Sun 2-5pm. Closed Mondays. Visits by appointment only.
Cost: Free.
Transport: Colindale tube.
Amenities: Wheelchair access.

The collections provide a rich source of inspiration for artists, designers and print makers, and include wallpapers, textiles, designs, books, catalogues and magazines, from the late 19th to the late 20th centuries. They're a great resource if you're interested in the history of domestic interiors or are seeking inspiration for creative projects.

The museum offers touring exhibitions (see website for a schedule) and the collections can also be viewed on-line. Visits to the centre to see particular items from the collections are by appointment.

The Museum of Domestic Design & Architecture (MoDA) was established in 2000 and is located at the Middlesex University in Colindale. The collections developed from a number of acquisitions made by Middlesex University between the late '60s and the '90s, the first and most important of which was the Silver Studio, which was given to what was then the Hornsey College of Art in 1966. Further acquisitions followed, including the Crown Wallpaper Collection in 1989 and the Charles Hasler Collection in 1993.

42 MUSEUM OF GREAT ORMOND STREET HOSPITAL

> **Address:** Great Ormond Street, WC1N 3JH (☎ 020-7405 9200, 🖥 gosh.nhs.uk/about-us/our-history/museum-and-archive-services).
> **Opening hours:** Mon-Fri, 9.30am to 5pm, by prior appointment only.
> **Cost:** Free. Maximum of 12 people for groups.
> **Transport:** Russell Square tube.
> **Amenities:** Wheelchair access.

Great Ormond Street Hospital (GOSH) for children – the UK's most famous hospital – was created in response to the shocking mortality rate in the mid-19th century, which meant that only half of all babies born into poverty lived to celebrate their first birthday. Desperate to save children's lives in the capital, Dr Charles West campaigned for a specialist hospital to be built. In 1852 he got his wish, and with ten beds, two physicians and five nurses, the GOSH was born. The old GOSH was replaced by a new hospital in the '90s.

The hospital's archives are public records and available for research. They include a photographic collection, the personal medical library of the hospital's founder Dr West, and a collection of *Peter Pan* editions in many languages resulting from Sir J M Barrie's copyright gift (he left the rights to his books to the hospital). Charles Dickens was another great supporter and friend of GOSH.

The hospital also has a small permanent exhibit relating its history, with display panels, and examples of historical medical and other equipment used.

43 PARASOL UNIT

> **Address:** 14 Wharf Road, N1 7RW (☎ 020-7490 7373, 🖥 parasol-unit.org).
> **Opening hours:** Tue-Sat, 10am to 6pm; Sun noon-5pm. Closed Mondays.
> **Cost:** Free.
> **Transport:** Angel tube or Old Street tube/rail.
> **Amenities:** Limited wheelchair access

The Parasol Unit Foundation for Contemporary Art (to give it its full name) was founded in 2004 and is a registered educational charity. The gallery is housed in a classic old warehouse building (next door to the excellent Victoria Miro Gallery), renovated to a design concept by the Italian architect Claudio Silvestrin which appears mundane until you spot the architecturally curious grey-and-glass shoebox perched on top. The interior's 5,000ft² (465m²) of exhibition space has an impressive minimalist design and features exciting multi-disciplinary exhibitions.

Internationally recognised for its forward-thinking and challenging exhibition programme, Parasol has introduced a host of international artists to London's public and been instrumental in launching the careers of artists such as Michaël Borremans, Yang Fudong and Charles Avery.

The foundation stages four challenging and thought-provoking exhibitions a year by contemporary artists working in various media, and also organises a variety of other artistic projects. Each exhibition is accompanied by a publication and related educational events. Parasol also runs an alfresco art scheme called Parasol Public.

RUDOLF STEINER HOUSE 44

Address: 35 Park Road, NW1 6XT (☎ 020-7723 4400, 🖳 rsh.anth.org.uk).
Opening hours: See website for exhibitions, special events, and library, bookshop and café opening hours.
Cost: Free, except for lectures and performances, for which the fees vary. There are regular talks on Tue and Fri (see website for details).
Transport: Baker Street tube or Marylebone tube/rail.
Amenities: Café, shop, library, wheelchair access.

For the majority of people, Rudolf Steiner House will be of more interest aesthetically – as an attractive, innovative piece of architecture – than for the person it's named after or the philosophy he espoused. Situated near Regent's Park, the house is a unique example of Germanic Expressionist architecture with a hint of the Modernista, which reminds some commentators of the buildings of Barcelona and Palma.

Now Grade II listed, it was designed by Montague Wheeler and built in two phases, the first in 1924, the second in 1931. It has curves, cleverly placed asymmetrical windows with stone frames, a coved hood at the entrance and a bookshop front, a free-form twisting concrete staircase and other details that make it unique. The rounded door and window frames have something of a Hobbit-house style about them, an interesting contrast with the building's Art Nouveau leanings.

Rudolf Steiner House promotes the anthroposophical philosophy of Rudolf Steiner (it's the UK HQ of the Anthroposophical Society), through its bookshop and cultural centre, and hosting performances and workshops. However, for most visitors the attraction is the architecture.

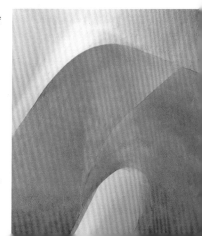

45 SHOWROOM GALLERY

Address: 63 Penfold Street, NW8 8PQ (☎ 020-7724 4300, 🖥 theshowroom.org)
Opening hours: Wed-Sat, noon to 6pm.
Cost: Free.
Transport: Edgware Road tube.
Amenities: Wheelchair access.

The Showroom was one of London's first East End galleries, which marked its first 20 years as a publicly-funded venue with a move to its present spacious home (3,000 ft²/279m²) in 2008. It reopened in September 2009 with a new programme that accommodates commissioned projects, as well as an expanded educational facility hosting workshops, conferences and events for artists, writers and curators.

The Showroom is a space for contemporary art committed to commissioning emerging artists who haven't previously had significant exposure in London. The gallery presents just four shows a year, which allows artists the time to develop and realise their work on site. Solo shows have featured Claire Barclay, Marc Chaimowicz, Subodh Gupta, Mona Hatoum, Jim Lambie, Christina Mackie, Simon Starling, Eva Rothschild and Sam Taylor-Wood. Significant commissions in recent years have included Lawrence Abu Hamdan, Can Altay, Petra Bauer, Emily Wardill and The Otolith Group.

46 WEMBLEY STADIUM TOUR

Address: Wembley Way, HA9 0WS (☎ 0844-800 2755, 🖥 wembleystadium.com/wembley-tours.aspx).
Opening hours: Tours (75mins) take place on selected days, usually between 10am and 4pm starting on the hour and half hour. Tours must be pre-booked (see website).
Cost: £16 adults, £9 concessions (over 60s) and children (5-16), £41 families.
Transport: Wembley Park or Wembley Central tube or Wembley Stadium rail.
Amenities: Shop, wheelchair access (not all areas).

The new Wembley Stadium opened in 2007 (replacing the original which dated from 1923) and is the national stadium of England and the home venue of the England national football team. With a capacity of 90,000, it's the second-largest stadium in Europe (after Camp Nou, Barcelona).

Tours include the opportunity to see the England team's changing rooms and warm-up areas, the players' tunnel and dugouts, to climb the 107 trophy winners' steps and hold an FA Cup replica in the Royal Box. Exhibits on display include the famous crossbar from the 1966 World Cup Final and the trophy awarded to the

1966 team by FIFA to commemorate their win. (The original Jules Rimet World Cup trophy was kept by Brazil after their third World Cup tournament win in 1970, but it was stolen soon after and has never been recovered.)

You can also see match-worn items and medals from the likes of David Beckham, David Villa, Steven Gerrard and Graeme Souness, as part of the Exhibition of Champions, featuring Champions League memorabilia.

ZABLUDOWICZ COLLECTION 47

Address: 176 Prince of Wales Road, NW5 3PT (☎ 020-7428 8940, 🖥 zabludowiczcollection.com/london).
Opening hours: Thu-Sun, noon-6pm
Cost: Free.
Transport: Chalk Farm tube or Kentish Town West rail.
Amenities: Café, library, no wheelchair access.

F ounded in 1994 by Poju and Anita Zabludowicz, this dynamic and growing collection spans four decades, from the '70s to today (and also exhibits in the US and Finland). The gallery (opened in 2007) – also known simply as 176 – is housed in a former (Grade II listed) Methodist chapel, built between 1867 and 1871 in the Corinthian style.

Inaugurated in 2007, the Zabludowicz Collection's London project space presents exhibitions of collection works and new commissions by artists linked to the collection. The gallery usually stages three major exhibitions a year, covering a wide variety of art forms, along with pieces from the Collection, comprising over 1,000 works by some 350 artists from 33 countries.

Its varied programme includes group and solo exhibitions, commissions, residencies and the Zabludowicz Collection Curatorial Open and Testing Ground – an annual initiative for higher education in the arts and curating. It also has a programme of free public events, ranging from talks and performances by artists and academics to community-based festivals and education. There's also a library and a café.

WEST LONDON

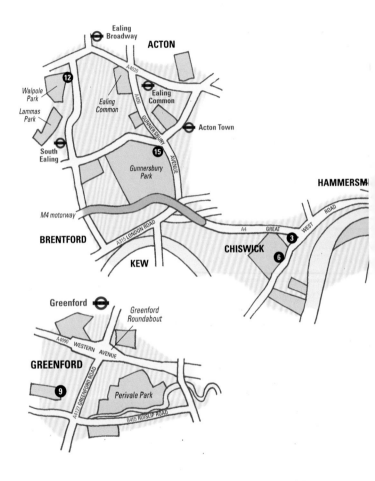

1. Royal Hospital Chelsea
2. Saatchi Gallery
3. William Hogarth's House
4. 7 Hammersmith Terrace
5. 18 Stafford Terrace/Linley Sambourne House
6. Chiswick House
7. Fulham Palace
8. Leighton House Museum
9. London Motorcycle Museum
10. Museum of Brands
11. National Army Museum
12. Pitzhanger Manor Gallery & House
13. Thomas Carlyle's House
14. Couper Collection
15. Gunnersbury Park Museum
16. Kelmscott House
17. Louise Blouin Foundation
18. Royal British Society of Sculptors

1 ROYAL HOSPITAL CHELSEA

Address: Royal Hospital Road, SW3 4SR (☎ 020-7881 5298,
🖳 chelsea-pensioners.co.uk).
Opening hours: Courtyards, chapel and museum, Mon-Fri, 10am to noon and
2-4pm (the Great Hall opens at 11am). The grounds open later in summer months
(see website) but are closed in May for the Chelsea Flower Show (see 🖳 rhs.org.uk/
shows-events for dates).
Cost: Free.
Transport: Sloane Square tube.
Amenities: Café (next door), shop, garden, wheelchair access.

The Royal Hospital Chelsea is a retirement and nursing home for British soldiers – commonly referred to as 'Chelsea pensioners' or 'In-Pensioners' – who are unfit for further duty due to injury or age. This may sound rather uninspiring but the Hospital is one of London's most historic and interesting buildings, housing some superb works of art and a small museum.

The Hospital is set back from the embankment on the north shore of the Thames and occupies a beautiful, red-brick, Grade I listed building, which is widely regarded as London's second-loveliest façade on the Thames (after Greenwich). The grounds are also attractive and have hosted the Chelsea Flower Show since 1913; this is the ultimate (worldwide) event in the gardening calendar and is also a major fixture on the London social scene.

The Hospital was founded in 1682 by Charles II for veteran soldiers; a

gilt statue (by Grinling Gibbons) of the monarch in the guise of a Roman general stands in Figure Court. It has been suggested that Charles was persuaded to build a hospital for veterans by his mistress, Nell Gwynn, whose father had been made destitute by the Civil War. Sir Christopher Wren was tasked with building the hospital, which was finally completed in 1692, when the first 476 'pensioners' were admitted.

 FOOD & DRINK

Tangerine Café: The next door Chelsea Physic Garden has an excellent café, where you can dine al fresco in the beautiful garden.

Chelsea Royal Hospital was built around three courtyards, the centre one opening to the south, the side ones to the east and west. The building remains almost unchanged, except for minor alterations by Robert Adam between 1765 and 1782, and the stables, which were added by Sir John Soane in 1814. The hospital is thus the work of three of Britain's finest architects. Even the stable block is regarded as an architectural gem, one Soane's finest exteriors,

Chelsea pensioners

👁 **DON'T MISS!**

The Hospital's chapel is a fine and rare example of Wren's pure ecclesiastical work, built between 1681 and 1687. Designed to accommodate around 500 people, it rises 42ft (13m) high. The half dome of the apse contains a fine painting (1714) of the Resurrection by Sebastiano Ricci, assisted by his nephew Marco. It's thought that the work was a donation from Queen Anne. Visitors are welcome to attend the Sunday 'Choral Matins' service at 11am.

although it's little-known or recognised by the general public.

The Hospital contains a small museum dedicated to its history, originally opened in the Great Hall in 1866. It features military artefacts and memorabilia donated by former pensioners, including items associated with the Duke of Wellington – six French 'Eagles', George Jones' panorama of the Battle of Waterloo (1820) and a portrait of the Duke by John Simpson – and other uniforms, medals (over 2,000), weapons, paintings and models. It also features a diorama depicting the Royal Hospital as it appeared in around 1742.

Today the Hospital is home to around 400 pensioners – including women since 2009 – who receive board, lodging, nursing care and a distinctive uniform. The museum features a reconstruction of one of the pensioners' berths, the actual rooms are private. Much of the rest of the buildings are accessible, however, including the Great Hall, Octagon, chapel, courtyards and gardens. The site of the 18th-century pleasure gardens, Ranelagh Gardens, now forms part of the Hospital grounds and is also open to the public (except in May when it hosts the Chelsea Flower Show). The Hospital also has a small souvenir shop.

2 SAATCHI GALLERY

Address: Duke of York's HQ, King's Road, SW3 4RY (☎ 020-7730 8135, 🖥 saatchi-gallery.co.uk).
Opening hours: Daily, 10am to 6pm.
Cost: Free.
Transport: Sloane Square tube.
Amenities: Restaurant, café, bar, shop, wheelchair access.

The Saatchi Gallery was founded by advertising guru (and husband of TV cook Nigella Lawson) Charles Saatchi in 1985 to exhibit his private collection of contemporary art. It has occupied various premises, first in north London, then at County Hall on the South Bank by the Thames, before moving to its current home, the Duke of York's HQ in Chelsea, in October 2008.

ALLOW...

The Saatchi Gallery is much less daunting than larger galleries such as the Tate Modern, and is clearly laid out, so a morning or afternoon should be enough to take in an exhibition.

The Duke of York's Headquarters (Grade II* listed) was completed in 1801 to the designs of John Sanders (1768-1826), and is of outstanding historic and special architectural interest. It was originally called the Royal Military Asylum, a school for the children of soldiers' widows, but in 1892 was renamed the Duke of York's Royal Military School. In 1909 the school moved to new premises and the building was renamed the Duke of York's Barracks. The site was purchased by Cadogan Estates in 2000 and redeveloped to include a public square, upmarket housing and retail outlets, part of which is now home to the Saatchi Gallery.

The gallery is an ideal environment to view contemporary art, with large rooms and high ceilings, and has been acclaimed as one of 'the most beautiful art spaces in London'. It's arranged over three floors, providing some 70,000ft² (6,500m²) of space, with 15 well-proportioned and equally-sized exhibition spaces. It's the only completely free, contemporary art museum of its size in the world, thanks to its sponsorship

Ghost, Kadir Attia

by art auction house Phillips de Pury & Company (💻 phillipsdepury.com).

Saatchi's collection (and hence the gallery's shows) has had distinct phases, starting with US artists and minimalism, moving to the Damien Hirst-led 'Young British Artists', followed by shows purely of painting and then returning to contemporary art from America in USA Today at the Royal Academy in London. The gallery's move to the Duke of York's HQ was marked by an exhibition of new Chinese painters entitled 'The Revolution Continues: New Art from China'.

The gallery has been a major influence on art in Britain since its opening and has had a history of media controversy – which it has courted – with extremes of critical reaction. Love it or hate it, the Saatchi never fails to provoke a reaction and has gone from strength to strength. It hosted seven of London's ten most visited exhibitions in 2009-11 and attracted over 1.2m visitors in 2011.

Many artists on display are unknown, not only to the general public but also in the commercial art world, and showing at the gallery has provided a springboard for many artists to launch their careers. One of the Saatchi Gallery's strength's is its ever-changing exhibitions – there's no permanent collection – with galleries given over to a single exhibition that normally runs for around three months. Successful exhibitions in recent years have included: The Empire Strikes Back: Indian Art Today (2010); Newspeak: British Art Now (2010/11); Gesamtkunstwerk: New Art from Germany (2011/12); Ink: The Art of China (2012); The Google Photography Prize 2012; Korean Eye 2012; and Art from Russia (2013).

 FOOD & DRINK

Gallery Mess: The Saatchi's restaurant/café/bar has attracted enthusiastic reviews for its beautiful setting, atmosphere and good food.

Peter Jones: If you're looking for something a bit quieter, then Peter Jones in nearby Sloane Square has a Brasserie and the Top Floor restaurant (☎ 020-7112 8984) with panoramic views.

Real Special Very Painting, Barry-Reigate

3 **WILLIAM HOGARTH'S HOUSE**

Address: Hogarth Lane, Great West Road, Chiswick, W4 2QN (☎ 020-8994 6757, ⌨ hounslow.info/arts/hogarthshouse/index.htm).
Opening hours: Tue-Sun, noon to 5pm. Closed Mondays (except Bank Holidays), Good Friday, Easter Sunday and 25-26th December.
Cost: Free.
Transport: Turnham Green tube or 190 bus to Hogarth Roundabout.
Amenities: Garden, wheelchair access (ground floor only).

Hogarth's House (Grade I listed) is the former country home of the famous 18th-century English painter, engraver and satirist William Hogarth (1697-1764), where he lived (with his wife, wife's cousin, mother-in-law and sister) from 1749 until his death. It provided a quiet summer retreat from the bustle of city life around Hogarth's main house and studio, in what is now Leicester Square. And while the house has now been swallowed up by London – the A4 traffic thunders past its front door – it's still a surprisingly tranquil spot.

👁 DON'T MISS!

After visiting the house, take a few minutes to visit Hogarth's tomb in the graveyard of nearby St Nicholas' church. The monument carries an obituary by his great friend, the actor David Garrick.

The house was built between 1713 and 1717 in the corner of an orchard belonging to the Downes family. Its first occupant was the Rev George Andreas Ruperti, the pastor of St Mary's Lutheran church in the Savoy (where the hotel now stands). Hogarth purchased it in 1749 and extended it the following year, adding the projecting Venetian-style oriel window on the first floor (an identical window appears in one of his prints, *The Times*).

Hogarth was born near Smithfield Market in London, where his childhood was blighted by his father's imprisonment for debt. He was apprenticed to a silver engraver, and thus learned the skills which helped him to paint and produce prints. But his background meant that he hated injustice, snobbery and pretension, and deplored the degradation suffered by the poor.

His fame rests in particular on his series of paintings telling contemporary stories, his 'modern moral subjects' such as *A Harlot's Progress*, *A Rake's Progress* and *Marriage-a-la-Mode*. These began as paintings full of detail, theatrical in style and showing the follies and foibles of humanity, which still strike a chord today – *Gin Lane* has come to represent the worst aspects of slum life in 18th-century London. Hogarth was a shrewd businessman. He displayed his artworks to an enthusiastic audience, taking advance

William Hogarth, self-portrait

orders for engravings of the same images. He also sold his prints at modest prices, ensuring he reached a much wider audience than the few who could afford his original paintings.

Hogarth's House was opened to the public in 1904 (making it one of London's oldest house museums) by a local landowner and Hogarth enthusiast, Lieutenant-Colonel Robert William Shipway (1841-1925), who gave the house to Middlesex County Council in 1907. It was damaged in 1941 during the Second World War, but was repaired and reopened in 1951, and was restored again for the Hogarth Tercentenary in 1997. It closed for refurbishment in September 2008, during which it was badly damaged by fire in August 2009, and only reopened in November 2011.

Two floors of the house are open to the public and include the most extensive collection of Hogarth's prints on permanent public display. The panelled rooms also house some replica pieces of 18th-century furniture. An exhibition documents Hogarth's life and work and there are also periodic special exhibitions relating to the surrounding area.

Take time to visit the attractive walled garden where there's an ancient mulberry tree that's at least 300 years old. Hogarth had a 'painting room' at the bottom of this garden and continued to work there until a few days before his death.

🍴 **FOOD & DRINK** 🍷

Chiswick House Café: A short walk from Hogarth's House is **Chiswick House** (see page 198) and its excellent café, which has an exceedingly tempting array of cakes.

4 | 7 HAMMERSMITH TERRACE

> **Address:** 7 Hammersmith Terrace, W6 9TS (☎ 020-8741 4104,
> 🖳 emerywalker.org.uk).
> **Opening hours**: April to September (dates vary – see website) for pre-booked
> guided tours (1hr). Three tours (1hr) daily on Sat – other times by appointment.
> **Cost**: £10 adults, £5 concessions and students.
> **Transport**: Stamford Brook tube.
> **Amenities**: Shop, garden, wheelchair access (ground floor only).

Walker moved into 7 Hammersmith Terrace in 1903, although he had already spent 25 years at number 3, and many of its contents were relocated down the road. After his death, his daughter Dorothy inherited number 7 and it later passed to her nurse-companion Elizabeth de Hass who was instrumental in setting up the trust which manages the house.

From the outside, it's a traditional Georgian dwelling, but inside the decor and furnishings have been preserved as they were in Walker's lifetime, from its William Morris furniture, textiles, linoleum and wallpaper, to its Middle Eastern and North African ceramics and textiles. There's furniture and glass by Philip Webb, ceramics by William de Morgan and furniture by Ernest Gimson, as well as a crewelwork bedcover made by Morris's daughter May. Outside, a pretty, walled garden adjoins the river.

This is Britain's last authentic Arts & Crafts interior, the former home of printer and collector Emery Walker (1851-1933) who was friend and mentor to design guru, William Morris. It's one of a terrace of 17 tall, narrow houses built in the 1750s between Chiswick Mall and Lower Mall, Hammersmith on the north bank of the Thames, an area which became popular with artists and other creative types. Barely changed since the '30s, the house has been dubbed 'an internationally important Arts & Crafts time warp'.

Emery Walker was a coachbuilder's son who found success by developing new printing techniques. He befriended William Morris who lived in nearby Upper Mall; it was Walker who gave Morris the idea for his famed Kelmscott Press.

 FOOD & DRINK

The Black Lion: Iconic riverside pub down the road from Walker's house, with a menu ranging from Spanish tapas to fish and chips.

18 STAFFORD TERRACE/LINLEY SAMBOURNE HOUSE

5

> **Address:** 18 Stafford Terrace, W8 7BH (☎ 020-7602 3316, 🖥 rbkc.gov.uk/subsites/museums/18staffordterrace.aspx).
>
> **Opening hours**: Mid-September to mid-June. Closed in summer and December 25-26th and January 1st. Visits by guided tour only, on Wed at 11.15am and 2.15pm, and Sat-Sun at 11.15am. Booking strongly advised.
>
> **Cost**: £8 adults, £6 over-60s and full-time students, £3 children under 16.
>
> **Transport**: High Street Kensington tube.
>
> **Amenities:** No wheelchair access.

Tucked away behind the shops of Kensington High Street, 18 Stafford Terrace is one of London's hidden gems: a unique, beautifully preserved late Victorian townhouse, classical Italianate in style, with most of its original decor and furnishings. While preserved Victorian exteriors aren't uncommon, it's rare to have an almost original interior.

The house is also known as Linley Sambourne House, after Edward Linley Sambourne (1844-1910) who lived here with his wife Marion and two children from 1875 to his death. Sambourne was a photographer, book illustrator and the chief political cartoonist of the (now defunct) satirical magazine *Punch*, and an ancestor of the Earl of Snowdon, who married Queen Elizabeth's sister, Princess Margaret.

 ALLOW...

Tours take around 90 minutes. At weekends there's the option of a costumed tour based on Marion Sambourne's diaries, led by 'Marion' or one of her servants (see website for details).

The house was originally decorated by the Sambourne family, following the principles of the then-fashionable Aesthetic Movement which encouraged the use of 'exotic' influences in interior décor. Thus the William Morris wallpaper, heavy velvet curtains and stained glass windows are juxtaposed with exotic Turkish carpets, ebonised wardrobes and vast numbers of ornaments, including objects from Africa, the Middle East and Japan – an interesting and attractive jumble. There's a notable collection of Chinese export porcelain, from the 17th to 19th centuries, displayed throughout the house, along with a number of Sambourne's cartoons, drawings and sketches.

Sambourne's descendants preserved the property in its original style until its opened to the public in 1980 and it paints a vivid picture of intellectual, late-Victorian tastes and lifestyle.

Note that 18 Stafford Terrace is spread over five floors, with steep external and interior stairs, and is unsuitable for visitors with restricted mobility.

6 CHISWICK HOUSE

Address: Burlington Lane, W4 2RP (☎ 020-8742 3905, 🖳 chgt.org.uk).
Opening hours: April to October, Sun-Wed and Bank Holidays, 10am to 5pm.
Closed 1st November to 21st December (except for pre-booked tours) and from
22nd December to 31st March.
Cost: £5.70 adults, £5.10 concessions, £3.40 children (5-15, under-5s free), £14.80
families. Access to the gardens is free.
Transport: Turnham Green tube or Chiswick rail.
Amenities: Café, conservatory, gardens, wheelchair access (ground floor only).

Nestled unexpectedly in affluent, mock-Tudor Chiswick suburbia is a glorious piece of Palladian extravagance surrounded by beautiful gardens. Chiswick House was completed in 1729, the vision of the third Earl of Burlington, who'd been inspired by the architecture he saw during his 'grand tours' of Italy. It's one of England's finest examples of neo-Palladian design, i.e. modelled on the architecture of ancient Rome and 16th-century Italy.

👁 DON'T MISS!

Chiswick House gardens were the birthplace of the English Landscape movement. With their combination of grand vistas and hidden pathways, architectural delights and dazzling planting, they are a unique oasis in this corner of London.

It wasn't built as a private residence so much as a showcase for art and a venue for entertaining; the Earl played host to the luminaries of the day, including Alexander Pope and Handel. The design of the house echoes that of classical temples, and is the result of a collaboration between the Earl and the architect William Kent.

There's much to see in the house, including eight beautiful landscape views of Chiswick House and its gardens by the 18th century Flemish artist Pieter Andreas Rysbrack and statues of the architects Palladio and Inigo Jones by Rysbrack's brother Michael. Other notably statuary includes carvings of the pagan god the Green Man in the fireplaces of the Green Velvet Room, and a rather splendid lead sphinx.

There are some glorious objects on display, including the Chiswick Tables – some of the best examples of English neo-Palladian furniture – and two porphyry urns purchased by Lord Burlington on his Grand Tour of 1714. But some of the most magical sights are overhead: the coffered dome in the Upper Tribunal, the beautiful, half-moon apses in the gallery and the ornate ceiling of the Blue Velvet Room Ceiling, portraying the goddess of architecture.

FULHAM PALACE

7

Address: Bishop's Avenue, SW6 6EA (☎ 020-7736 8140, 🖥 fulhampalace.org).
Opening hours: Sat-Wed, 1pm to 4pm. Gardens daily, dawn to dusk. Guided tours of the palace's most historic rooms are held on the 2nd and 4th Sundays and the 3rd Tuesday of each month at 2pm.
Cost: Free. Tours £5 per person.
Transport: Putney Bridge tube or Putney rail.
Amenities: Gallery, café, shop, garden, wheelchair access.

Fulham Palace is a well-kept local secret, an unexpected, tree-surrounded haven in a tranquil Thameside location. It's one of London's oldest and most historically significant buildings, yet strangely little-known outside the local area.

Much of the surviving palace building dates from 1495 and is Grade I listed. (It's said to be haunted by the ghosts of Protestant heretics, who were persecuted in the Great Hall.) It encompasses a variety of building styles and ages on one site, while the extensive gardens (the grounds used to extend to over 30 acres, but now cover just 12) have a range of international plant species, some dating from the 18th century. The palace once had England's longest moat (which was filled in 1924). It still has an exquisite walled garden, recently restored, which can be viewed as part of a historic garden walk (see website for dates).

The palace was the country home of the Bishops of London for many centuries, and excavations have revealed evidence of settlement dating back to Roman and Neolithic times. The land is recorded as belonging to the Bishop of London in 700 AD; the palace was the Bishops' country house from at least the 11th century (possibly earlier) and their main residence from the 18th century until 1975.

Two rooms at Fulham Palace are set aside for a museum that interprets the site's long history with displays of archaeological finds, models and paintings. There's also a shop, a contemporary art gallery and a café.

👁 DON'T MISS!

One of the more unusual objects in the gardens is the Bishop's Tree, the stump of a Cedar of Lebanon which features sculptures by Andrew Frost depicting some of the bishops. Look out for Bishop Compton (1675-1713), who established the gardens, peering out from the crown of the 'tree'.

8 LEIGHTON HOUSE MUSEUM

Address: 12 Holland Park Road, W14 8LZ (☎ 020-7602 3316, 🖥 rbkc.gov.uk/subsites/museums/leightonhousemuseum.aspx).
Opening hours: Daily except Tue, 10am to 5.30pm. Closed from around 25th December to 2nd January.
Cost: £5 adults, £3 concessions (over 60s, 16 and under and full-time students). Tickets are valid for one year. Free guided tours on Wednesday and Sunday at 3pm.
Transport: High Street Kensington tube.
Amenities: No wheelchair access.

This unjustly-obscure museum is on the edge of Holland Park, in the former home of painter and sculptor Frederic, Lord Leighton (1830-1896). It's one of the 19th-century's most remarkable buildings – from the outside it's elegant rather than striking, but it has one of London's most original interiors. Leighton was associated with the Pre-Raphaelite Brotherhood (although he later looked to contrast with them) and his work depicted biblical, classical and historical subjects; he's most famous for his painting *Flaming June*.

ALLOW...

About an hour is long enough to take in the splendours of Leighton House. The one-hour guided tour includes special access to the servant quarters in the basement and the models staircase.

The first part of the house was designed in 1864 by George Aitchison and resembles an Italianate villa. It's of red Suffolk brick with Caen Stone dressings in a restrained classical style. Subsequently, the building was extended over 30 years by Aitchison, to create a private art palace for Leighton. The house's centrepiece is a remarkable two-storey Arab Hall, designed to display Leighton's priceless collection of over 1,000 Islamic tiles, dating from the 13th to 17th centuries and collected during his trips to the Middle East. The interior of this pseudo-Islamic court gives a stunning impression of the Orient – with gilded ceilings, peacock blue tiles, red walls and intricate black woodwork – including a dome and a fountain.

With all this architectural and decorative finery, it would be easy to overlook the permanent collection, which would be a pity as there are works by various members of the Pre-Raphaelite Brotherhood, including Edward Burne-Jones, John Everett Millais and George Frederick Watts, in addition to 81 oil paintings by Leighton himself and a number of his sketches, watercolours, prints, personal documents and mementos.

Frederic Leighton, self-portrait

LONDON MOTORCYCLE MUSEUM 9

Address: Ravenor Farm, 29 Oldfield Lane, Greenford, UB6 9LD (☎ 020-8575 6644, 🖥 london-motorcycle-museum.org).
Opening hours: Sat-Sun and Bank Holidays, 10am to 4.30pm. Pre-booked school visits Mon-Thu, 10am to 3pm.
Cost: £5 adults, £2.50 concessions, £1 children (5 to 14), under 5s free.
Transport: Greenford tube.
Amenities: Café, shop, wheelchair access.

The London Motorcycle Museum (LMM) is London's only motorcycle museum focusing on Britain's long and distinguished biking history and heritage. Between 1960 and 1973, the museum's founder Bill Crosby (b 1932) hoarded many choice bikes which were originally displayed (until 1979) in Syon Park alongside a collection of vintage cars; after 1979 the collection was shown at a number of temporary venues before finding its present home in 1997.

The ever-growing collection (see website for an inventory) includes a 1902 Ormonde (a past participant in the Pioneer Run) and a 1903 Clyde (with a SIMS magneto). There's also a number of unique prototypes and 'media stars' and a wealth of iconic British machines, including racers and road bikes from ABC to Zenith, plus the Crosby collection of Triumphs including the last Triumph T140 out of the Meriden gates in 1983 and a 1991 Norton rotary in Paramedic livery. Among the ever-changing exhibits are a 1930s Coventry Eagle 1,000cc Flying 8, a 1911 Rudge TT, a 1907 Brown Precision, the Triumph P1 prototype Trident (owned by the Trident & Rocket 3 Owners Club), an immaculate 1959 Norton 'Dommie' 99, an equally perfect 1959 Velocette Venom, a 1966 BSA Lightning works production racer, and several other rarities and prototypes from biking's golden era when roads were less congested. Less nobly, there's even a Sinclair C5!

Bikes also regularly appear at community events, county shows and carnivals, as well as the museum's own special events and ride-ins. Some have also 'starred' in television series, such as *EastEnders* and *Dad's Army*.

FOOD & DRINK

Greenford Broadway: There are a number of pubs, cafes and fast-food outlets on this shopping street, just a short walk south of the museum. If the weather's good, why not take a picnic and enjoy it in nearby Ravenor Park?

10 MUSEUM OF BRANDS

> **Address:** 2 Colville Mews, Lonsdale Road, W11 2AR (☎ 020-7908 0880,
> 🖳 www.museumofbrands.com).
> **Opening hours**: Tue-Sat, 10am to 6pm; Sun 11am to 5pm. Closed 25-26th
> December, 1st January and during the Notting Hill Carnival (August Bank Holiday
> weekend).
> **Cost**: £6.50 adults, £4 concessions, £2.25 children (aged 7-16), £15 families.
> **Transport**: Notting Hill Gate tube.
> **Amenities**: Café, shop, wheelchair access.

Packaging and Advertising) is the result of the work of Robert Opie, an author and consumer historian who was eager to record the history of the products around us. He began collecting at the age of 16 (with a packet of Munchies), and it has extended to all aspects of daily life: design, fashion, magazines, souvenirs, technology, toys, travel and much more. As well as the permanent collection, there are a series of exhibitions (see website for details).

The permanent collection features over 12,000 items from the Robert Opie Collection and explores the history of consumer culture over the past 200 years through household products, from Victorian times to the present day. The collection shows how famous brands have evolved through their creative use of packaging and advertising, from Fry's and Kellogg's to Oxo and Heinz.

Anyone connected with the creative industries – advertising, art, branding, design, fashion, graphic design, packaging et al – will find this museum educational and inspirational, and you can take some of it home with you, as the shop sells merchandise related to the Robert Opie Collection.

This is one of London's smaller, specialist museums that at first sight might appear dull or too obscure, but is actually fascinating. A recent addition to the roster of London museums (from 1984 to 2001, the collection was housed in a museum in Gloucester, moving to London in 2005), it's situated near buzzy, visitor-choked Portobello Market (it's tucked away in a mews, so consult a map before heading here).

The Museum of Brands (its full name is the Museum of Brands,

 ALLOW...

An hour is enough for a quick tour but it's easy to become caught up in nostalgia for 'your' decade and find that several hours have swept by.

NATIONAL ARMY MUSEUM 11

Address: Royal Hospital Road, SW3 4HT (☎ 020-7881 6606, 🖳 nam.ac.uk).
Opening hours: Daily, 10am to 5.30pm. Closed 24-26th December and 1st January.
Cost: Free.
Transport: Sloane Square tube.
Amenities: Café, shop, wheelchair access.

The National Army Museum (NAM) is often overlooked in favour of the more famous **Imperial War Museum** (see page 267) which has a wider theme – it includes the war experiences of British civilians and military personnel – but a much narrower timeframe (after 1914). The NAM covers a much longer period, commencing around 1066.

Four main permanent exhibitions 'tell the ordinary and extraordinary stories of the men and women who served in Britain's armies across the globe and how they helped shape the world of today': Changing the World 1784-1904 (the role of the Army in the expansion and defence of British trade and empire); World Wars 1905-1945; Conflicts of Interest 1969 to Present (including Northern Ireland, the Falklands, Iraq and Afghanistan); and the Art Gallery, with paintings from 1630 to 2000, including work by such luminaries as Sir Thomas Gainsborough, Sir Joshua Reynolds and Rex Whistler.

Army from medieval times to the 18th century, and 'National Service' which recounts the experiences of men in the post-war call-up.

The museum also has a Kids' Zone which allows children to 'live in a soldiers' tent, defend a castle from invasion and look after the king's horses'.

There are regular activities, events and talks, including free lunchtime lectures on Thursdays at 12.30pm, and 'celebrity lectures' for which fees vary (usually around £15 to £20 per head). There's also a shop and the aptly named Base Café.

👁 DON'T MISS!

One of the more unusual exhibits in the 'Changing the World' gallery is the skeleton of Napoleon's warhorse, Marengo. He was brought back to Britain after Napoleon went into exile and lived to the ripe old age of 38.

Just as fascinating are the special displays which include 'The Making of Britain', which tells the story of the

14 COUPER COLLECTION

> **Address:** The Couper Collection Barges, Battersea Beach, Thames Riverside Walk, Hester Road, SW11 4AN (🖥 coupercollection.org.uk, ✉ info@coupercollection.org.uk).
> **Opening hours:** Tue-Fri, 10am to 4pm and by appointment.
> **Cost:** Free.
> **Transport:** Bus routes: 19, 49, 239, 319, 345 to the south side of Battersea Bridge.
> **Amenities:** No wheelchair access.

The Couper Collection exhibits artwork and installations by London artist Max Couper, as well as hosting exhibitions and events by other artists. However, what makes the gallery unique is that the artworks are created and displayed on board a fleet of permanently-moored Thames' barges – a secret world of fictional charts, sculptures and artefacts that take inspiration from the River Thames. The Collection's barges are London's last remaining fleet of historic Thames barges on their ancient moorings, which were continuously in use from the 18th century until the '80s.

The Collection includes work shown in 1996 and 1997 at Couper's one-man exhibitions at The Museum of Contemporary Art (Antwerp), The Lehmbruck Museum of Sculpture (Duisberg), and The Sprengal Museum of Modern Art (Hanover), plus work shown in New York and London installations since 1978. The Collection opened on the site in 1998 as a permanent public trust in association with Wandsworth Council.

There's also a changing programme of live events, new artists' exhibitions, discussions, educational collaborations and ecology.

15 GUNNERSBURY PARK MUSEUM

> **Address:** Popes Lane, W3 8LQ (☎ 020-8992 1612, 🖥 hounslow.info/arts-culture/historic-houses-museums/gunnersbury-park-museum).
> **Opening hours**: Daily, 11am to 5pm (11am to 4pm, November to March). Closed 25-26th December and 1st January.
> **Cost**: Free.
> **Transport**: Acton Town tube.
> **Amenities:** Park, gardens, wheelchair access.

Gunnersbury Park in Brentford covers 186 acres (75ha) and contains two early 19th-century mansions, one of which (the Large Mansion) is Grade II* listed and home to Gunnersbury Park Museum. In 1760, the house and estate were purchased for Princess Amelia, favourite daughter of George II, as a country summer retreat, and she landscaped the park in the 18th-century style. After Amelia died

in 1786, it had a number of owners until being purchased 1835 by merchant and financier Nathan Mayer Rothschild (1777-1836).

The estate was sold to Ealing & Acton Councils in 1925 and the house was opened to the public in 1926 by Neville Chamberlain, then Minister of Health. Since 1929, it has been the home of the local history museum for the London boroughs of Ealing and Hounslow. The museum contains a wide range of objects, paintings and photographs reflecting life in Ealing and Hounslow, from prehistory to the present day, including material from local businesses, such as Hoovers from the famous Hoover factory and posters from the original Ealing Film Studios.

KELMSCOTT HOUSE 16

Address: 26 Upper Mall, W6 9TA (☎ 020-8741 3735, 🖥 williammorrissociety.org).
Opening hours: The house is privately-owned, but the basement and coach house are open to visitors on Thu and Sat, 2-5pm, and at other times by appointment.
Cost: Free. Tours (min. 8 and max. 16 people) by appointment, suggested £6 donation.
Transport: Ravenscourt Park tube.
Amenities: Shop, library, wheelchair access (limited).

Kelmscott House is an attractive Georgian building where William Morris lived from 1879 until his death in 1896. Built in around 1780 it was originally called The Retreat, but Morris renamed it after his home in Oxfordshire, Kelmscott Manor, and sometimes travelled between the two by boat (those were the days!). In 1891, Morris set up the Kelmscott Press at number 16. Today, the William Morris Society occupies the basement of Kelmscott House, the entrance of which is down steps leading from the driveway.

There's a small, interesting museum, with a collection of Morris's drawings, some lovely furniture and his printing press. The photographs of Morris himself are especially revealing – he looks rather more approachable and lively than many of his Victorian contemporaries appear to have been. The coach house was used for meetings for the socialist groups that William Morris was involved with, and the likes of Keir Hardie and George Bernard Shaw lectured here. Kelmscott House also has a shop offering tasteful gifts with a Morris theme.

17 LOUISE BLOUIN FOUNDATION

Address: 3 Olaf Street, W11 4BE (☎ 020-7985 9600, 🖥 ltbfoundation.org).
Opening hours: Gallery: Mon-Fri, 9.30am to 5.30pm. Exhibitions: Mon-Fri 10am to 6pm, Sat noon to 5pm.
Cost: Free.
Transport: Latimer Road tube.
Amenities: Café, wheelchair access.

The Louise Blouin Foundation is one of London's largest non-government funded, not-for-profit cultural spaces in London, featuring exhibitions of both established and emerging international contemporary artists alongside a lively programme of lectures and events. It's housed in the former '20s headquarters of Barker & Co., coach-builders for the classic English auto-manufacturers Bentley, Daimler and Rolls-Royce, which was transformed at a cost of £20m into a dramatic 5,000ft² (465m²) gallery space with a café.

The Foundation was established in 2005 by Louise Blouin – chairwoman and CEO of Louise Blouin Media, the leading global media company focused on the promotion of the arts, culture and luxury – with the philosophy of experimentation, questioning, debate, and learning. It presents the work of individual artists through temporary exhibitions, installations, performances and screenings, and promotes a lively programme of events such as lectures, debates, workshops, think tanks and summits. Recent presentations have included a retrospective on the French writer, director and photographer Chris Marker and an exhibition based around editing an issue of *Modern Painters* magazine.

ROYAL BRITISH SOCIETY OF SCULPTORS **18**

Address: Dora House, 108 Old Brompton Road, SW7 3RA (☎ 020-7373 8615, 🖵 rbs.org.uk).
Opening hours: Wed-Fri, noon-5.30pm.
Cost: Free.
Transport: Gloucester Road or South Kensington tube.
Amenities: Garden, wheelchair access (via ramps).

The Royal British Society of Sculptors is a registered charity (since 1963) whose aims are to promote and support sculpture. Founded in 1904, it received its royal charter in 1911, and is the oldest and largest organisation dedicated to sculpture in the UK. It has a worldwide membership of over 500 professional sculptors, who may use the post-nominal ARBS or FRBS. Queen Elizabeth II is patron of the Society.

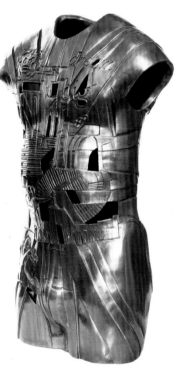

Committed to the pursuit of excellence in the art form, it aims to inspire, inform and engage people with sculpture/three dimensional art. The Society offers opportunities to see and experience the extraordinary diversity of contemporary work and to learn from those who make it through their exhibition programme. It supports sculptors by providing bursaries to newly emergent artists, professional development seminars, a mentoring scheme, and a growing number of awards and residencies.

In the '90s it began an active exhibition programme by opening a gallery at its beautiful home in Kensington and mounting large off-site shows.

SOUTHWEST LONDON

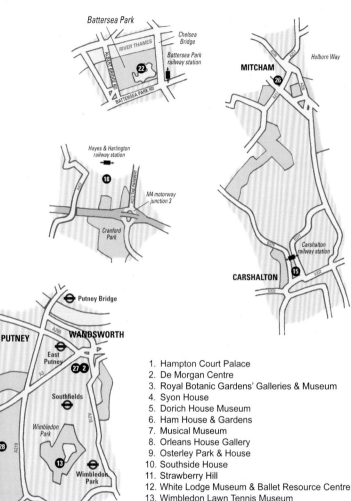

1. Hampton Court Palace
2. De Morgan Centre
3. Royal Botanic Gardens' Galleries & Museum
4. Syon House
5. Dorich House Museum
6. Ham House & Gardens
7. Musical Museum
8. Orleans House Gallery
9. Osterley Park & House
10. Southside House
11. Strawberry Hill
12. White Lodge Museum & Ballet Resource Centre
13. Wimbledon Lawn Tennis Museum
14. World Rugby Museum
15. Honeywood Museum
16. Kew Bridge Steam Museum
17. Kingston Museum
18. London Motor Museum
19. Marble Hill House
20. Museum of Richmond & Riverside Gallery
21. National Archives
22. Pump House Gallery
23. Royal Military School of Music Museum
24. Stanley Picker Gallery
25. Twickenham Museum
26. Wandle Industrial Museum
27. Wandsworth Museum
28. Wimbledon Windmill & Museum

1 HAMPTON COURT PALACE

Address: Hampton Court Palace, East Molesey, KT8 9AU (☎ 0844-482 7777/020-3166 6000, 🖳 hrp.org.uk/hamptoncourtpalace).

Opening hours: Daily, April to Oct 10am to 6pm, Nov to March 10am to 4.30pm (dates and times may vary, so check website).

Cost: £16.95 (£14.40 online) adults, £14.30 (£12) concessions, £8.50 (£7.20) children under 16, £43.46 (£36.50) families (max. two adults and six children). Tickets include access to the palace, gardens and maze. The maze (year round) and formal gardens (April-Sept only) can be also visited separately.

Transport: Hampton Court rail.

Amenities: Three cafés, four shops, gardens, wheelchair access.

Hampton Court Palace (Grade I listed) is a vast royal palace covering 6 acres (2.5ha) situated on the River Thames at Hampton Court. It was built in 1514 for Cardinal Thomas Wolsey – Lord Chancellor and favourite of Henry VIII – and was appropriated by the King in 1529 when Wolsey fell from favour. Henry made it his main London residence and greatly enlarged it. Further massive rebuilding by William III in the following century (intended to rival Versailles) was halted in 1694, leaving the palace in two distinct contrasting architectural styles: domestic Tudor and Baroque.

Hampton Court remains a royal palace – one of only two surviving palaces previously occupied by Henry VIII (the other is St James's) – but hasn't been inhabited by the British royal family since the 18th century, when George II was resident (his son, George III, never set foot there as king). It's maintained by an independent charity, Historic Royal Palaces, and is a major tourist attraction. It receives no funding from the government or the crown, hence the eye-watering admission prices. The palace's Home Park is the site of the annual Hampton Court Palace Festival and the RHS Hampton Court Palace Flower Show.

Works of Art: The palace houses a wealth of art and furnishings from the Royal Collection, mainly dating from the early Tudor and late Stuart to early Georgian eras. The single most important works are Andrea Mantegna's *Triumphs of Caesar* (1484 to 1492) – one of the most famous sets of paintings in the whole history of European art – now housed in the Lower Orangery. The Cartoon Gallery on the south side of the Fountain Court was designed by Christopher Wren to display another famous collection, the Raphael Cartoons; the originals are now at the Victoria and Albert Museum and copies painted in the 1690s by a minor artist, Henry Cooke, are displayed in the gallery.

Queen's Drawing Room

remains, including tables by Jean Pelletier, 'India back' walnut chairs by Thomas Roberts and clocks and a barometer by Thomas Tompion. Several state beds are still in their original positions, as is the Throne Canopy in the King's Privy Chamber. This room also contains a crystal chandelier (ca. 1700), possibly the first such in Britain.

The King's Guard Chamber contains almost 3,000 pieces of armoury: muskets, pistols, swords, daggers, powder horns and pieces of armour. They are arranged on the walls in decorative patterns and the existence of bills dated 1699 for payment to a John Harris for the arrangement suggest that they have hung in the same place for more than 300 years.

Other highlights of the palace include:

Great Hall: Situated in Henry VIII's State Apartments, the Great Hall was England's last and greatest medieval hall. It's spanned by a large and sumptuously decorated hammer-beam roof, while its walls are hung with Henry VIII's most splendid Flemish tapestries

---

👁 DON'T MISS!

Astronomical Clock: This rare clock in the Main Gatehouse is one of the most significant late-medieval clocks in Europe; only a handful of earlier such timepieces still survive. It was designed by Bavarian horologist Nicholas Kratzer (a friend of court painter Hans Holbein) and installed around 1540. Working with French clockmaker Nicholas Oursian, Kratzer created not only a marvel of Tudor engineering with complex mechanics, but also an enviable work of art. It also had great practical use showing the time, month and day as well as the position of the sun in the zodiac and the phase and age of the moon. It also determined the time at which the moon would cross the meridian and therefore the time of high water at London Bridge, useful if – like the king – you travelled to London by royal barge.

Much of the original furniture from the late 17th and early 18th centuries

Triumphs of Caesar, Mantegna'

depicting *The Story of Abraham*. William Shakespeare's company – the 'King's Men' – performed in the hall for James I over Christmas and New Year in 1603-4.

ALLOW...

It's easy to spend the whole day at Hampton Court Palace – and it's a good way to justify the high cost of admission! There's plenty to keep children amused, whether getting lost in the maze or following the ghost trail in search of Catherine Howard (Henry's fifth wife, who was arrested at the palace and later beheaded) and the 'Grey Lady'.

Chapel Royal: The double height chapel was begun by Wolsey and completed under Henry VIII, and has been in continuous use for over 450 years. Its timber and plaster ceiling, a Gothic vault with Renaissance pendants completed by models of trumpeting boys, is considered the 'most important and magnificent in Britain.' The altar is framed by a massive oak reredos in Baroque style carved by Grinling Gibbons (Britain's greatest wood carver) during the reign of Queen Anne. Opposite the altar, at first floor level, is the royal pew where the royal family would attend services isolated from the general congregation seated below. A reconstruction of Henry VIII's crown (the original was melted down on the orders of Oliver Cromwell) is displayed here.

Visitors are welcome to attend religious services at the chapel. On Sundays in theory it's closed to all but worshippers, although it can be seen after Evensong – between 16.45-17.15pm – and when there are no Choral Services.

Henry VIII's Kitchens: For many people, Hampton Court Palace **is** Henry VIII, and his abiding reputation remains as a 'consumer of food and women'. So it's no surprise that the Tudor kitchens are a major draw. They were conceived in 1530 to feed the Court of Henry VIII (at least 600 people!) twice a day; a vast operation larger than any modern hotel, and one that had to cope without modern conveniences. For a taste of what was on the menu in Henry's day, there are monthly cookery

maze

Hampton Court maze – designed by George London and Henry Wise and commissioned around 1700 by William III – is the most famous in the world, covering a third of an acre. Other features of the gardens are the Great Vine, planted in 1768 by the celebrated gardener 'Capability' Brown (and still producing an annual crop of grapes) and Henry VIII's Privy Garden, which has been recreated based on a design of 1702.

demonstrations (see website for dates).

Young Henry VIII Exhibition: This permanent exhibition introduces you to the 'pin-up' prince, before he became fat old Henry VIII. It includes paintings and interactive displays and explores the stereotypes that still over-shadow the true characters and stories of Henry, Cardinal Wolsey and Katherine of Aragon.

Park, Gardens & Maze: Hampton Court Park (also called Home Park) covers 750 acres (304ha), including 60 acres (26ha) of formal gardens, set within a loop of the River Thames. The spectacular gardens feature sparkling fountains and glorious displays of over 200,000 flowering bulbs, while

 FOOD & DRINK

Tiltyard Café & Deli: Serves homemade hot dishes, beverages, cakes and organic ice cream – why not buy a picnic and eat it in the gardens?

The Privy Kitchen: Located in the heart of the Tudor palace, the Privy Kitchen café was originally Elizabeth I's private kitchen.

King's Arms Hotel: A 300-year-old inn perched on the Lions Gate of the palace, rich in atmosphere, décor and history

Chapel Ceiling

2 DE MORGAN CENTRE

> **Address:** 38 West Hill, SW18 1RX (☎ 020-8871 1144, 🖥 demorgan.org.uk).
> **Opening hours:** Tue-Fri 1-5pm; Sat 11am to 5pm (open until 9.30pm on the first Thursday of each month).
> **Cost:** £4 adults, children free.
> **Transport:** East Putney tube.
> **Amenities:** Café, shop, wheelchair access.

The splendid 'De Morgan Centre for the Study of 19th-Century Art and Society' houses the world's largest collection of the work of William De Morgan (1839-1917) – the most important ceramic artist, potter and tile designer of the Arts and Crafts Movement – and his wife, the painter Evelyn De Morgan (1855-1919). William is credited with the rediscovery of the art of lustre (his work was heavily influenced by the Islamic tiles he saw at the South Kensington Museum – now the Victoria & Albert Museum), while Evelyn was a prolific artist and symbolist painter, whose style was notable for its rich use of colour, allegory, and emphasis on strong female subjects.

In 1859, De Morgan was admitted to the Royal Academy School and studied alongside Frederick Walker and Simeon Solomon. In 1863, he was introduced by Henry Holiday to the painter Edward Burne-Jones and designer and polymath William Morris. As Morris hadn't been very successful with ceramics, De Morgan took over the tile production side of his business and soon began designing his own tiles. A lifelong friend of William Morris, he designed tiles, stained glass and furniture for Morris & Co from 1863 to 1872.

** DON'T MISS!**

One of William De Morgan's most spectacular creations (shown below) is the Galleon Tile Panel, an exotic scene of sailing ships, birds and sea creatures comprised of 40 ceramic tiles and measuring 5ft (152cm) across. It was originally a commission for the P&O shipping company in the late 19th century and intended to decorate the SS Malta, but ended up with an American collector in Colorado, and was purchased for the De Morgan collection at a Sotheby's auction in 2006.

Galleon Tile Panel

Punchbowl

His tiles were often based on medieval designs or Persian patterns, and he experimented with innovative glazes and firing techniques. Ships and fish were popular motifs, as were 'fantastical' birds and other animals. Many of De Morgan's tile designs were planned to create intricate patterns when several tiles were laid together. (One of his earliest commissions was working on the Arab Hall at **Leighton House** in Kensington, now a museum – see page 200.)

William and Evelyn married in 1887 and, in addition to their art, became involved in many of the leading issues of the day, including prison reform, pacifism, the Suffragette movement and spiritualism – all documented in the Centre.

The Centre's collection was assembled by Evelyn De Morgan's sister, Mrs Wilhelmina Stirling, who wrote a number of books under the name AMW Sterling, including the De Morgans' biography. She inherited some pieces from the De Morgans and actively sought out other works to add to the collection, which she assembled at her home, Old Battersea House in London. Following her death in 1965 (at the age of 99) she bequeathed the collection to be looked after in trust for perpetuity, which gave rise to the De Morgan Foundation Charity in 1967. Parts of the collection have been

displayed at a number of locations with associations with William De Morgan, but since 2002 it's (recently refurbished) home has been the former West Hill Reference Library in Wandsworth. Appropriately, this is an Arts and Crafts building dating from 1887 – the year the De Morgans were married – and also houses the **Wandsworth Museum** (see page 240).

The Centre's collection includes ceramics (vases, tiles and panels), oil paintings, drawings and lustre-ware, and it hosts a wide-ranging programme of temporary exhibitions by contemporary designers (see website).

 FOOD & DRINK

Museum café: The museum has a café with a small lunch menu.
L'Auberge: A lovely hidden gem of a French restaurant (☎ 020-8874 3593) just a few yards from the gallery.

The Prisoner, Evelyn De Morgan

3 ROYAL BOTANIC GARDENS' GALLERIES & MUSEUM

Address: Royal Botanic Gardens, Kew, TW9 3AB (☎ 020-8332 5655, 🖳 kew.org/collections).

Opening hours: Daily, except for December 24-25th. Gardens open at 9.30am and closing between 3.45pm (winter) and 7.30pm (summer weekends); see website for exact dates and times.

Cost: £14.50 adults, £12.50 concessions, children (16 and under) free when accompanied by an adult. Fee includes admission to most RBG attractions.

Transport: Kew Gardens tube.

Amenities: Two restaurants, two cafés, two shops, wheelchair access.

Palm House

The Royal Botanic Gardens, Kew (a UNESCO World Heritage Site since 2003) – usually referred to simply as Kew Gardens – comprises around 300 acres (121ha) of gardens and botanical greenhouses. The gardens were created in 1759 and welcome some 2m visitors annually. The site includes no fewer than four Grade I listed buildings and 36 Grade II listed structures. Among Kew's many attractions are a number of galleries and a museum, described below:

👁 DON'T MISS!

One of Kew's most popular attractions is the **Xstrata Treetop Walkway** which takes visitors along a 200m (660ft) long stroll through the treetops, 18m (59ft) above the ground. There are lifts to get you up there but don't be surprised if you sway in the breeze.

Marianne North Gallery: Recently restored and refurbished, the Marianne North Gallery first opened in 1882, and is the only permanent solo exhibition by a female artist in Britain. Marianne North (1830-1890) – naturalist and botanical artist – was a remarkable Victorian woman who travelled the globe to satisfy her passion for recording the world's flora with her paint brush. Although she had no formal training and was rather unconventional in her methods, North had a natural artistic talent and was very prolific: the gallery contains 833 paintings – depicting over 900 plant species – all completed in 13 years of world travel.

Shirley Sherwood Gallery of Botanic Art: Opened in April 2008, the gallery displays paintings owned by Kew and by botanical art collector Dr Shirley Sherwood, many of which have never been seen by the public before. It features works by artists and illustrators

Marianne North Gallery

such as Georg Dionysius Ehret, the Bauer brothers and Walter Hood Fitch.

🍴 FOOD & DRINK 🍸

Orangery Restaurant: Kew's self-service restaurant, operated by the acclaimed Peyton & Byrne.

Pavilion Restaurant: With its gorgeous vine-sheltered terrace, the Pavilion is a great spot for an al fresco summer lunch.

Cafes: If you're after a quick snack, try the Victoria Gate or White Peaks cafés.

Museum No. 1: Near the Palm House is a building known simply as Museum No. 1 (despite being Kew's only museum), designed by Decimus Burton and opened in 1857. It houses Kew's economic botany collections, including tools, ornaments, clothing, food and medicines. The upper two floors comprise an education centre, while the ground floor has the Plants+People exhibition, which highlights the variety of plants and the ways that people use them.

Cambridge Cottage: Also known as Kew Gardens Gallery, the cottage displays exhibitions of botanical art by past and contemporary artists and other subjects, including iconic London Transport posters which since 1908 regularly featured trips to Kew.

Nash Conservatory: Originally designed for Buckingham Palace, the Nash Conservatory was moved to Kew in 1836 by William IV. With an abundance of natural light the building is used to house displays of photographs and educational exhibitions.

Kew Palace & the Royal Kitchens: Built by Samuel Fortrey, a Dutch merchant in around 1631, the recently restored Kew Palace (aka 'The Dutch House') was leased by George III in the 18th century and was a place of sanctuary for him and his family during his 'madness'. The nearby royal kitchens remain intact, almost 200 years after they were last used by George III's wife, Queen Charlotte, who died at the palace in 1818.

Other Attractions: Kew's wealth of attractions include the **Chokushi-Mon** or 'Imperial Envoy's Gateway', a scale replica of the gateway of the Nishi Hongan-ji temple in Kyoto; **Minka House**, a Japanese wooden house originally erected in around 1900 in a suburb of Okazaki (Japan); **Queen Charlotte's Cottage**, given to Queen Charlotte as a wedding present on her marriage to George III; **The Palm House**, an icon of the gardens, designed by Decimus Burton and engineered by Richard Turner between 1844 and 1848; the **Pagoda**, a ten-storey octagonal structure 163ft/50m high, constructed in 1762; and the **Orangery**, designed by Sir William Chambers in 1761 and the largest classical style building in the Gardens.

Museum No. 1

4 SYON HOUSE

Address: Syon Park, Brentford, TW8 8JF (☎ 020-8560 0882, ⌨ syonpark.co.uk).
Opening hours: House; mid-March to end of October, Wed, Thu, Sun & Bank Holidays 11am to 5pm. Gardens; daily, March to October, 10.30am to 5pm (4pm Fri-Sat). See website for other dates and times.
Cost: House, gardens and Great Conservatory, £11 adults, £9.50 concessions, £4.50 children (aged 5-16), £25 families. Gardens and Great Conservatory only, £6 adults, £4.50 concessions, £3 children, £13 families.
Transport: Gunnersbury or Ealing Broadway tube then 237 or 267 bus to Brent Lea Gate bus stop, or E2 or E8 bus to Brentford.
Amenities: Café, shop, conservatory, park, gardens, wheelchair access.

Syon House and its 200-acre (80ha) park (both Grade I listed) have a rich history and comprise one of England's finest estates. The name derives from Syon Abbey (named after Mount Zion in the Holy Land), a medieval monastery of the Bridgettine Order (established in the 14th century by the great Swedish mystic St Bridget) which was founded nearby in 1415 by Henry V. It moved to the site now occupied by Syon House in 1431 and was dissolved in 1539, during the Dissolution of the Monasteries. Syon Abbey is where Catherine Howard was imprisoned in 1541 by Henry VIII before her final trip to the Tower.

In 1594, Henry Percy, 9th Earl of Northumberland, acquired Syon House through his marriage to Dorothy Devereux, and the Percy family have lived there ever since. In 1750, Sir

Hugh Smithson inherited the Percy estates through his wife, Elizabeth Seymour, and they revived the Percy name, when Sir Hugh became Earl and then 1st Duke of Northumberland in 1766. In 1761, he commissioned architect and interior designer Robert Adam (1728-1792) and landscape designer Lancelot 'Capability' Brown (1716-1783) to redesign the house and estate. While Adam's architecture was inspired by classical Rome, Brown took the medieval deer park as his model.

Adam's plans for the interior of Syon House included a complete suite of rooms on the principal level, together with a rotunda in the main courtyard (not built). In the event, only five main rooms on the west, south and east sides of the House, from the Great Hall to the Long Gallery, were designed in the Neo-classical style. Nevertheless, Syon House is feted as Adam's early English masterpiece and is the finest surviving evidence of his revolutionary use of colour.

The house contains a sumptuous collection of period furniture and paintings, not least in the print room, which now accommodates a magnificent collection of portraits of many of the people who contributed to the history of Syon. These include a portrait of Lady Jane Grey – although now thought to be an early and

DON'T MISS!

Two rooms sum up Robert Adam's genius: the grand scale and splendour of the Great Hall, which resembles the Imperial Rome of a Hollywood epic, and – in dramatic contrast – the richly-decorated Ante Room or Vestibule, with its riot of coloured marble, which is one of Adam's most ingenious and original designs.

The Great Hall

rare portrait of Elizabeth I – as well as a stunning likeness of Joseph Brant, the celebrated chieftain of the Mohawk tribe, by the American artist Gilbert Stuart, and Thomas Gainsborough's portrayal of Hugh Smithson, 1st Duke of Northumberland.

The park includes 40 acres (16ha) of gardens and an ornamental lake, and is famous for its extensive collection of rare trees and plants. The crowning glory of the gardens is the Great Conservatory, designed by Charles Fowler (1792-1867) and completed in 1830, which was the first large-scale conservatory to be built from metal and glass. It was said to be the inspiration for Joseph Paxton in his designs for the Crystal Palace.

Syon House remains the London home of the Duke of Northumberland and is the last surviving ducal residence complete with its country estate in Greater London. It has provided the backdrop for a number of films and television series, most notably Robert Altman's 2001 period comedy-drama, *Gosford Park*.

FOOD & DRINK

Garden Centre Refectory: Syon House's café serving drinks, snacks and light lunches, plus the inevitable cream tea.

Coach and Horses (183 London Road, ☏ 020-8181 5627): Old coaching house, now a Young's pub with an interesting gastro-pub menu; recommended for Sunday lunch.

The Ante Room

5 DORICH HOUSE MUSEUM

Address: 67 Kingston Vale, Kingston-upon-Thames, SW15 3RN (☎ 020-8417 5515, 🖳 dorichhousemuseum.org.uk and dorichhouse.com).
Opening hours: Monthly open days (see website), 11am to 5pm, with guided tours at 11.30am and 2.30pm. Private curator's tours and school visits by appointment.
Cost: £4 adults, £3 concessions, children under 16 free. Private tours (min. 10 people) £9 per head.
Transport: Kingston or Putney rail, then 85 bus.
Amenities: No wheelchair access.

Built in 1936 and restored by Kingston University in 1994, Dorich House is a fine example of Art Deco design, its severe exterior concealing magnificent interiors. It was the studio, gallery and home of the sculptor Dora Gordine (1895-1991) and her husband the Hon. Richard Hare (1907-1966), a professor of Russian literature. After her death, Dora left the house and its collections in trust for the British public, and it was restored and opened in 1996, becoming a museum in 2004.

Trained in Tallinn and Paris, Dora Gordine achieved almost overnight critical acclaim in the mid-'20s, and when London's Leicester Galleries hosted her solo show in 1928, every piece was sold. By the mid-'30s she was being feted by some experts as the finest woman sculptor in the world, and she remained a major presence in European sculpture until the late '60s.

She married Richard Gilbert Hare (second son of the 4th Earl of Listowel) in 1936 and they settled at Dorich House. Educated at Oxford, the Sorbonne and Berlin University, Hare had a lifelong interest in the study and collection of Russian art and culture.

The museum now houses the world's largest collection of Dora Gordine's bronzes and plaster sculptures, as well as many paintings and drawings, spanning her early years in Paris to her last works created in the '60s and '70s. It's also home to Hare's Russian art collection, including icons, paintings, ceramics, glassware, metalwork, folk art and furniture, dating from the early 18th century to the early 20th century. All are displayed in the unique surroundings of this studio-home, described as 'one of Kingston's hidden treasures'.

 DON'T MISS!

Dora Gordine's bronze, *Head of a Chinese Philosopher,* is one of her most important sculptures, exhibited at the Salon des Tuileries in Paris in 1926.

HAM HOUSE & GARDENS

6

Address: Ham Street, Ham, Richmond-upon-Thames, TW10 7RS (☎ 020-8940 1950, 🖳 nationaltrust.org.uk/ham-house).

Opening hours: House: 2nd April to 30th October, daily (closed Fri) noon to 4pm. Garden, shop & café, 11am to 4.30pm (closed Fri). For 'winter' opening times, see website.

Cost: House & Garden: £9.90 adults, £5.50 children, £25.30 families. Garden only: £3.30 adults, £2.20 children, £8.85 families (reduced prices Nov to late Feb – see website). Free for National Trust members.

Transport: Richmond or Twickenham rail.

Amenities: Café, shop, wheelchair access.

Ham House is an unusually complete surviving sample of 17th-century fashion and power, located on the Thames. Rich in atmosphere and history, it's one of London's architectural and horticultural gems, but often overlooked, despite being only a short journey from central London.

The house was built in 1610 for Sir Thomas Vavasour, Knight Marshal to James I, but was later leased by Charles I to one of his favourite courtiers, William Murray (literally the king's whipping boy, who took the punishment for the young royal's misdemeanours). Murray created much of its grandeur, and it was further extended and refurbished as a palatial villa under the ownership of his daughter Elizabeth, Lady Dysart. It remained within the Dysart family until the National Trust took it over in 1948.

Ham House has rooms of sumptuous splendour, including walls hung with tapestries, rich fabrics and rococo mirrors. Meticulous restoration has created an atmosphere redolent of its original splendour. There are spectacular collections of furniture, textiles and paintings, including a portrait of Elizabeth and her second husband the Duke of Lauderdale by Sir Peter Lely. Ham also has a notable collection of statues made from Coade stone, a hard ceramic stoneware named after its inventor, Eleanor Coade. The statue of Father Thames at the front of the house is one of the largest pieces of Coade ever produced.

One of the most remarkable aspects of the house is its 17th-century formal garden. Most such gardens were replaced in the following two centuries by then-fashionable natural landscapes, but Ham's gardens have changed little in over 300 years, and include Britain's oldest orangery and a lovely, trellised cherry garden.

 FOOD & DRINK

Orangery Café: Sample home-made salads, vegetable tarts and pasties, all made from produce grown in Ham's 17th-century kitchen garden, which produces everything from purple-podded peas to salsify.

7 MUSICAL MUSEUM

Address: 399 High Street, Brentford, TW8 0DU (☎ 020-8560 8108, 🖳 musicalmuseum.co.uk).
Opening hours: Tue-Sun, 11am to 5.30pm, including most Bank Holidays. Closed Mondays. Live presentations on Tue (2.30pm), Fri (11.30am) and Sat-Sun (2.30pm).
Cost: £8 adults, £6.50 concessions, children under 16 free accompanied by an adult.
Transport: Kew Bridge rail.
Amenities: Café, shop, wheelchair access.

The unique museum contains one of the world's largest collections of automated musical instruments. It was founded in 1963 by the late Frank Holland (1910-1989), who believed passionately that self-playing musical instruments should be preserved and not lost to future generations. Holland was a pioneer in this field and his collection eventually consumed all the space in his flat from where it moved to a redundant church in Brentford, before finding a permanent home in 2008 in the purpose-built museum you see today.

From a tiny clockwork musical box (first made in the late 18th century) to the 'Mighty Wurlitzer' concert organ, the collection embraces an impressive and comprehensive array of sophisticated reproducing pianos, pianolas, cranky barrel organs, orchestrions and orchestrelles, residence organs and violin players. The museum is also

 ALLOW...

A live presentation at the Musical Museum lasts around an hour, but you should allow a couple of hours for your visit.

home to the world's largest collection (30,000!) of historic musical rolls and an extensive archive of related material. The ground floor galleries display instruments once found in the large houses of the wealthy as well as in cafes and pubs, while the street setting reproduces shop windows with displays of musical toys and street instruments. You can experience the actions and sounds of the instruments on the guided live presentations.

Upstairs is a concert hall seating 230, complete with an orchestra pit from which the Wurlitzer organ console (formerly resident at the Regal Cinema, Kingston) rises to entertain you, just as it did in the '30s. The concert hall offers a range of musical entertainment, spanning organ recitals, concerts, cabaret, classical music and light opera, with performers from throughout the UK and overseas, as well as film screenings.

The museum has a pleasant tea room and a fascinating shop.

ORLEANS HOUSE GALLERY   8

Address: Riverside, Twickenham, TW1 3DJ (☎ 020-8831 6000, ⌨ richmond.gov.
uk/orleans_house_gallery).
Opening hours: April to September, Tue-Sat 1-5.30pm, Sun and Bank Holidays
2-5.30pm; October to March closes at 4.30pm. Closed Mondays and over Christmas
(24-27th Dec) and New Year (31st Dec-2nd Jan).
Cost: Free.
Transport: St Margaret's rail.
Amenities: Café, shop, wheelchair access.

The Orleans House Gallery is one of Greater London's finest small galleries, located within woodland overlooking the Thames. It opened in 1972 and is home to the London borough of Richmond-upon-Thames' art collection, one of the most outstanding fine art collections in London outside the city's national collections, comprising some 3,200 paintings, drawings, photographs, prints and objects dating from the early 18th century to the present day. The collection contains oil paintings, watercolours, drawings and prints by notable artists, including Peter Tillemans (1684-1734), Samuel Scott (1702-1772), Jean-Baptiste-Camille Corot (1796-1875) and the illustrator Eric Fraser (1902-1983).

The original Thameside house was built in 1710 as a home for James Johnston (1655-1737), Joint Secretary of State for Scotland. However, its name comes from Louis-Phillippe, Duc D'Orleans and later King of France, who lived there between 1813 and 1815.

The Orleans House Gallery has a reputation for innovative exhibitions and hosts five a year in the main gallery, ranging from historical exhibitions of works from the permanent collection to contemporary exhibitions of painting, photographs, crafts and ceramics. The nearby Stables Gallery (opened in 1994) is housed in the evocative 19th-century stable buildings, and exhibits work by up-and-coming, avant-garde artists, local artists, and community groups and organisations.

There's also the Coach House Education Centre, an artist in residence studio, a shop and the North Stables café.

👁 DON'T MISS!

One of the house's most appealing features is the ornate baroque Octagon Room, designed as a garden pavilion in around 1720 by the renowned architect James Gibbs (1682-1754). The simple exterior belies the stunning baroque interior, decorated by the celebrated Swiss stuccatori (plaster artists) Guiseppe Artari and Giovanni Bagutti, who also decorated St Martin-in-the-Fields church in central London.

9 | OSTERLEY PARK & HOUSE

Address: Jersey Road, Isleworth TW7 4RB (☎ 020-8232 5050, 🖥 nationaltrust.org. uk/osterley-park).

Opening hours: House: 30th March to 30th October, Wed-Sun, noon to 4.30pm (garden, 11am to 5pm). For 'winter' opening times, see website. The park is open year round.

Cost: House & garden: £8.70 adults, £4.35 children, £21.75 families. Garden only, £3.80 adults, £1.90 children. Car park: £3.50. Free for National Trust members.

Transport: Osterley tube or Isleworth rail.

Amenities: Café, shop, gardens, wheelchair access.

This is a large, striking, National Trust-owned mansion set in gardens, park and farmland. It's one of London's last surviving country estates, once called 'the palace of palaces'. The property is an original Tudor (1576) redbrick house of square design with four towers, built for Sir Thomas Gresham, an Elizabethan tycoon (who, among other things, was financial adviser to Elizabeth I).

The property was remodelled by the fashionable architect and designer Robert Adam for the Child family between 1760 and 1780. His vast entrance portico is especially striking, an expression of classical refinement. The interiors are one of the most complete surviving examples of Adam's work, with beautiful plasterwork, splendid carpets and fine furniture (some by Chippendale), all designed by Adam specifically for Osterley Park House. The rooms are an ornate visual treat and remain much as they were in the mid-18th century. Although it isn't noted for its art collection, the house (particularly the Long Gallery) contains many fine paintings, including a number by Raffaelo Vanni.

The house is set in 357 acres (144ha) of gardens and parkland, making it one of west London's largest open spaces. It isn't, however, the most tranquil, as the M4 motorway cuts across the middle of it and you can hear aircraft at nearby Heathrow airport. However, there's some lovely planting, notably in the Pleasure Gardens where the floral displays are at their best between June and September. The grounds also boast three lakes: the Garden Lake, Middle Lake and North Lake, which are important wildfowl habitats.

Osterley Park was the location of the first training school for the Home Guard (Dads' Army) in 1940, set up by Captain Tom Wintringham, where volunteers learned such skills as hand-to-hand combat and making home-made explosives.

 DON'T MISS!

The house features a 'downstairs' exhibit which reveals how Osterley Park's servants lived, in stark contrast to the glories of Adam's 'upstairs' rooms.

SOUTHSIDE HOUSE 10

Address: 3-4 Woodhayes Road, Wimbledon, SW19 4RJ (☎ 020-8946 7643, 💻 southsidehouse.com).

Opening hours: Guided tours (1¼ hrs), Wed, Sat, Sun and Bank Holidays at 2pm, 3pm and 4pm, from Easter Saturday to the last Sunday of September. Closed for Wimbledon tennis fortnight and during winter.

Cost: £9 adults, £6 students, £12 families (up to 4 people including children under 12).

Transport: Wimbledon tube/rail, then a 93 bus to the Rose and Crown pub in Wimbledon Village.

Amenities: Garden, no wheelchair access.

Southside House is a 17th-century property situated (appropriately) on the south side of Wimbledon Common. The house was built in the late 1680s by Robert Pennington, who commissioned Dutch architects to build it, incorporating an existing farmhouse into the design (Pennington had shared Charles II's exile in Holland). Two niches on either side of the front door contain statues of Plenty and Spring, which are said to bear the likenesses of Pennington's wife and daughter.

Southside was later rebuilt in the William and Mary style, but behind the long façade are the old rooms, still with much of the Pennington's original 17th-century furniture, and a superb collection of art and historical objects reflecting centuries of ownership. The Music Room was prepared for the entertainment of Frederick, Prince of Wales, who visited in 1750, and there have been many more famous guests, including Sir William and Lady Emma Hamilton, Lord Nelson and Lord Byron. The house passed down through the Pennington-Mellor family, eventually coming into the possession of Malcolm Munthe, a hero of the Second World War, who spent much of his later life restoring it.

Described by connoisseurs as an unforgettable experience, Southside House provides an enchantingly eccentric backdrop to the lives and loves of generations of the Pennington-Mellor-Munthe families. Maintained in traditional style without intrusive refurbishment and crammed with centuries' of family possessions, it offers a wealth of fascinating stories.

Today, Southside House serves partly as a residence but also as a museum, administered by the family trust. It hosts tour groups – including special candlelit tours – and cultural events such as lectures, concerts and literary discussions.

👁 DON'T MISS!

Southside's gardens are just as glorious as the house and include wilderness, woodland, secret pathways, classical follies and water features, as well as a poignant pet cemetery.

11 STRAWBERRY HILL

Address: 268 Waldegrave Road, Twickenham, TW1 4ST (☎ 020-8744 1241, 🖥 strawberryhillhouse.org.uk).
Opening hours: 31st March to 31st October, Mon-Wed 2pm to 4.20pm, Sat-Sun noon to 4.20pm. Booking advisable. Closed Thu-Fri. For December opening and Twilight tours, see website.
Cost: £8 adults, £7 concessions, £5 children 5-18, £20 families.
Transport: Strawberry Hill rail.
Amenities: Café, shop, garden, wheelchair access.

Strawberry Hill is a Gothic castle of undoubted charm and originality and, as its website claims, visiting it is a 'truly theatrical experience'. Built in 1698, it was originally a modest house, but from 1747 was transformed by Horace Walpole (1717-1797), son of Britain's first Prime Minister, into Britain's finest example of Georgian Gothic architecture and interior design.

Walpole was a dedicated collector, and Strawberry Hill was created to house his huge assortment of 'treasures'. Whereas nearby houses such as Marble Hill (see page 234) were based on classical traditions, Walpole used the architecture of Gothic cathedrals as his inspiration. Between 1747 and 1797, he doubled the size of Strawberry Hill, creating rooms and adding battlements and towers as he saw fit. The project evolved in the way medieval cathedrals did – over time and with no fixed overall design. The exterior resembles a wedding cake; while inside, the gloomy hall and staircase – where Count Dracula wouldn't look out of place – provide a dramatic contrast to magnificent rooms bedecked in gold and crimson.

 DON'T MISS!

One particular attraction of Strawberry Hill's gardens was a seat carved to resemble a large Rococo style sea shell – one of Walpole's favourite inventions. It's been recreated in the gardens, which are being remodelled to their original design.

By the end of the 20th century the house had fallen into disrepair and was closed for restoration. It reopened in October 2010 after the first phase of an £9m restoration project, including the conservation of the huge collection of painted renaissance glass. Later phases will see contents added, as the house returns to its original 1790s splendour.

Interestingly, Strawberry Hill was a tourist attraction in Walpole's time, although he only allowed four visitors a day (no children!). He even wrote his own guide book – an abridged version is provided to today's visitors.

WHITE LODGE MUSEUM & BALLET RESOURCE CENTRE

12

Address: White Lodge, Richmond Park, Richmond, TW10 5HR (☏ 020-8392 8440, 🖥 royal-ballet-school.org.uk/wl_museum.php?s=1).
Opening hours: Tue-Thu, 1.30-3.30pm during term time (see website for dates). Booking is essential.
Cost: Free.
Transport: Mortlake rail or car to Sheen Gate. Access to the museum is only via a free park and ride service from the Sheen Gate entrance of Richmond Park.
Amenities: Wheelchair access.

White Lodge in Richmond Park is a fine example of the Neoclassical English Palladian style of architecture. Formerly a royal residence, today it houses the Royal Ballet Lower School for students aged 11-16, and the White Lodge Museum and Ballet Resource Centre. The house was designed by Roger Morris as a hunting lodge for George II, shortly after his accession to the throne in 1727. The name White Lodge first appeared in the 18th century after Princess Amelia (daughter of George II) added two white wings to the main lodge.

There followed a succession of distinguished occupants. Queen Victoria and Prince Albert chose it as a home for the young Edward VII (when he was still Prince of Wales), while Edward VIII was born there in 1894. Later, in 1932 it was transformed into a charming home for Prince Albert (the future George VI) and Elizabeth, and the Princesses Elizabeth and Margaret.

In 1955, the Sadler's Wells Ballet School (it became the Royal Ballet School in 1956) was given the use of White Lodge on a permanent basis. The lodge has recently undergone an extensive £22m redevelopment.

The White Lodge Museum and Ballet Resource Centre is the first dedicated ballet museum in the UK, displaying material from the Royal Ballet School collections, including Margot Fonteyn's ballet shoes, the death mask of Anna Pavlova and school reports of famous alumni. Visitors also learn about the daily life of students at the school, the history and development of classical ballet, and the appealing story of White Lodge itself.

  FOOD & DRINK

Richmond Park: There are several places to eat, including the tea rooms at Pembroke Lodge, to the west of White Lodge, and the Roehampton Cafe at Roehampton Gate. The park is also a great place for a picnic.

13 WIMBLEDON LAWN TENNIS MUSEUM

Address: The All England Lawn Tennis Club, Church Road, Wimbledon, SW19 5AE
(☎ 020-8944 1066, 🖥 wimbledon.com/visiting/museum).
Opening hours: Daily, 10am to 5pm. Tours between 10.30am and 3.30pm; check website for times – booking advisable. Closed during the Championships, except for ticket holders.
Cost: Museum: £11 adults, £9.50 concessions, £6.75 children; Museum & Tour: £20 adults, £17 concessions, £12.50 children.
Transport: Wimbledon, Southfields or Tooting Broadway tube, then 493 bus.
Amenities: Café, shop, library, gardens, wheelchair access.

The Wimbledon Lawn Tennis Museum is the captivating museum of the All England Lawn Tennis Club (AELTC), otherwise known simply as Wimbledon. The Wimbledon tournament (or Championships) is the oldest tennis competition in the world – considered by many to be the most prestigious – held at the AELTC since July 1877.

Opened in 1977, Wimbledon Lawn Tennis Museum is the largest tennis museum in the world with some 15,000 objects dating back to 1555! The current museum opened in 2006 and is now a high-tech spectacular with many hands-on exhibits. Wimbledon's rich history is recorded on paper, captured in photos and on film, and presented through objects, memorabilia and interactive displays.

change seasonally. Highlights include the championship trophies; a tour by a John McEnroe 'ghost' of normally off-limit areas; a 200 degree cinema capturing the 'Science of Tennis'; film and video footage of the most memorable and exciting tournament matches; treasures from the first Championship to the most recent, including donations from players; 'CentreCourt360', which allows you to sample the atmosphere of Centre Court; and 'Viewpoint', a 3D cinematic experience which captures the sights, sounds and people of Wimbledon.

Guided tours take visitors behind the scenes at the club and take in the Centre Court, No 1 Court, the picnic terraces (aka Henman Hill or Murray Mound) and water gardens, the Millennium Building and the press box.

 ALLOW...

The Wimbledon tour takes 90 minutes and the website recommends allowing an extra hour to view the museum.

The game's evolution is traced from a garden party pastime to a multi-million dollar professional sport, with interactive displays, touch screens, films and audio guides in ten languages. Memorabilia from many famous players from Victorian times to the present day are included in several different exhibits, which

WORLD RUGBY MUSEUM 14

Address: Twickenham Stadium, Rugby Road, Twickenham TW1 1DZ (☎ 020-8892 8877, 🖥 rfu.com/museum).
Opening hours: Tue-Sat, 10am to 5pm; Sun, 11am to 5pm. Tours are held Tue-Sat at 10.30am, noon, 1.30pm and 3pm, and at 1 and 3pm on Sundays. Closed Mondays, most Public Holidays and match days (see website).
Cost: Museum: £7 adults, £5 concessions and children (under 16), under 5s free. Tours & Museum: £15 adults, £9 concessions and children, £45 families (2 adults, up to 3 children).
Transport: Twickenham rail.
Amenities: Shop, wheelchair access.

The World Rugby Museum at Twickenham Stadium (usually known simply as Twickenham or 'Twickers') is the ultimate visitor experience for rugby enthusiasts. Twickenham is the home of English rugby and of the game's governing body – the Rugby Football Union (RFU) – whose museum houses the finest collection of rugby memorabilia in the world. It takes visitors through the history of the sport from its origins to the present day; more than simply a collection of interesting artefacts, the museum is 'an inspirational journey through the history of the ultimate team game'.

Since the birth of the RFU in 1871, a wealth of rugby memorabilia has been accumulated, including dusty minute books, faded letters, early match programmes and tickets for memorable games. More recently the collection has developed to include historical and contemporary photographs, videos, artworks, equipment and other miscellaneous objects – a total of some 10,000 from all over the globe.

Stadium Tours last around 40 minutes and take you behind the scenes to visit the most exciting and prestigious parts of the stadium. You can soak up the atmosphere in the England dressing room, imagine the roar of the crowd as you emerge onto the hallowed turf through the players' tunnel, and see the breath-taking view from the very top of the stands.

👁 DON'T MISS!

One of the highlights of the museum is a close-up look at the original Calcutta Cup, which has been awarded to the winner of the annual Six Nations Championship match between England and Scotland since 1880. The trophy, which has handles modelled on king cobras, was made in Kolkata in 1878 using the melted down silver rupees that constituted the savings of the disbanded Calcutta Rugby Club, from whom it derives its name.

15 HONEYWOOD MUSEUM

Address: Honeywood Walk, Carshalton, SM5 3NX (☎ 020-8770 4297,
💻 friendsofhoneywood.co.uk and sutton.gov.uk/index.aspx?articleid=1253).
Opening hours: Wed-Fri, 11am to 5pm; Sat-Sun and Bank Holiday Mondays, 10am to 5pm. Closed Mondays and Tuesdays.
Cost: Free.
Transport: Carshalton rail.
Amenities: Café, shop, garden, wheelchair access.

Honeywood Museum (Grade II listed) is Sutton borough's heritage centre and local history museum, occupying a lovely 17th-century building on the banks of Carshalton's scenic ponds. In 1883 the building was purchased by London merchant John Pattinson Kirk, probably as a country retreat. In 1903, he added a large Edwardian wing to the south end of Honeywood, which was pebble-dashed and decorated in mock Tudor style.

During the late '80s it was converted into a heritage centre, opening in 1990, since when it has been repainted in the 1903 decorative scheme and completely refurbished. It now has new exhibition rooms in the north corridor and on the ground floor, including a scullery, a magnificent Edwardian billiards room, a Second World War room and a nursery. The collection contains over 6,000 items – mainly from the 19th and 20th centuries – representing the history of local communities.

The museum also has a shop, café and garden, plus an art gallery with changing exhibitions and a programme of special events throughout the year.

16 KEW BRIDGE STEAM MUSEUM

Address: Green Dragon Lane, Brentford, TW8 0EN (☎ 020-8568 4757,
💻 kbsm.org).
Opening hours: Tue-Sun, 11am to 4pm. Closed Mondays except for Bank Holidays.
Cost: £10 adults, £9 concessions, £4 children aged 5-15.
Transport: Kew Bridge rail or Gunnersbury tube.
Amenities: Café, shop, garden, free parking, wheelchair access.

Kew Bridge Steam Museum (est. 1975) is a unique museum of water supply, housing a magnificent collection of steam engines and diesel-powered water pumping machines. It's a fascinating museum which allows visitors to see how London's water supply has evolved over the last 2,000 years, from Roman times to the present day. It's housed within Georgian and Italianate buildings in the Kew Bridge

Pumping Station – opened in 1838 by the Grand Junction Waterworks Company – which supplied west Londoners with water for over 100 years until the engines were retired in 1944.

The museum houses the world's largest collection of Cornish beam engines, including the largest working beam engine, the spectacular Grand Junction 90 Engine, which was used to pump water for 98 years. In 2008, the museum completed the restoration of its Bull Engine (built in 1856), which is one of only four known examples in the world. The Cornish beam engines are steamed on one weekend each month (check website for dates).

The museum is also home to London's only operating steam railway, and has a café and a pleasant garden for picnics.

KINGSTON MUSEUM 17

Address: Wheatfield Way, Kingston-upon-Thames, KT1 2PS (☎ 020-8547 5006, 🖳 kingston.gov.uk/museum).
Opening hours: Tue, Fri and Sat, 10am to 5pm; Thu 10am to 7pm. Closed Mondays, Wednesdays, Sundays, Public Holidays, and between Christmas and New Year.
Cost: Free.
Transport: Kingston rail.
Amenities: Shop, wheelchair access.

Kingston Museum (built 1904) is one of the richest local museums in London, if not the whole of the UK. The collections cover most aspects of the history of the Royal Borough of Kingston-upon-Thames, from prehistoric times to the present.

The museum has three permanent galleries – Ancient Origins, Town of Kings and the Eadweard Muybridge Gallery – plus a gallery for temporary and art exhibitions. Ancient Origins covers the time-span up to Saxon times, and features Mesolithic flint tools, Neolithic axe heads, Roman artefacts and a Pagan Saxon human burial. Town of Kings examines the town's royal connections – seven Saxon kings were believed to have been crowned in Kingston – and displays items from the Saxon period, including an important metalwork cache of swords, spearheads and shield bosses. There are also items reflecting Kingston's social and civic history.

One of the town's most famous sons was Eadweard Muybridge (1830-1904), famous for his pioneering work in motion picture projection and animal locomotion. He bequeathed his equipment to the museum, including his original zoopraxiscope moving image projector and discs.

18 LONDON MOTOR MUSEUM

Address: 3 Nestle's Avenue, Hayes, UB3 4SB (☎ 0800-195 0777,
🖥 londonmotormuseum.co.uk).
Opening hours: Daily, 10am to 6pm.
Cost: £10 adults, £5 students & seniors, children (3-10 yrs), £20 families (2 adults
and up to 3 children).
Transport: Hayes & Harlington rail.
Amenities: Café, shop, wheelchair access.

The London Motor Museum is the only custom car museum in Europe and home to a unique collection of privately-owned American and European classic and custom cars from the '30s to the '80s. The collection numbers over 100 vehicles, including hot rods and 'famous' cars from films and television – like the DeLorean from *Back To The Future*, a signed Ford Torino (*Starsky and Hutch*) and, of course, the Batmobile. All have been lovingly restored with their own individual modifications, making each vehicle unique.

The museum's founder Elo stars in MTV's car-pimping series *Slips* and is a regular on the Gumball (see 🖥 gumball3000.com) rally scene; he first drove with Gumball founder Maximillion Cooper in the rally's first outing in 1999.

The museum provides hire services and its cars have featured in fashion shoots and music videos such as those of the Black Eyed Peas. Its website suggests it's a big hit with celebrities – the photo gallery features 50 Cent and Kelly Rowland among others.

19 MARBLE HILL HOUSE

Address: Richmond Road, Twickenham, TW1 2NL (☎ 020-8892 5115,
🖥 english-heritage.org.uk/daysout/properties/marble-hill-house).
Opening hours: 1st April to 31st October, Sat 10am to 2pm, guided tours (1½ hrs)
only at 10.30am and noon; Sun 10am to 5pm, tours at 10.30am, noon, 2.15pm and
3.30pm. See website for 'winter' opening times.
Cost: £5.50 adults, £5 concessions, £3.30 children, £14.30 families. Free for English
Heritage members.
Transport: Richmond tube/rail and St Margarets rail.
Amenities: Café, shop, gardens, wheelchair access.

Marble Hill House is a beautiful Palladian villa on the north bank of the Thames, the last intact survivor of the lovely villas and gardens that bordered the river between Richmond and Hampton Court in the 18th century. Owned by English Heritage, the house is little known – despite its proximity to Hampton Court Palace – but fine enough to be included in Simon Jenkins's book, *England's Thousand Best Houses*.

Its grand interiors have been beautifully restored, and conjure up the atmosphere of fashionable Georgian life better than almost anywhere else in Britain. Built in 1724-1729 for Henrietta Howard, mistress of George II, who entertained guests such as Jonathan Swift and Alexander Pope. The Great Room has five architectural *capricci* by the Italian painter Giovanni Paolo Pannini and ornate gilded decoration, while the dining parlour displays hand-painted Chinese wallpaper. There's also a collection of early Georgian furniture and Chinoiserie as well as some fine paintings.

The gardens of Marble Hill House are linked to **Ham House** (see page 223) by a ferry across the Thames.

MUSEUM OF RICHMOND & RIVERSIDE GALLERY

20

> **Address:** Old Town Hall, Whittaker Avenue, Richmond-upon-Thames, TW9 1TP (☎ 020-8332 1141, 🖳 museumofrichmond.com).
> **Opening hours:** Tue-Sat, 11am to 5pm. Closed Sundays, Mondays and Public Holidays.
> **Cost:** Free.
> **Transport:** Richmond rail/tube.
> **Amenities:** Shop, wheelchair access.

For centuries Richmond has been a centre of fashion and the arts, as well as home to several of Britain's monarchs. This interesting small museum celebrates the rich heritage of the old pre-1965 Borough of Richmond, which comprised Richmond, Ham, Petersham and Kew, as well as neighbouring areas.

The museum (on the second floor of the renovated Old Town Hall) was opened by the Queen in 1988 and spans the medieval period to the present day. The foundation of the collection came from the Borough collection then stored at Orleans House, but has grown considerably over the years. Highlights include a fragment of 16th-century stained glass from Richmond Palace, bearing the monogram of Henry VII and Elizabeth of York, and a workhouse clock dating from 1819.

The **Riverside Gallery**, on the ground floor of the Old Town Hall (☎ 020-8831 6000, 🖳 richmond.gov. uk, Mon-Fri 10am to 5pm or 6pm, Sat 10am to 1.30pm), has a year-round programme of exhibitions including paintings, prints and photographs. A variety of local artists are featured and work is usually for sale.

21 NATIONAL ARCHIVES

Address: Kew, Richmond, TW9 4DU (☎ 020-8876 3444, 🖥 nationalarchives.gov.uk).
Opening hours: Tue and Thu, 9am to 7pm; Wed, Fri-Sat, 9am to 5pm. Closed Mondays and Sundays. Note that you need a reader's ticket to access original documents (see website).
Cost: Free.
Transport: Kew Gardens tube.
Amenities: Restaurant, café, shop, wheelchair access.

The National Archives (NA) is the official archive of the UK government (and of England and Wales) and the guardian of some of the country's most iconic national documents dating back over 1,000 years. Anyone aged 14 or over can access original documents after producing two acceptable proofs of identity and obtaining a free reader's ticket.

The interactive museum showcases some of the diverse treasures of the archives, which range from the Magna Carta to Jane Austen's will. It stages exhibitions on selected subjects from its records, and also traces the history of the National Archives and record keeping. The museum was in the process of being upgraded in 2012 to provide a brighter and more welcoming experience – although this will limit access to more fragile documents such as the Domesday Book – and you should check the website before visiting. It's an excellent resource which provides access to many documents online.

The National Archives stages a range of events, from free public talks on records of interest to training courses for archivists. There's an excellent bookshop, a café and a lovely outside area with a pond.

22 PUMP HOUSE GALLERY

Address: Battersea Park, SW11 4NJ (☎ 020-8871 7572, 🖥 pumphousegallery.org.uk).
Opening hours: Wed-Sun, 11am to 5pm. Closed Mon-Tue.
Cost: Free.
Transport: Battersea Park or Queenstown rail.
Amenities: Park, wheelchair access (ground floor only).

The Pump House Gallery is a public contemporary exhibition space housed in a four-storey (Grade II listed) water tower built in 1861 to supply water to the lake and cascades in Battersea Park. Derelict for many years, the Pump House was painstakingly restored between 1988 and 1992, becoming a permanent gallery space in 1999 with a year-

round programme of contemporary visual arts exhibitions.

In recent years it has been recognised, both nationally and (increasingly) internationally, as a centre of excellence in the provision of contemporary visual art. The programme integrates exhibitions of work by emerging and more established contemporary artists, touring exhibitions and projects created locally through educational initiatives. The Pump House also hosts a comprehensive schedule of workshops, talks, film screenings, education and outreach projects.

One of London's most idyllically located galleries, overlooking the lake in one of the capital's most interesting and varied public parks.

ROYAL MILITARY SCHOOL OF MUSIC MUSEUM 23

Address: Kneller Hall, Kneller Road, Twickenham TW2 7DU (☏ 020-8744 8679, 🖳 army.mod.uk/music/23294.aspx).
Opening hours: Open prior to concerts and by appointment.
Cost: £4 adults, £3 concessions, £2 children (under 12).
Transport: Whitton rail.
Amenities: Wheelchair access.

The Royal Military School of Music (RMSM) at Kneller Hall – the home of army music since its foundation in 1857 – trains musicians for the British Army's 29 bands and is part of the Corps of Army Music. The RMSM museum houses a fascinating collection of instruments and other interesting articles associated with military music, ranging from bugles to saxophones, some of which are over 100 years old. There's also a wide variety of paintings, photographs and original music manuscripts, all relating to military music.

The museum is a working part of the Royal Military School of Music and split over three levels within Kneller Hall, an 18th-century stately home which was once the country house of court painter Sir Godfrey Kneller. A number of interactive and video displays further demonstrate army music, and if you visit during the working day there's a chance you may hear (and possibly see) a military band in action, as the musicians are all trained at the hall.

The museum is open prior to the Kneller Hall Concerts in the Park and by appointment.

24 STANLEY PICKER GALLERY

Address: Faculty of Art, Design & Architecture, Kingston University, Knights Park, Kingston-upon-Thames, KT1 2QJ (☎ 020-8417 4074, 🖳 stanleypickergallery.org),
Opening hours: Mon-Sat 11am to 5pm (open until 7pm Wed). Closed Sundays.
Cost: Free.
Transport: Kingston rail.
Amenities: Wheelchair access.

The Stanley Picker Gallery is the exhibition space of Kingston University's Faculty of Art, Design & Architecture, which opened in February 1997. It was a gift from the Stanley Picker Trust, established by New Yorker Picker to support young artists. Picker moved to the UK to run his family's cosmetics business, although his first love was art.

The gallery holds a rolling programme of lectures and exhibitions and is a public venue dedicated to the research, development, production and presentation of contemporary arts. It has hosted work by such diverse talents as animator Damian Gascoigne, film-maker Rachel Davies and curator Alexandra Stara, among others, and initiated Muybridge in Kingston, in partnership with Kingston Museum, to investigate and celebrate pioneering photographer and inventor Eadweard Muybridge (🖳 muybridgeinkingston.com/home.html).

The gallery has developed a strong national and a growing international reputation for its diverse and challenging programme of research fellowships, contemporary commissions, exhibitions, participatory activities and public events. At the heart of its activities, the Stanley Picker Fellowship programme supports young artists across all art and design disciplines.

25 TWICKENHAM MUSEUM

Address: 25 The Embankment, Twickenham, TW1 3DU (☎ 020-8408 0070, 🖳 twickenham-museum.org.uk).
Opening hours: Tue and Sat, 11am to 3.00pm, Sundays 2-4pm.
Cost: Free.
Transport: Twickenham rail.
Amenities: Wheelchair access.

The first local museum in Twickenham was opened as long ago as 1860, although the current museum, housed in a Georgian building (ca. 1720 and Grade II listed) facing the river, only dates from 2001. The museum's permanent exhibition records and celebrates the history, life and growth of the various settlements in the area, which have a rich history going back thousands of years; these include Twickenham, Whitton, Teddington and the Hamptons, and the many smaller villages which once formed the Borough of Twickenham. The museum also has an on-going programme of exhibitions and displays; recent themes have included the history of local public houses and the area's sporting heritage.

The museum's website is a rich resource, including a Timeline which allows visitors to trace events from the earliest days of 'Tuican hom' (the earliest recorded settlement in 704 AD) to the present or explore the themed 'exhibitions' to discover historical sites and the stories behind the people, places and events of the area. The website also contains an archive of photographs, maps, documents and paintings.

WANDLE INDUSTRIAL MUSEUM 26

Address: The Vestry Hall Annex, London Road, Mitcham, CR4 3UD (☎ 020-8648 0127, 🖥 wandle.org)
Opening hours: Wed, 1-4pm, Sun 2-5pm (except Bank Holiday weekends).
Cost: 50p adults, 20p children and concessions.
Transport: Morden or Colliers Wood tube, Tramlink to Mitcham, or bus routes 118, 127, 200, 201 and 280.
Amenities: Wheelchair access, no public toilets.

The Wandle Industrial Museum is a unique and remarkable museum established in 1983 to preserve and interpret the heritage and history of the industries and people of the Wandle Valley. The fast-flowing River Wandle has been used by people living along its banks since prehistoric times, first as a source of water and fish, and later for power to drive water wheels. In its heyday in the 18th and 19th centuries there were around 50 working mills on the Wandle, which was then the most industrialised river in the world, fuelling the production of everything from snuff to dye. The coming of the Industrial Revolution meant that many of the mills added steam power, but a number of waterwheels survived into the 20th century.

The museum has displays on some of the many businesses that used the river's power, including William Morris's and Liberty's silk printing works at Merton, Connolly Leather which produced the best leather in the world – used in Spitfire planes, luxury liners and still found in both Chambers of the Houses of Parliament – and Young's Brewery.

27 WANDSWORTH MUSEUM

Address: 38 West Hill, SW18 1RX (☎ 020-8870 6060,
🖥 wandsworthmuseum.co.uk).
Opening hours: Tue-Fri, 10am to 5pm; Sat & Sun 11am to 5pm (late opening first
Thursday of the month until 9.30pm). Closed Mondays.
Cost: £4 adults, £3 concessions, children aged under 6 free.
Transport: East Putney tube.
Amenities: Café, shop, wheelchair access.

In 1885, Putney Lodge, a late Georgian Mansion house, became only the second public library in London. A huge success it also served for over 120 years as a local museum, displaying locally discovered artefacts alongside the books. It closed in 2007, a victim of local budget cuts, but was rescued by local residents Michael and Dorothy Hintze, who pledged £2m to refurbish and modernise the facility.

The new state-of-the-art museum and gallery was reopened in 2012 and presents the history of the Wandsworth area in three distinct interwoven story lines spanning 25,000 years. The Natural Landscape tells the story of the shaping of the land, the environment and the ecology of the region; the Cultural Landscape reveals how humans have modified the region's terrain; and the Human Story records the rich and detailed lives of the people who have lived and passed through Wandsworth. There are also regular temporary exhibitions, a pleasant café and shop.

The Wandsworth Museum shares its home with the **De Morgan Centre** (see page 216).

WIMBLEDON WINDMILL & MUSEUM

28

Address: Windmill Road, Wimbledon, SW19 5NR (☎ 020-8947 2825,
🖥 wimbledonwindmill.org.uk).
Opening hours: End of March to October; Sat 2-5pm; Sundays and Bank Holiday
Mondays, 11am to 5pm.
Cost: £2 adults, £1 children and concessions, £5 families (two adults and up to four
children).
Transport: Wimbledon train or tube, then 93 bus to Windmill Road.
Amenities: Café (next door), shop, free parking, wheelchair access (ground floor
only).

The Wimbledon Windmill Museum is – reassuringly and appropriately – housed in a windmill in the middle of Wimbledon Common, and offers an enjoyable day out for families. The windmill was built by Charles March in 1817 to grind flour for local residents, and operated until 1864; it was later converted into living accommodation.

In 1976 the building became a museum and the sails were later restored to working order and are occasionally run when there's sufficient wind. The ground floor exhibits relate mainly to the development and construction of windmills, and include a model room with operating models of different types of windmill, tracing the development of windmills from early Greek and Persian mills to modern wind farms, including some unusual and experimental mills. There's also a magnificent collection of millwright's tools. Upstairs, exhibits explain how the windmill worked and how grain was milled to produce flour. Children can try their hand at milling their own flour.

A small shop sells souvenirs, books, postcards and even Wombles – who, of course, live on Wimbledon Common – and there's a café next door.

SOUTHEAST LONDON

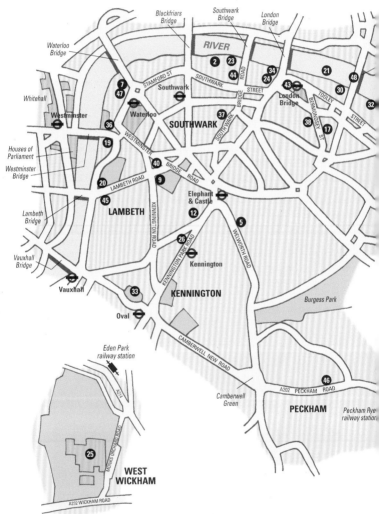

SEE OVER PAGE FOR KEY

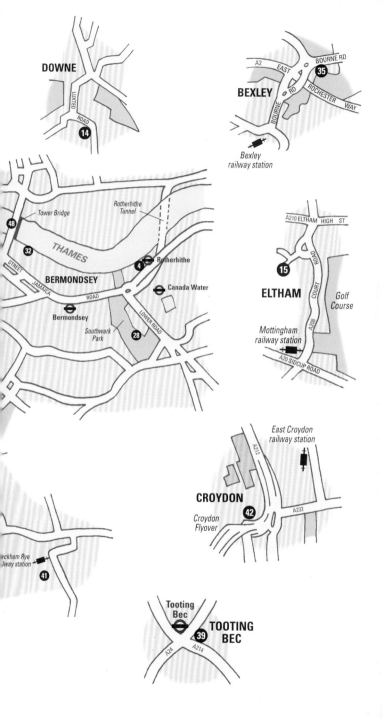

DOWNE

LUXTED ROAD

14

A2 EAST BOURNE RD

BOURNE RD

ROCHESTER WAY

35

BEXLEY

Bexley railway station

Tower Bridge

Rotherhithe Tunnel

48

32

THAMES

STREET

JAMAICA

BERMONDSEY

ROAD

Bermondsey

Southwark Park

LOWER ROAD

4 Rotherhithe

Canada Water

28

A210 ELTHAM HIGH ST

15

COURT ROAD

ELTHAM

Golf Course

A208

Mottingham railway station

A20 SIDCUP ROAD

ckham Rye lway station

41

East Croydon railway station

A212

CROYDON

42

A232

Croydon Flyover

Tooting Bec

TOOTING BEC

39

A24 A214

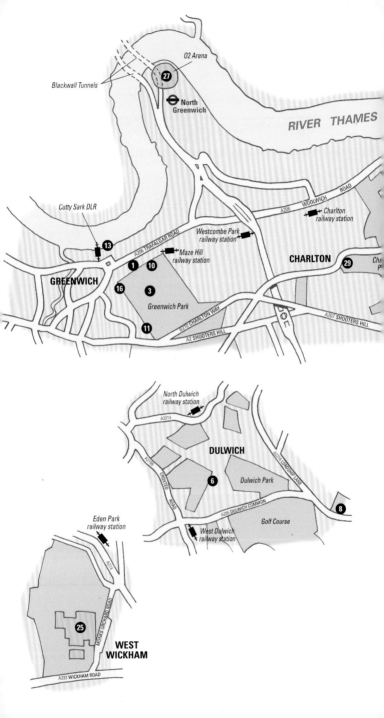

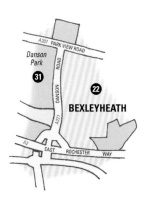

1. National Maritime Museum
2. Tate Modern
3. Royal Observatory
4. Brunel Museum
5. Cuming Museum
6. Dulwich Picture Gallery
7. Hayward Gallery
8. Horniman Museum
9. Imperial War Museum London
10. The Queen's House
11. Ranger's House & Wernher Collection
12. Cinema Museum
13. Cutty Sark
14. Down House (Home of Charles Darwin)
15. Eltham Palace
16. Fan Museum
17. Fashion & Textile Museum
18. Firepower: Royal Artillery Museum
19. Florence Nightingale Museum
20. Garden Museum
21. HMS Belfast
22. The Red House
23. Shakespeare's Globe Theatre Exhibition
24. Winchester Palace & Clink Prison Museum
25. Bethlem Royal Hospital Museum
26. Black Cultural Archives
27. British Music Experience
28. Café Gallery & Dilston Grove
29. Charlton House
30. City Hall Art Gallery
31. Danson House
32. Design Museum
33. Gasworks
34. Golden Hinde
35. Hall Place
36. London Film Museum
37. London Fire Brigade Museum
38. London Glassblowing Studio & Gallery
39. London Sewing Machine Museum
40. Morley Gallery
41. Museum of Contemporary Art
42. Museum of Croydon
43. Old Operating Theatre & Herb Garret
44. Rose Theatre
45. Royal Pharmaceutical Society Museum
46. South London Gallery
47. Topolski Century Gallery
48. Tower Bridge Exhibition

1 NATIONAL MARITIME MUSEUM

Address: Park Row, Greenwich, SE10 9NF (☎ 020-8858 4422, 💻 rmg.co.uk/
national-maritime-museum and ornc.org).
Opening hours: Daily, 10am to 5pm. Closed 24-26th December.
Cost: Free.
Transport: Cutty Sark DLR or Greenwich rail.
Amenities: Restaurant, two cafés, shop, library, wheelchair access.

The National Maritime Museum (NMM) was officially opened in 1937 and is the UK's leading maritime museum and the largest museum of its kind in the world. The historic buildings (mostly Grade I listed) form part of the Maritime Greenwich World Heritage Site and incorporate the Royal Observatory and the 17th-century Queen's House (which are covered separately in this chapter).

Since the earliest times, Greenwich has had associations with the sea and navigation. It was a landing place for the Romans; Henry VIII had his favourite palace here; the navy has its roots on the waterfront; and Charles II founded the Royal Observatory here in 1675. The home of Greenwich Mean Time and the Prime Meridian since 1884, Greenwich has long been a centre for astronomical study, while navigators across the world have set their clocks according to its time of day.

Greenwich began to develop as a cultural visitor destination with Sir James Thornhill's completion of the Painted Hall (see box), and from 1823 a 'National Gallery of Naval Art' – eventually to include some 300 portraits, paintings and artefacts – was created in the Hall, the first of its kind. A separate Naval Museum was established within the Royal Naval College after its founding in 1873. The College took over the site of the Royal Hospital for Seamen, established in 1694 as a home for injured sailors, and was the 'Navy's university' until 1998.

Baltic Exchange Memorial Glass

The NMM was formally established by Act of Parliament in 1934 within the 200-acre (81ha) Greenwich Royal Park, in buildings dating from 1807 formerly occupied by the Royal Hospital School (before it moved to Holbrook in Suffolk). The museum has the most important holdings in the world on the history of Britain at sea comprising some 2.5m items. These include maritime art (both British and 17th-century Dutch); cartography; manuscripts, including official public records; ship models and plans; scientific and navigational instruments; and instruments for time-keeping and astronomy (based at the Observatory). Its British portraits collection is exceeded in size only by that of the **National Portrait Gallery** (see page 29) and its holdings relating to Vice-Admiral Horatio Nelson and Captain James Cook, among many other individuals, are unrivalled.

The museum also has the world's largest maritime historical reference library (100,000 volumes), including books dating from the 15th century. An active loans programme ensures that items from the collection are seen in the UK and abroad.

By virtue of its pairing with the Royal Observatory, the NMM enjoys a unique conjunction of subjects (history, science and the arts), enabling it to trace the movement and accomplishments of people and the origins and consequences of empire. Visiting the NMM gives you a unique understanding of British economic, cultural, social, political and maritime history and its consequences in the world today.

The museum's galleries and exhibitions trace 500 years of Britain's encounters with the world at sea and include the following (in route order from ground to second floor):

👁 DON'T MISS!

The Painted Hall

The Painted Hall (1708-1727) within King William Court in the Old Royal Naval College is often described as the 'finest dining hall in Europe'. Designed by Sir Christopher Wren but completed by Nicholas Hawksmoor and Sir John Vanbrugh, it was originally intended as an eating space for naval veterans who lived at the Royal Hospital for Seamen. Its exuberant wall and ceiling decorations are by James Thornhill (1675-1734) and pay tribute to British maritime power. In 1806 the body of Horatio Nelson lay in state in the Hall.

◆ **Voyagers: Britons and the Sea.** A dynamic and inventive new gallery, Voyagers tells the story of Britain and the sea, illustrating the contemporary significance of

The Painted Hall

Captain James Cook, Nathaniel Dance

maritime histories and the personal stories of this island nation.

◆ **Maritime London: 1700 to now.** Traces London's importance as a port and a centre of commerce and industry for over 300 years. One of the highlights is a selection of Nelson artefacts, including the uniform he wore at Trafalgar.

◆ **Explorers: the Americas and the North-West Passage.** Discover a brief history of world exploration, from Columbus to today.

◆ **Arctic Convoys, 1941-45:** An exhibition marking the 70th anniversary of the first Allied Arctic convoys to Russia, described by Churchill as 'the worst journey in the world'.

◆ **Traders: the East India Company and Asia.** Looks at Britain's maritime trade with Asia, focusing on the pivotal role played by the East India Company.

◆ **The Atlantic: Slavery, Trade, Empire.** How the movement of people, goods and ideas across

and around the Atlantic Ocean from the 17th century to the 19th century shaped the modern world.

◆ **Environment Gallery:** Explores how our everyday lives depend and impact on the health and survival of the world's oceans.

◆ **Baltic Exchange Memorial Glass:** The newly-restored glass windows from the old Baltic Exchange, which were created as a memorial to members of the Exchange who died in the First World War.

👁 DON'T MISS!

Chapel

The Chapel, constructed by Thomas Ripley (1682-1758) to the designs of Sir Christopher Wren, was the last major part of the Royal Hospital for Seamen to be built. Following a disastrous fire in 1779, it was redecorated by James 'Athenian' Stuart (1713-1788) in the Greek revival style, and is a wonderful example of a complete neoclassical interior. There are regular concerts in the Chapel and worshippers are welcome to attend services.

◆ **The Upper Deck Gallery:** A display of over 400 of the museum's

Admiral Lord Nelson, Lemuel Francis Abbot

In 2011 the National Maritime Museum opened the Sammy Ofer Wing, the largest development in the museum's history. This ultra-modern extension includes a special exhibitions gallery, allowing the museum to stage a full programme of temporary shows; a permanent gallery (Voyagers); a café and restaurant; and a state-of-the-art library and archive. It also includes the Compass Lounge, which has free wi-fi and provides a resource to examine the museum's vast collection and plan your visit. The collections website is also invaluable for exploring the many treasures of the museum (collections.rmg.co.uk).

treasures, including swords, globes and astrolabes.

◆ **Ships of War: Models 1660-1815.** Scale models of ships which played an important role in the Royal Navy's shipbuilding advances and helped it to emerge as the world's leading naval force.

◆ **The Children's Gallery and Ship Simulator:** Great fun for younger visitors who can learn about navigation and captain their own ship.

 FOOD & DRINK

16 Seconds West Brasserie: Modern British fare in an appropriate location, exactly 16 seconds west from the Prime Meridian line.

Museum Café: All-day food, including salads, sandwiches and afternoon teas.

Trafalgar Tavern: Late Regency pub overlooking the Thames, and officially the Tavern serves 'whitebait suppers'.

Le Bretagne, Jules Achille Noël

2 TATE MODERN

Address: Bankside, SE1 9TG (☎ 020-7887 8888, 🖳 tate.org.uk/visit/tate-modern).
Opening hours: Daily, 10am to 6pm (Fri and Sat 10am to 10pm). Open on Bank Holidays but closed 24-26th December.
Cost: Free, except for special exhibitions.
Transport: Southwark or Mansion House tube and Blackfriars or London Bridge rail.
Amenities: Restaurant, café, coffee bar, three shops, wheelchair access.

The Tate Modern is one of the runaway success stories of the British arts scene. Created to provide a dedicated space in which to show off the Tate's burgeoning collection of 20th-century art – from Matisse and Picasso to Warhol and Damien Hirst – it's now the most-visited modern art gallery in the world. The Tate empire's *enfant terrible* attracts almost 5m visitors a year, three times as many as Tate Britain upriver at Millbank (see page 257) to which it's connected by high-speed boat (16 mins).

 ALLOW...

You'll need a day at the very least to do Tate Modern justice – a couple of days is even better – and a stout pair of walking shoes. There's a lot to get around and see, although £4 hires you a multi-media guide for the day: a small handheld computer that covers the best of the displays and includes videos, music and interactive games.

Tate Modern's location, in the former Bankside Power Station overlooking the City of London, is as visually arresting as the art inside. Originally designed by Sir Giles Gilbert Scott (also famous for Liverpool Cathedral, Waterloo Bridge, Battersea Power Station and the iconic red telephone box), the building with its 99m (325ft) central tower was built in the post-war years and was in service until 1981. It was almost demolished before the Tate took it over in 1994 and commissioned architects Herzog & de Meuron to convert it. The giant machinery was stripped out but much of the internal structure remains, and the scale and grandeur of the building complements its contents.

The new gallery opened in 2000, just as the Young British Artists of the '90s were developing into the new establishment. It was the perfect space in which to display installations and live art, which were becoming as important as traditional painting and sculpture. It's constantly evolving to meet demand and in 2009 began a new project which will include a separate extension and tower.

Endless Rhythm, Robert Delaunay

Max Liebermann, self-portrait

member (from £60 a year) and admission is free.

Some interesting things to see among the permanent collections are listed below:

Structure & Clarity (level 4): This wing looks at the development of abstract art from the '20s onwards, and includes cubism and minimalism, explored in paintings, sculpture, photography and digital art. Featured artists include Henri Matisse, Bridget Riley, Oskar Fischinger, Lewis Baltz, Charlotte Posenenske and Pedro Cabrita Reis.

The Tate Modern's collections consist of works of international modern and contemporary art dating from 1900 to the current day. The permanent collections are displayed on levels two to four of the building, while temporary exhibitions and events take place on levels one to three and in the Turbine Hall and the Tanks – three converted oil tanks now dedicated to live art. There's a restaurant on the top floor and a café on level one, plus the usual tempting gift shops.

Collections are grouped in genres and influences, rather than in chronological order, making it easy to concentrate on a couple of areas, maybe take in a special exhibition, and leave the rest for another visit. Many of the temporary exhibitions are free, though the big names – which in 2012 included Damien Hirst and Edvard Munch and in 2013 will feature a major retrospective on the comic-strip illustrator, Roy Lichtenstein – cost between £10 and £15. Become a Tate

FOOD & DRINK

Restaurant at Tate Modern: On the top floor with wonderful views across the Thames towards St Paul's. A two-course set lunch is £29, afternoon tea from £10.95.

Borough Market: Plenty of lunchtime choices at the foodies' favourite off Southwark Street, a short walk away, where there's also a great pub, The Market Porter.

Important exhibits include Matisse's *The Snail*, Carl Andre's bricks sculpture *Equivalent VII*, Picasso's cubist *Seated Nude* and Bridget Riley's undulating *Deny II*. Minimalism is illustrated by Larry Bell's *Untitled* boxes and Kim Ku-lim's ladder-like *Intervals*; constructionism by Mary Martin's *Expanding Form*. Kandinsky's *Swinging* and Mondrian's unmistakable *Compositions* always draw crowds, but allow time to study the cool monochrome modernist photography

Whaam! Roy Lichtenstein

of Werner Mantz and Paule Vézelay's exquisitely simple *Five Forms*.

Energy & Process (level 4): On the opposite wing, this zone presents art using ordinary materials in extraordinary ways. Featured artists include Kasimir Malevich, Richard Serra, Cy Twombly, Bruce Nauman, Abraham Cruzvillegas and Marisa Merz. The latter has some surprising untitled sculptures on display, including a suspended jungle of beaten aluminium and a delicately worked little shoe.

There's a room dedicated to Italian Arte Povera and anti-form – look for Mario Merz's *Lingotto* sculpted from brushwood and Gilberto Zorio's *Terracotta Circle* – while Cruzvillegas takes things a step further by making *Shit Models* out of sheep dung and steel. Meanwhile, Beyond Painting is a room dedicated to conceptual art, such as Niki

Claes Oldenburg's oversized apple

Damien Hirst Retrospective, 2012

de Saint Phalle's *Shooting Picture* where spectators were invited to fire guns at the canvas to release its colours.

Transformed Visions (level 3): This area takes an in-depth look at abstract painting after the Second World War, when artists began to include human figures in their works. Some reflect their creators' reactions to war, while others are purely escapist. Thomas Hirschhorn, Kara Walker, Mark Rothko, Mark Ruwedel and Ursula Schulz-Dornburg are among the artists featured, and there's a surprise appearance by one JMW Turner.

Highlights are Rothko's paintings of red or black on maroon and Barnett Newman's *Moment*, which contrast well with Turner's sun-dazzled seascape *Yacht Approaching the Coast*. A room entitled New Images of Man presents Jean Dubuffet's *The Tree of Fluids*, Jean Fautrier's (who was arrested by the Nazis in 1943 because of his Resistance connections) *Head of a Hostage* and Alberto Giacometti's *Man Pointing*.

Poetry & Dream (level 2): A celebration of surrealism in all its forms, from still life and landscapes, to portraits and nudes. Salvador Dali's *Metamorphosis of Narcissus* and Picasso's *Nude Woman with Necklace* are instantly recognisable, but there are many more weird and wonderful creations to enjoy. To single out just a few, seek out Joan Miró's *Painting*, Francis Bacon's *Figures in a Garden* and Edward Wadsworth's *The Beached Margin*, as well as paintings by André Masson, Max Ernst (*Dadaville*) and Francis Picabia (*The Fig-Leaf*). Some exhibits are extraordinary for their use of colour – like the holiday hues of Ellsworth Kelly's *Méditerannée* – while others are full of (unintentional?) humour, such as E.L.T. Mesens' *The Staff*, composed of cigarette cards of footballers with blanked-out eyes.

These rooms also feature a homage to realism, which includes Sir Stanley Spencer's *The Centurion's Servant* and Dora Carrington's *Spanish Landscape with Mountains*, as well as what, for many, must be the ultimate surrealistic painting: Giorgio de Chirico's *The Uncertainty of the Poet*.

Autumn, Henri Laurens

3 ROYAL OBSERVATORY

Address: Blackheath Avenue, Greenwich, SE10 8XJ (☎ 020-8858 4422, 🖳 rmg.co.uk/royal-observatory).
Opening hours: Daily, 10am to 5pm. Closed 24-26th December.
Cost: Free entry to the Astronomy Centre and Altazimuth Pavilion. **Royal Observatory**, £7 adults, £5 concessions, £2 children 6-15 (under-6s free), £15 families (2 adults, 2 children) or £8 (1 adult, 3 children). **Planetarium**, £6.50 adults, £4.50 children (3-15), £17.50 families. You can save money by purchasing a combined (Astro) ticket for the Royal Observatory and Planetarium.
Transport: Cutty Sark DLR or Greenwich rail.
Amenities: Café, tea house, shop, park, wheelchair access.

The Royal Observatory, Greenwich (formerly called the Royal Greenwich Observatory), situated on a hill in Greenwich Park, is one of the most important historic scientific sites in the world. It's best known as the 'home' of Greenwich Mean Time (GMT) and the Prime Meridian, i.e. a line of longitude which is defined as 0°, established in 1851. Greenwich is the official starting point for each new day, year and millennium (at the stroke of midnight GMT, as measured from the Prime Meridian), adopted by international decree in 1884. (Nowadays the Prime Meridian is marked by a powerful green laser that shines north across the London night sky.)

The Observatory was commissioned in 1675 by Charles II and designed by Sir Christopher Wren, and was the first purpose-built, scientific research facility in Britain. Charles II also created the position of Astronomer Royal, which was initially filled by John Flamsteed (1646-1719). The Observatory was built to improve navigation at sea and 'find the much-desired longitude of places' – one's exact position east and west – while at sea and out of sight of land, by astronomical means. This was inseparable from the accurate measurement of time, for which the Observatory became most famous in the 19th century.

The Observatory building was completed in the summer of 1676 and soon came to be known as Flamsteed House, which was eventually made official. In 1953, the Old Royal Observatory became part of the National Maritime Museum and Flamsteed House was opened to visitors in 1960. The scientific work of the observatory was relocated elsewhere in stages in the first half of the 20th century, and the Greenwich site is now maintained solely as a tourist attraction.

Today, the buildings include a museum of astronomical and

navigational tools and include the following galleries:

◆ **Weller Astronomy Galleries:** Located in the Astronomy Centre in the Observatory South Building. Here you can touch a 4.5 billion-year-old meteorite, watch how the universe was formed, unravel the mysteries of the cosmos and guide a space mission. **Note that this is the only free gallery.**

👁 DON'T MISS!

The bright red Time Ball on top of Flamsteed House is one of the world's earliest public time signals, distributing time to ships on the Thames and to many Londoners. It was first used in 1833 and still operates today. The ball is dropped from its top position each day at 1pm to signal to ship's navigators to reset their marine chronometers.

◆ **Time and Longitude (Flamsteed House):** Explores two British solutions to the longitude problem. One was based on detailed mapping measurements of the night sky at Greenwich, while the other was the development of an accurate, portable clock that worked on board ships – the celebrated Harrison marine timekeepers, named after their inventor, John Harrison.

◆ **Time and Greenwich (Flamsteed House):** Looks at the historical need to develop increasingly accurate timekeeping, the machines that measured time, how time was shared and distributed, and the people who 'used the time'.

◆ **Time for the Navy (Great Equatorial Building):** Tells the story of the provision of accurate timekeepers for the Royal Navy. Virtually all ships used marine chronometers and deck watches for navigation from the 1820s until the 1950s.

◆ **Time and Society (Meridian Building):** Examines the role of timekeeping in our everyday lives – from sundials and wristwatches to calendars and clocks.

Other Royal Observatory attractions include:

◆ **Greenwich Meridian Line:** You can stand astride **this line**, which represents the Prime Meridian and divides the eastern and western hemispheres of the Earth, just as the equator divides north from south.

◆ **Flamsteed House & the Astronomer Royal's Apartments:** See where the Astronomer Royal and his family lived and worked,

Thames tunnel construction

accomplishments included the Great Western Railway from Paddington station to Bristol; the Hungerford Suspension Bridge; the Water Towers for the spectacular fountains at Crystal Palace; and the *Great Eastern* and *SS Great Britain* steamships, the latter built at nearby Millwall on the Isle of Dogs.

Isambard's son, Henry Marc, was the structural engineer for Tower Bridge and co-designed Blackfriars Railway Bridge, both in partnership with Sir John Wolfe Barry, and he was also responsible for many other projects throughout Britain.

This fascinating museum is set in attractive landscaped grounds on three levels, circling Brunel's original shaft, and overlooking a pretty section of the Thames. There's also a café (see box) and bookshop. The museum also stages special events, concerts, guided walks and exhibitions throughout the year (see website for details).

navigable river. Originally designed for horse-drawn carriages, it's now part of the London Overground railway network.

Isambard Kingdom Brunel was even more famous than his father; he built dockyards and the fastest railway in the world, the 7ft broad gauge Great Western; constructed a series of steamships, including the first propeller-driven transatlantic steamship; and engineered numerous bridges and tunnels. His designs revolutionised public transport and modern engineering. In London, his first project was Thames Tunnel when, aged just 19, working as an assistant engineer to his father – a dangerous assignment during which he nearly drowned. Other

 FOOD & DRINK

Museum Café: The delightful café is also a gallery, hosting a series of exhibitions by talented local artists and photographers. On Sunday mornings, it serves a Turkish breakfast of olives, cheese and delicious pastries.

SS Great Britain

CUMING MUSEUM   5

Address: Old Walworth Town Hall, 151 Walworth Road, Southwark, SE17 1RY
(☏ 020-7525 2332, 🖳 southwark.gov.uk/cumingmuseum).
Opening hours: Tue-Sat, 10am to 5pm. Closed Sundays, Mondays, Bank Holidays
and over Christmas and New Year (see website for dates).
Cost: Free.
Transport: Elephant and Castle tube/rail or Kennington tube.
Amenities: Shop, wheelchair access.

This is another of the small, quirky and intriguing museums that help to make London such an interesting place. It houses the collection of the Cuming family and is also Southwark's history museum, containing the Southwark Art Collection and the Local History Library Collection.

The museum opened in 1906 and was the result of over a century of collecting by father and son Richard (1777-1870) and Henry (1817-1902) Cuming. Between 1782 (when Richard was given an old coin and some fossils on his fifth birthday, which inspired him to become a collector) and 1900, they collected around 100,000 objects from all over the world. The result is an intact 19th-century 'cabinet of curiosities', one of very few still in existence, which Henry bequeathed to the people of Southwark.

The Cuming collection is a diverse assortment of objects encompassing archaeology, ethnography, natural history and social history, among other things. The collection stems from a time when a London-based gentleman collector could buy objects from around the globe (Richard never

👁 DON'T MISS!

One of the more unusual bequests made to the Cuming Museum was the Lovett Collection, donated by Edward Lovett (1852-1933) in 1916. Lovett collected charms and other items connected to superstition, particularly those with a London connection. Among the many 'charms' is a cow's heart stuck with pins, which was used by a dairyman as a talisman against someone he believed had cursed his cows!

actually travelled abroad). He and Henry were like Victorian versions of Sir John Soane (see **Sir John Soane's Museum** on page 148), gathering anything and everything through auctions, private sales, gifts and donations. As a result, the collection has objects from Africa, the Americas, Asia, Europe and Oceania – everything from Maori nose flutes to a Hawaiian feathered cape. There are also natural history exhibits, objects relating to celebrities and royalty, and a section devoted to fakes and forgeries. Fake antiques flooded the market in the 19th century but Henry was expert at spotting them, exposing the fakers and then exhibiting the goods.

On a broader scale, the Cuming Museum also reflects the development of Southwark and its people. It's one of London's oldest and more ethnically diverse areas, and the Southwark gallery explores the story of the borough from Roman times to the present day across three themes: Settling Here, Visiting Southwark and World Connections. The Southwark Local History Library collection includes an extensive assortment of historic prints and photographs documenting the history and development of the borough, as well as maps, ephemera, works of art on paper and a wide range of historic documents. Some items are available to view at the library; others can only be viewed by appointment.

When it first opened, the Cuming Museum was dubbed 'the British Museum in miniature'. This is rather overegging the pudding, but the collectors' energy, enthusiasm and eccentricity shine through to this day, and it deserves to be much more widely known. Furthermore, it's a hands-on museum – great for kids – with crafts to attempt, costumes to try on, games to play and trails to follow. There's also a gallery showing an eclectic range of temporary exhibitions – a recent subject was Charles Dickens' experiences of Southwark – and a museum shop selling books and souvenirs.

👁 DON'T MISS!

The Southwark Art Collection (formerly housed at the South London Gallery) contains a variety of fine art, including some 250 Victorian oil and water-colour paintings and around 2,000 works on paper, including prints. The collection also includes contemporary art by artists connected with south London.

Cree Dolls

DULWICH PICTURE GALLERY

6

Address: Gallery Road, Dulwich, SE21 7AD (☎ 020-8693 5254,
💻 dulwichpicturegallery.org.uk).
Opening hours: Tue-Fri 10am to 5pm; Sat-Sun 11am to 5pm. Closed Mondays
except for Bank Holidays. Also closed 25-26th December and 1st January.
Cost: £5 adults, £4 seniors, free for the unemployed, students and under 18s. Free
guided tours of the permanent collection, 3pm Saturdays and Sundays.
Transport: West Dulwich or North Dulwich rail.
Amenities: Café, shop, garden, wheelchair access.

👁 DON'T MISS!

One of its smallest oils, Rembrandt's
Portrait of Jacob de Gheyn III,
has been dubbed the 'Takeaway
Rembrandt' as it has been stolen
from the museum four times! It has
variously been recovered from a
left-luggage office in West Germany;
returned anonymously; found on the
back of a bicycle; and discovered
under a bench in nearby Streatham.
The painting is now closely guarded
by an upgraded security system.

The tranquil south London suburb
of Dulwich is home to a quietly
revolutionary art gallery. Designed by
Sir John Soane (a noted architect,
most famous for designing the Bank
of England – see page 124 for his
museum) and opened in 1817, the
Dulwich Picture Gallery was England's
first purpose-built public art gallery and
has proved hugely influential on the
way we look at art. The building has
been called 'the world's most beautiful
art gallery' and is an elegant piece of
abstract classicism, made from brick
with Portland stone detailing.

The collection itself was mainly
bequeathed by Frenchman Noël
Desenfans (1745-1807) and his young
Swiss friend Sir Francis Bourgeois
(1753-1811), who together formed one
of the most successful art dealerships
of Georgian London. The highlight in
the career of the Bourgeois-Desenfans
partnership came in 1790 when they
were commissioned by Stanislaus
Augustus, King of Poland, to create
a Royal Collection-cum-National
Gallery in order to 'encourage the
progress of the fine arts in Poland'.
They devoted the next five years to
this task, during which time Poland

A Young Man, Rembrandt

paintings indirectly, to avoid damaging them with direct light. As the noted 20th-century architect Philip Johnson said, 'Soane has taught us how to display paintings'.

As for the collection itself, it's a small-but-beautifully-formed gem, mostly comprising a well-chosen assemblage of European old masters, mainly from the 17th and 18th centuries, including works by Canaletto, Constable, Gainsborough, Hogarth, Murillo, Rembrandt, Reynolds, Rubens and Van Dyck. The earliest picture in the collection, painted around 1500, is Piero Di Cosimo's portrait of *A Young Man*. It's an excellent example of High Renaissance portraiture, so much so that when first purchased it was incorrectly thought to be by Leonardo da Vinci.

was gradually partitioned by its more powerful neighbours, leading in 1795 to its complete disappearance as an independent state. The King was forced to abdicate and the dealers were left with a royal collection on their hands.

Bourgeois and Deschamps spent many years seeking a home for the collection, which was eventually left to Dulwich College, to be put on permanent public display in a specially-built gallery. Thus came into being England's first public art gallery, founded in 1811 on the death of Francis Bourgeois. Bourgeois, Noël Desanfans and his wife Margaret Desanfans are interred in a mausoleum at the centre of the west wing of the museum.

It's thought that Sir John Soane was chosen to design the museum because he was a friend of Bourgeois. His design, a series of simple interlinked rooms lit by natural light through overhead skylights, has been a major influence on the design of art galleries ever since. He cleverly designed the skylights to illuminate the

---

 FOOD & DRINK

Dulwich Picture Gallery Café: Hailed by the Square Meal Restaurant Guide as 'one of the top ten places in London for afternoon tea', the café also serves an excellent selection of main meals and snacks, and has an imaginative children's menu.

The gallery also regularly stages temporary exhibitions, which are often significant, and holds a comprehensive series of lectures and other educational events. It's surrounded by peaceful gardens, mainly lawns, with a number of old and unusual trees.

HAYWARD GALLERY

7

Address: Southbank Centre, Belvedere Road, SE1 8XX (☏ 020-7960 4200, 🖥 ticketing.southbankcentre.co.uk/find/hayward-gallery-visual-arts).
Opening hours: Daily, 10am to 6pm (Mon from noon, Thu-Fri until 8pm).
Cost: Fees vary, but are typically £10 adults, £9 concessions, £8 students, £7.50 12-18s. There's also a £1.75 online booking fee. Some events are free.
Transport: Waterloo tube/rail.
Amenities: Variety of restaurants, cafés and bars in the Southbank Centre, shop, wheelchair access.

The Hayward Gallery is part of the Southbank Centre, a complex of artistic venues on the South Bank of the Thames. It comprises three main buildings, the Royal Festival Hall, the Queen Elizabeth Hall and the Hayward Gallery, and is Europe's largest centre for the arts. The Centre attracts over 3m visitors annually, who attend almost a thousand paid performances of music, dance and literature, plus over 300 free foyer events and an education programme in and around the performing arts venues.

The Southbank Centre was built in 1951 as part of the Festival of Britain and the concert halls were originally funded and managed by the London County Council (LCC) and their successors, the Greater London Council (GLC). The Centre became an independent arts organisation in April 1988.

The Hayward Gallery (named after the late Sir Isaac Hayward, former

Tracey Emin's *Love is what you want*

The Stockbroker, George Condo

leader of the LCC) opened in 1968 and is an outstanding example of '60s Brutalist architecture. It's one of the UK's few remaining buildings of this style, designed by a group of young architects, including Dennis Crompton, Warren Chalk and Ron Herron. The design brief was for five gallery spaces, two levels of indoor galleries and three outdoor sculpture courts (the massive concrete trays on the upper level) designed to house the Arts Council collection, although in practice they have been little used (a rare exception was the *Blind Light* exhibition of works by Antony Gormley in 2007).

In 2011 the Hayward was added to the protected list by the World Monuments Fund, despite being refused listed building status in the UK. In common with the rest of the Southbank complex, people either admire its audacity or regard it as a concrete eyesore.

From 1968 to 1986, the gallery was managed by the Arts Council of Great Britain, after which management passed to the Southbank Centre. Unlike British galleries receiving state funding support, but in common with other temporary exhibitions at British national galleries, the Hayward charges admission fees for its major exhibitions. However, there are always a number of free events –

exhibitions, installations, readings and concerts – to enjoy at the Hayward and the other Southbank venues.

The gallery doesn't have a permanent collection but hosts three or four major contemporary exhibitions annually, and has a long history of presenting work by the world's most adventurous and innovative artists. The first Hayward Gallery show in 1968 was a retrospective of Matisse and its exhibition policy embraces visual art from all periods – past shows have included the works of Leonardo da Vinci, Edvard Munch and the French Impressionists. Recently the programme has tended to concentrate on surveys of contemporary art which complement the spaces and powerful concrete structure of the building, such as those by Dan Flavin and Antony Gormley. It has also hosted two surveys of works from the Arts Council Collections: *British Art 1940-1980* and *How to Improve the World: 60 Years of British Art*.

The gallery also runs Hayward Touring, a contemporary art organisation producing exhibitions that tour to galleries, museums and other publicly-funded venues throughout the UK. It collaborates with artists, independent curators, writers and partner institutions to develop and tour exhibitions which are seen by around half a million people in over 100 cities and towns each year.

 FOOD & DRINK

Concrete Café/Bar: The gallery's café/bar displays regularly changing works of contemporary art.

Riverside Terrace Café, Royal Festival Hall: A great place to have an alfresco snack or drink, while enjoying the riverside views.

Queen Elizabeth Hall Roof Garden Café/Bar: On a fine day in spring/summer, there's no better place to have a drink/snack than the Roof Gardens.

HORNIMAN MUSEUM 8

Address: 100 London Road, Forest Hill, SE23 3PQ (☏ 020-8699 1872, 🖥 horniman.ac.uk).

Opening hours: Daily, 10.30am to 5.30pm. Closed 24-26th December. Gardens: Mon-Sat 7.30am to sunset, Sun 8am to sunset; closed 25th December.

Cost: Free. Aquarium £2.50 adults, £1 children (under 3s free), £6 families (up to 2 adults and 2 children). Aquarium annual pass £6 (£15 families).

Transport: Forest Hill rail.

Amenities: Café, shop, gardens, wheelchair access.

It's well worth journeying out to the southern suburbs to see this interesting and varied collection. Opened in 1901, it's housed in a lovely Arts & Crafts and Art Nouveau-style building designed by Charles Harrison Townsend (1851-1928), who was also responsible for the striking **Whitechapel Art Gallery** (see page 139). The museum was founded by the Victorian tea trader Frederick John Horniman (1835-1906) to house his superb collection of cultural artefacts, ethnography, natural history and musical instruments, some collected personally on his travels (although he didn't leave Britain until he was 60), but most by his tea merchants.

 DON'T MISS!

Among the museum's more bizarre objects are a pair of Annang puppets from Nigeria depicting the wedding of Prince Charles and Lady Diana, and a 'torture chair' reputed to have been used in a dungeon in Cuenca in 17th-century Spain.

The Horniman's collection of over 350,000 objects (significantly added to since the original bequest) is neither dusty nor static, and is constantly being enlarged, researched and brought into public view. The ethnography and music collections have 'designated' status; i.e. are considered of great importance. The ethnographic collection is the third most important in the UK (after the British Museum and the Pitt-Rivers Museum, Oxford) and comprises approximately 80,000 items from around the world.

The museum has over 8,000 objects made to produce sound, the earliest dating from 1500 BC – a pair of Egyptian bone clappers in the form of human hands. Electric guitars and synthesizers are among the most recent acquisitions. The Horniman interprets instruments in a broad musical and cultural context, and aims to acquire sound and video recordings for each new instrument.

The Natural History collection contains over 250,000 specimens of local, national and worldwide origin. It's noted for its large collection of stuffed

Natural History Gallery

creatures, which include a walrus, an ostrich and an assortment of dogs' heads, including a Bloodhound, Bulldog and Pekingese. The museum also has one of London's oldest aquariums, dating from 1903, although there's a new, modern aquarium in the basement, presenting different aquatic environments from the British Isles to Fiji.

There are also many interesting archaeological and cultural exhibits from Africa, America, Europe, Asia and the Pacific. The African Worlds gallery was the first permanent exhibition in Britain dedicated to African art, while the museum also has some important British prehistoric material, some from significant sites such as Grimes Graves and Swanscombe. The website contains comprehensive information about the various collections.

The core collections are complemented by a separate Education Handling Collection containing over 3,700 objects. It's an excellent resource providing a unique opportunity to touch and study closely a wide selection of objects and specimens similar to those in the galleries.

The Horniman Museum is set in 16 acres (6.5ha) of award-winning, beautifully maintained gardens, which include a Grade II listed conservatory, bandstand, animal enclosure, nature trail and an ornamental garden. A 20ft (6.1m) totem pole sits outside the museum's main entrance; although dating only from 1985, it's one of the UK's few totem poles. There's also a grass-roofed Centre for Understanding the Environment building, constructed from sustainable materials.

Museum Conservatory & Café

IMPERIAL WAR MUSEUM LONDON 9

Address: Lambeth Road, SE1 6HZ (☎ 020-7416 5000, 🖥 iwm.org.uk/visits/iwm-london).

Opening hours: Daily, 10am to 6pm. Closed 24-26th December. Check in advance, as the museum was undergoing a major redevelopment in 2013 and was scheduled to close from January to July 2013.

Cost: Free.

Transport: Lambeth North or Elephant & Castle tube.

Amenities: Café, shop, library, park, wheelchair access.

The Imperial War Museum (IWM) was founded in 1917 and is the world's leading authority on conflict and its impact, focusing on Britain, its former Empire and the Commonwealth, from the First World War to the present (earlier conflicts are covered in the **National Army Museum** – see page 203). A family of five museums (including **HMS Belfast** – see page 282), the IWM illustrates and records all aspects of modern war and of the individual's experience of it, whether allied or enemy, service or civilian, military or political, social or cultural. The collections include archives of personal and official documents, photography, film and video material, and oral history recordings; an extensive library; a large art collection; and examples of military vehicles and aircraft, equipment and other artefacts.

 ALLOW...

IWM London is a huge museum and when all the exhibitions are open it can easily take two days to explore them all.

The galleries allow you to delve deeper into the stories of both world wars, exploring their complex origins and discovering what life was like for those who experienced war first hand, from the trenches of the Western Front to a Blitzed London street in 1940. The museum also traces the Nazi persecution and murder of Jews in the Holocaust Exhibition, and looks at extraordinary stories of bravery behind the Victoria Cross and George Cross medals.

The museum's permanent galleries include the following:

♦ **Large Exhibits Gallery:** The first gallery on show as you enter the museum houses some of the most important weapons and vehicles. Significant items on display include the 4-inch gun which fired the first British shot from *HMS Lance* in the First World War, a Supermarine Spitfire Mark 1A which flew in the Battle of Britain, and an unusual one-man *Biber* German submarine. It also includes some of the most destructive weapons of the Second World War, including a V1 and V2 rocket, and the 'Little Boy' atomic bomb of the type dropped on Hiroshima in 1945.

♦ **Secret War:** From the early days of MI5 and MI6 to the work of modern-

day 'spooks', this gallery reveals the clandestine world of espionage and covert operations. Exhibits include an original German Enigma cipher machine.

◆ **The Lord Ashcroft Gallery: Extraordinary Heroes.** This gallery houses the world's largest collection of Victoria Crosses (donated by Lord Ashcroft, KCMG) and a significant collection of George Crosses. It looks at some of the stories behind the medals, awarded from the Crimean War to the recent conflicts in Iraq and Afghanistan, which recognise acts of extreme bravery.

👁 DON'T MISS!

Art Gallery: Breakthrough is a powerful gallery dedicated to displaying IWM's own art in a changing programme of exhibitions. Featured artists include Evelyn Dunbar, Henry Moore, Paul and John Nash and Sir Stanley Spencer. One of the most significant paintings is *Gassed* by John Singer Sargent, which is permanently displayed in the Sargent Gallery.

◆ **The Holocaust Exhibition:** This chilling display traces the Nazi persecution and murder of Europe's Jews from 1933 to 1945 through photographs, documents and film, while toys, diaries, storybooks and hand-made mementos reveal people's efforts to survive. Testimonies from 18 survivors bring a moving and haunting perspective.

◆ **Crimes against Humanity,** provides an overview of genocide and ethnic warfare over the last 100 years, from Armenia to Rwanda.

The museum also stages temporary exhibitions, which in recent years have included: Cecil Beaton: Theatre of War; A Family in Wartime; and War Story: Serving in Afghanistan.

Over the next decade, IWM London is creating new gallery spaces. In 2012 this necessitated the temporary closure of the First World War, Second World War and Conflicts since 1945 galleries, and restricted access to others. **Before visiting, check the website or telephone to find out whether the museum is fully open.**

The museum has a café or you can picnic in Harmsworth Park.

THE QUEEN'S HOUSE 10

Address: Greenwich, SE10 9NF (☎ 020-8858 4422, 🖥 rmg.co.uk/queens-house).
Opening hours: Daily, 10am to 5pm.
Cost: Free.
Transport: Cutty Sark DLR or Greenwich rail.
Amenities: Wheelchair access.

The Queen's House (Grade I listed) is a former royal residence (originally part of Greenwich Palace) built between 1616 and 1619 for Queen Anne, wife of James I. It was a crucial early commission for Inigo Jones, who spent three years in Italy studying Roman and Renaissance architecture prior to designing the Queen's House. The result was the first consciously classical building to be constructed in Britain and a landmark in British architectural history. Reflecting Renaissance ideas of mathematical, classical proportion and harmony, the design was revolutionary at a time when even the best native buildings were still in red-brick, Tudor style.

the collection Charles I had purchased from the Gonzaga dukes of Mantua. Of this original splendour, all that survives in the house is the 'grotesque' style painted ceiling of the Queen's Presence Chamber, the ironwork of the 'tulip stairs' (the first centrally unsupported spiral stair in Britain), the much discoloured but original painted woodwork of the Great Hall and its geometric-patterned marble floor laid in 1635.

Today, the Queen's House is part of the National Maritime Museum and serves as a gallery for some of the NMM's fine art collection, consisting of contemporary art, miniatures, oil paintings, photography, prints, drawings, watercolours and sculpture. The collection includes over 4,500 oil paintings covering the period 1530 to 2000, the earliest of which is a Flemish artist's depiction of Portuguese ships from around 1530. It's essential viewing if you enjoy paintings of sea battles, noble vessels and famous naval commanders.

The Queen's House displays paintings by Gainsborough, Lely, Hogarth, Reynolds, Hodges and the van de Veldes, and has the following galleries:

👁 DON'T MISS!

The museum's most famous picture is Joseph Mallord William Turner's painting of the Battle of Trafalgar in 1805, painted for George IV in 1823 and Turner's largest artwork.

Leading European painters, including Jacob Jordaens and Orazio Gentileschi, were commissioned to provide decorative ceiling panels and other art works, while classical sculpture was provided from

Queen's Presence Chamber

◆ **Art for the Nation:** An excellent exhibition presenting 200 of the most important works in the NMM's collection. It includes portraits, paintings of historical events and, especially, marine painting and seascapes, on such themes as global exploration, shipwreck and battles at sea. Subjects range from a delightful portrait of Emma Lady Hamilton to Adam Willaerts' menacing depiction of *Jonah and the Whale.*

◆ **The Royal Hospital School Gallery:** Learn what life was like at the Royal Hospital School in Greenwich, Britain's largest school of seamanship between 1821 and 1933.

◆ **Historic Greenwich:** The Queen's House wasn't built to stand alone but was designed as an addition to the royal Palace of Placentia at Greenwich (Greenwich Palace). This gallery highlights the history of the house and its surroundings.

◆ **The Tudors at Greenwich:** The paintings displayed in this room are from the earliest period of English history covered by the NMM's art collection – from Henry VII to Elizabeth I, who was born there.

◆ **Art and the van de Veldes:** In 1673-4, Dutch artists Willem van de Velde the Elder and Younger (father and son) established a studio in the Queen's House, and their work influenced marine painting in the following two centuries.

You can enjoy the museum's collection of oil paintings, prints, drawings and watercolours online (see rmg.co.uk > collections > fine art).

 FOOD & DRINK

Goddard's Pie & Mash: The Cockney staple – eels are optional – from a family business dating back to 1890. Find the Greenwich branch in King William Walk.

  Black Vanilla: The best *gelato* outside Italy in College Approach by the entrance to Greenwich Market.

RANGER'S HOUSE & WERNHER COLLECTION 11

Address: Chesterfield Walk, Blackheath, SE10 8QX (☏ 020-8853 0035, tours 020-8290 2548, 🖵 english-heritage.org.uk/daysout/properties/rangers-house-the-wernher-collection and friendsofrangershouse.org.uk).
Opening hours: See website for tour times and details.
Cost: £6.50 adults, £5.90 concessions, £3.90 children. Free for English Heritage members.
Transport: Blackheath rail.
Amenities: Wheelchair access.

1912), a German-born railway engineer's son who became a diamond magnate. He was incredibly wealthy – the company he formed was later amalgamated with De Beers and Wernher left over £11m on his death – and was able to indulge his lifelong passion for collecting.

> **👁 DON'T MISS!**
>
> Giulio Bergonzoli's strikingly beautiful marble sculpture (in the Chesterfield Gallery), *Love of Angels*, depicting an angel kissing a semi-nude woman, which despite weighing two tons succeeds in appearing light and ethereal.

The Ranger's House is an elegant, red brick Georgian villa built in the Palladian style, adjacent to Greenwich Park, which dates from the early 1700s. It's a graceful building with panelled interiors that was first used as the official residence of the Ranger of Greenwich Park in 1816, when it was called Chesterfield House (named after its former owner, Lord Chesterfield).

The property alone is worth visiting, but all the more so because since 2002 it has housed the Wernher Collection of works of art (jewellery, paintings, porcelain, silver and much more) collected in the late 19th and early 20th centuries by Sir Julius Wernher (1850-

It's one of the best private collections of art ever assembled by one person and of international importance, including some of Europe's most spectacular jewellery. This makes it all the more surprising that it has such a low profile; in fact few people seem to have heard of it, although it has been run by English Heritage since 1986.

Nearly 700 works of art are on display, spread over 12 rooms, including early religious paintings, Dutch Old Masters, tiny carved Gothic ivories, fine Renaissance bronzes (the best collection in the world outside the major museums) and silver treasures – look out for the silver owl with a body made from a coconut. They demonstrate the many skills of

13 CUTTY SARK

Address: King William Walk, SE10 9HT (☎ 020-8312 6608,
🖳 rmg.co.uk/cuttysark).
Opening hours: Daily, 10am to 5pm.
Cost: £12 adults, £9.50 concessions, £6.50 children (5-15), £29 families (2 adults, 2 children).
Transport: Cutty Sark DLR or Greenwich rail.
Amenities: Café, shop, wheelchair access (limited to three per hour).

The *Cutty Sark* (Grade I listed) is one of the world's most famous sailing ships. A living museum, she's also home to a range of objects, including an extensive collection of figureheads, historic newspaper cuttings and artefacts relating to the ship's history.

The *Cutty Sark* was designed by Hercules Linton and built in Dumbarton, Scotland, for John Willis & Son, and launched on 22nd November 1869. She **was** destined to be a tea clipper, carrying tea from China to London, and was one of the fastest ships of her day. In her most celebrated race, against *Thermopylae* in 1872, both ships left Shanghai together on 18th June, but the *Cutty Sark* lost her rudder and had to improvise. She arrived in London on 18th October, just one week later than the fully seaworthy *Thermopylae*, a feat more astonishing than actually winning the 'race'!

Between 1885 and 1895, under Captain Richard Woodget, the *Cutty Sark* won the 'wool race' between Australia and London ten years in a row, once even out-pacing a steamship. Soon after, she was sold and endured an ignominious few decades until being saved for posterity in 1922 by Captain Wilfred Dowman. She saw service as a training ship in Falmouth and Greenhithe, Kent, before becoming a museum ship in Greenwich in 1957.

After a devastating fire in 2007, the *Cutty Sark* was restored to her former glory at a cost of £50m and re-opened to the public in April 2012. Visitors can now walk underneath the ship to better appreciate her elegant lines.

👁 DON'T MISS!

Florence Nightingale, Disraeli and Hiawatha are among the characters immortalised as figureheads in the *Cutty Sark*'s collection. The ship's own figurehead, a young witch named Nannie, is a character in Robert Burns' 1790 poem, *Tam O'Shanter*. The ship's name is Scots for the short chemise or undergarment that Nannie wore.

DOWN HOUSE (HOME OF CHARLES DARWIN)

14

Address: Luxted Road, Downe, BR6 7JT (☎ 01689-859119 or 0870-333 1181, 🖥 english-heritage.org.uk/daysout/properties/home-of-charles-darwin-down-house).

Opening hours: Summer/autumn (April to October), open daily including Bank Holidays (see website for times). Winter/spring (November to March), weekends 10am to 4pm,

Cost: £9.90 adults, £8.90 concessions, £5.90 children, £25.70 families. Free to English Heritage members.

Transport: Bromley South rail, then 146 bus.

Amenities: Tea room, shop, gardens, wheelchair access.

Down House and its 18-acre (7.2ha) estate was the home of the celebrated English naturalist Charles Darwin (1809-1882) and his family, from 1842 until his death. When he moved to Down House it was a plain and sturdy 18th-century block. Darwin made extensive alterations to the house, extending and enlarging it, while the grounds became his 'open-air laboratory'.

👁 DON'T MISS!

Darwin did much of his thinking in the Down House gardens and you can follow in his footsteps along the wooded Sandwalk track, and explore his beloved greenhouses with their carnivorous plants and exotic orchids. It's worth visiting in spring when the orchids are in bloom.

Situated in rural Kent (now the London borough of Bromley), the house offered the peace and privacy that Darwin needed to work on his revolutionary scientific theories. It was at Down that he developed his landmark views on evolution by natural selection and wrote his ground-breaking work, *On the Origin of Species* (1859) – a book that shook the Victorian world and has influenced scientific thinking ever since.

After the death of Darwin's widow Emma in 1896, the house was let on a series of short-term tenancies – between 1907 and 1921 it was a girls' school – and then languished empty for a number of years, until Sir Arthur Keith (1866-1955), curator of the Hunterian Museum, encouraged the British Association for the Advancement of Science (BAAS) to preserve it as a national memorial to Darwin. Down House was maintained as a museum by the BAAS for 60 years, until the house and contents were purchased by English Heritage in 1996.

Today you can see Darwin's famous study, recreated as it would have appeared in the 1870s. It features a replica of his cabin on HMS *Beagle* and his journal compiled during his epic five-year voyage.

Charles Darwin

15 ELTHAM PALACE

Address: Court Yard, Eltham, SE9 5QE (☎ 020-8294 2548 or 0870-333 1181,
🖥 english-heritage.org.uk/daysout/properties/eltham-palace-and-gardens).
Opening hours: See website for opening times, which are restricted from November to Match.
Cost: £9.60 adults, £5.80 children, £8.60 concessions, £25 families.
Transport: Eltham or Mottingham rail.
Amenities: Tea room, shop, gardens, wheelchair access.

Hidden away in a southeast London suburb is an unexpected treat that combines one of England's best Art Deco interiors with some of the few significant remains of an English medieval royal palace. Initially a moated manor house set in extensive parkland, the palace was given to Edward II in 1305 and was a royal residence until the 16th century – Henry VIII lived there as a young prince. It was eclipsed by the rebuilding of Greenwich Palace – which was more easily accessible from the Thames – although hunting deer in its enclosed parks remained popular. However, the parks were almost stripped of deer – and trees – during the English Civil War, while the palace and its chapel were badly damaged.

👁 DON'T MISS!

Lady Courtauld's bathroom is the last word in luxury, somewhere between a Hollywood boudoir and a Roman bath, boasting golf-leaf mosaic, onyx and a statue of a goddess.

The current building dates from the '30s, when Sir Stephen and Lady Virginia Courtauld were granted a lease. They restored the Great Hall, which boasts England's third-largest hammer-beam roof, gave it a minstrels' gallery and incorporated it into a sumptuous home with a striking interior in a variety of Art Deco styles. Among many notable features are the ebonised doors in the dining room, featuring animal motifs, and the stunning circular entrance hall by Swedish designer Rolf Engströmer. The latter boasts an impressive glazed dome that floods it with light, highlighting the lush, figurative parquetry.

The red brick and Bath stone exterior is modelled on Wren's work at Hampton Court Palace, and the extensive gardens feature a 15th-century bridge spanning the 14th-century moat, which is planted with lilies. The gardens are an important example of '30s garden design and an ideal picnic spot. There's also a tea room and gift shop.

FAN MUSEUM

16

Address: 12 Crooms Hill, Greenwich, SE10 8ER (☎ 020-8305 1441, 🖥 thefanmuseum.org.uk).
Opening hours: Tue-Sat, 11am to 5pm; Sun and Bank Holidays noon to 5pm. Closed Mondays.
Cost: £4 adults, £3 concessions and children 8-15, under 7s free. Tue from 2pm, free entry for pensioners and disabled visitors.
Transport: Cutty Sark DLR or Greenwich rail.
Amenities: Tea room, shop, garden, wheelchair access.

The Fan Museum opened in 1991 and is the only museum in the world devoted entirely to fans and fan-making. It's housed in a pair of Grade II* listed early Georgian houses built in 1721, which have been lovingly restored to their original character and elegance. An Orangery, faithful to the architecture of the period, has been added with a spectacular mural, overlooking a Japanese-style garden with a fan-shaped parterre, pond and stream – an oasis of tranquillity.

The museum's collection numbers over 4,000 fans, fan leaves and related ephemera, with the oldest fan dating from the 11th century. It's the world's most important collection of fans, with many extremely rare and exquisite examples – and some bizarre ones, such as a fan with a built-in ear trumpet, one that doubles as a bonnet and one with an in-built repair kit. The stars of the collection are undoubtedly the rare and beautiful 18th- and 19th-century European fans.

 FOOD & DRINK

The Orangery: Served twice a week (Tuesdays and Sundays at 2:30pm and 3:45pm, open to museum visitors only), the Orangery's afternoon tea has been praised for its value by the *Daily Telegraph* – a real treat for just £6. If you plan to sample it while visiting the museum, be sure to book well in advance.

Fans from the collection and those on loan from other collections are displayed in changing themed exhibitions, presented in their historical, sociological and economic contexts. There's also a permanent educational display about fans, including their history, the materials used, the manufacturing process and the different kinds of fan. Fans have been used for many purposes over the centuries: cooling devices, ceremonial tools, fashion accessories, status symbols, commemorative presents and advertising giveaways.

The museum also has a conservation unit and gift shop and runs workshops in the art of fan-making.

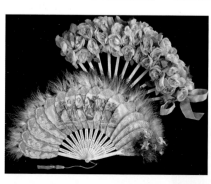

17 FASHION & TEXTILE MUSEUM

Address: 83 Bermondsey Street, Bermondsey, SE1 3XF (☎ 020-7407 8664, 🖥 ftmlondon.org).
Opening hours: Exhibition space and shop: Tue-Sat, 11am to 6pm. Closed Sundays and Mondays.
Cost: For changing exhibitions: £7 adults, £5 students and senior citizens, under 12s free.
Transport: London Bridge tube/rail.
Amenities: Café, shop, wheelchair access.

Appropriately sited in the heart of trendy Bermondsey village, the Fashion & Textile Museum is an exhibition centre devoted, as you might expect, to fashion and textile design. It was founded in 2003 by one of Britain's most famous fashion designers, Zandra Rhodes, who was part of the new wave of designers who launched London into the forefront of the international fashion scene in the '70s. Zandra Rhodes Enterprises is based a couple of doors down the road (at 81 Bermondsey Street), although the museum has been taken over by Newham College. It's housed in a striking building designed by Mexican architect Ricardo Legorreta, with an eye-catching egg

yolk yellow and pink exterior – a tourist attraction in itself.

DON'T MISS!

Check out the gift shop for an interesting range of accessories by talented young designers on their way to becoming the next Zandra Rhodes. The jewellery is especially tempting.

The website declares it 'a cutting edge centre for contemporary fashion, textiles and jewellery'. The museum has a small permanent collection which highlights the changing face of contemporary fashion from 1947 to the present day, and includes a number of key garments from designers such as Christian Dior, Balenciaga, Biba, Mary Quant and Vivienne Westwood – and, of course, Zandra Rhodes.

It also hosts exhibitions exploring elements of fashion, textiles and jewellery. Like fashion itself, which by its nature is constantly evolving, so do the exhibitions. Past ones have included The Little Black Dress, The Evolution of Underwear, Sampling the '70s and Tommy Nutter: The Rebel on the Row, about the noted Savile Row tailor. The museum also holds a series of fashion-related events and talks (see website for details).

There's also an Academy which runs courses and an archive that can be visited by appointment, plus a café open seven days a week.

FIREPOWER: ROYAL ARTILLERY MUSEUM

18

Address: Royal Arsenal, Woolwich, SE18 6ST (☎ 020-8855 7755, 🖥 firepower.org.uk).
Opening hours: Tue-Sat, 10.30am to 6pm. Closed Sundays and Mondays.
Cost: £5.30 adults, £4.60 concessions, £2.50 children, £12.50 families (maximum 4 people).
Transport: Woolwich Arsenal DLR or rail.
Amenities: Café, shop, wheelchair access.

Firepower is one of the world's oldest military museums and tells the story of the Royal Regiment of Artillery (RA) and the Royal Arsenal. The history of the RA goes back to 1716, when the first two permanent companies of artillery were formed at Woolwich. It has been involved in most British actions during the past 200 years and over 2m men and women have served in the regiment since its formation; their stories of courage and sacrifice make Firepower much more than just a regimental museum.

👁 DON'T MISS!

An important place at Firepower is reserved for the two Chinese guns which have provided bronze gunmetal to Hancock's Jewellers for the manufacture of the Victoria Cross, over 800 of which have been made from these guns.

The Royal Arsenal, where Firepower is located, was Britain's principal ordnance manufacturing facility from the early 18th century until 1967. It was one of the most important centres in the world for munitions production, and many of the guns and carriages on display were made there.

Firepower tells its powerful stories through a series of galleries, including History, which explores 700 years of artillery from slings and arrows to shrapnel shells – displays also include instruments, uniforms, illustrations and personal accounts – and the Medals gallery, which shows some of the thousands of medals won by members of the RA.

The Gunnery Hall is crammed with weapons and vehicles from the 20th century: anti-aircraft, anti-tank, coastal defence, light and medium artillery, self-propelled guns and missile launchers. You can experience their power at the 'ground-shaking' Field of Fire audio-visual show, which places you in the midst of battle, as shells whiz overhead and guns roar.

When you need a break from loud noises, the museum has a tranquil café and a shop.

19 FLORENCE NIGHTINGALE MUSEUM

Address: St Thomas' Hospital, 2 Lambeth Palace Road, SE1 7EW (☎ 020-7620 0374, 🖥 florence-nightingale.co.uk).
Opening hours: Daily, 10am to 5pm. Closed Good Friday and 25-26th December.
Cost: £5.80 adults, £4.80 children and concessions, £16 families (2 adults and up to 5 children).
Transport: Waterloo or Westminster tube.
Amenities: Café (in hospital), shop, wheelchair access.

The Florence Nightingale Museum tells the engrossing story of one of Britain's greatest heroines. From the slate she used as a child to the Turkish lantern she carried in the Crimean War – which earned her the sobriquet 'The Lady with the Lamp' – the collection spans the life of Florence Nightingale (1820-1910) and her nursing legacy.

👁 DON'T MISS!

Among the medical kit, uniforms and other memorabilia is a Little Owl, stuffed and mounted in a cabinet. This was Florence's pet owl Athena, rescued as a fledgling and carried everywhere in her mistress's pocket.

Florence Nightingale

Nightingale was born in Florence on 12th May 1820, the daughter of wealthy landowner William Nightingale. In 1851, her father reluctantly gave permission for her to train as a nurse and she travelled to Kaiserwerth (Germany) to study at the Institute of Protestant Deaconesses. The Crimean War began in 1853, and there were soon reports describing the desperate lack of proper medical facilities and care for wounded soldiers. The following year, Nightingale led a team of 38 nurses who cared for thousands of soldiers during the war and helped save the British army from medical disaster.

In 1860 she established the Nightingale Training School for nurses at London's St Thomas' Hospital. Once trained, nurses were sent to hospitals throughout Britain, where they introduced her ideas and established nursing training. Her theories, published in *Notes on Nursing* (1860), were hugely influential and her concerns for sanitation, military health and hospital planning established practices which are still in use today.

Florence was a visionary health reformer, a brilliant campaigner and the second most influential woman in Victorian Britain, after Queen Victoria. The Nightingale Pledge taken by new nurses was named in her honour, and International Nurses Day is celebrated throughout the world on her birthday to this day.

GARDEN MUSEUM

20

Address: St Mary-at-Lambeth, Lambeth Palace Road, SE1 7LB (☎ 020-7401 8865, 🖥 gardenmuseum.org.uk).

Opening hours: Sun-Fri, 10.30am to 5pm; Sat 10.30am to 4pm. Closed first Monday of the month (except Bank Holidays) and over the Christmas and New Year period (see website for details).

Cost: £7.50 adults, £6.50 seniors, £3 students, free for under-16s and disabled people's carers. Free tours last Tuesday of the month at 2pm.

Transport: Lambeth North tube or Waterloo tube/rail.

Amenities: Café, shop, library, wheelchair access.

Despite being described by the *Daily Telegraph* as 'one of London's best small museums', the Garden Museum (which used to be called the Museum of Garden History but was renamed and revamped in 2008) is sometimes overlooked. Ironically, this is partly due to its splendid riverside location, next to Lambeth Palace and almost directly opposite the Houses of Parliament.

It's the world's first museum dedicated to the history of gardening, and celebrates British gardens and gardening through its collection, temporary exhibitions, events, symposia and garden. The permanent collection comprises three main categories: tools, ephemera (including prints, photographs and catalogues, giving an insight into the social as well as practical history of gardening) and a library. The tools range from Neolithic implements to a Victorian cucumber straightener, while one of the more unusual plants is the Vegetable Lamb of Tartary, thought until the 18th century to be a cross between an animal and a vegetable (it's actually the stem of a variety of fern).

The museum is based in the deconsecrated church of St Mary-at-Lambeth, dating from the 14th century (restored in 1850). It was established to rescue the church from demolition following the discovery there of the graves of two 17th-century royal gardeners and plant hunters, John Tradescant (father and son). Anne Boleyn's mother Elizabeth also rests here, as does William Bligh, captain of the *Bounty*.

In the churchyard is a lovely, recreated 17th-century knot garden, in a formal, geometric style with authentic period planting (seeds for which can be purchased in the museum shop).

 FOOD & DRINK

Garden Café: This much-loved (rated no. 6 in *Gourmet* magazine's world's best museum restaurants in 2012) oasis specialises in vegetarian food – soups, tarts and splendid cakes – making the most of the museum's kitchen garden. Lunch is served from noon to 3pm and on Sundays the focus is on an all-day afternoon tea. **Free access.**

21 HMS BELFAST

Address: The Queen's Walk, SE1 2JH (☎ 020-7940 6300, 🖥 iwm.org.uk/visits/hms-belfast).
Opening hours: Daily, March to October 10am to 6pm, November to February 10am to 5pm. Closed 24th-26th December.
Cost: £14.50 adults, £11.60 concessions, children under 16 free.
Transport: London Bridge tube/rail.
Amenities: Café, shop, no wheelchair access.

now open. Exploring her is a challenge as you negotiate a maze of low-slung doorways and steep ladders, but it provides a real sense of the claustrophobic atmosphere on board.

A visit to HMS *Belfast* consists of three broad sections: Life on Board reveals everyday life for her crew, from the Messdeck where they ate and slept, to the Provision Issue Room where the daily measures of rum were poured. Life at War looks at what it was like to serve on the ship on active service, while Inner Workings visits the nerve centres of *Belfast*, including the Operations Room and Engine Room.

H MS *Belfast* is a remarkable museum ship – originally a Royal Navy light cruiser – permanently moored on the Thames and operated by the **Imperial War Museum** (see page 267). Named after the city where she was built, *Belfast* was launched on 17th March 1938 and commissioned in August 1939, just before the outbreak of the Second World War. She struck a mine and was out of service for three years but when she returned to action in November 1942, *Belfast* was the most powerful cruiser in the Royal Navy.

She saw action escorting Arctic convoys to the Soviet Union in 1943 and assisted in the destruction of the German battleship *Scharnhorst*, and in 1944 took part in Operation Overlord supporting the Normandy landings. She was placed in reserve in 1963 and in 1967 a campaign was initiated to preserve her as a museum ship. *Belfast* opened to the public in 1971.

In the early days, visitors were limited to the upper decks and forward superstructure, but nine decks are

---

DON'T MISS!

The Gun Turret Experience recreates the atmosphere for sailors during a sea battle, as you're bombarded with lights, imagery, smoke effects, vibrations, sounds and smells, while enclosed in a cramped gun turret.

Visitors' rations are available in the Walrus Café.

THE RED HOUSE 22

Address: Red House Lane, Bexleyheath, DA6 8JF (☎ 020-8304 9878,
🖥 nationaltrust.org.uk/redhouse).
Opening hours: March to October, Wed-Sun 11am to 5pm; November to mid-
December, Fri-Sun 11am to 5pm. Until 1.30pm, visits are by pre-booked guided
tours only. See website for details and exact dates and times.
Cost: £7.20 adults, £3.60 children, £18 families. Garden only: £2 adults, £1 children,
£5 families. Free for National Trust members.
Transport: Bexleyheath rail.
Amenities: Café, shop, garden, no wheelchair access.

The Red House (Grade I listed) is a gem, described by the Pre-Raphaelite painter Dante Gabriel Rossetti as 'more a poem than a house' and by the designer and artist Edward Burne-Jones as 'the beautifullest place on earth'. It was designed by the architect Philip Webb and William Morris (see also **Kelmscott House** on page 207 and the **William Morris Gallery** on page 116), founder of the Arts and Crafts movement which was influential in the later 19th and early 20th centuries.

Morris and his family only lived in the Red House for five years (1860-1865), but the building is a significant landmark in English domestic architecture, being designed as both a home and an artists' workshop. It embodies the aesthetic principles that Morris upheld, and is a clever blend of the practical and the romantic, with Gothic and medieval influences.

The Red House is a large, elegant building, made of warm, red bricks and with substantial chimneys, a tall tiled roof, and a beautiful stairway, making it striking both externally and internally. It retains a wealth of Arts and Crafts features – original and restored – including furniture designed by William Morris and Philip Webb, and stained glass and paintings by Edward Burne-Jones.

The garden is also significant. It was planned to harmonise with the building – 'to clothe the house' – and was one of the first gardens to be designed as a series of rooms.

The Red House was acquired by the National Trust in 2002 and has a tea-room and gift shop.

👁 DON'T MISS!

A trio of gorgeous frescos by Burne-Jones is one of the highlights of the Red House. Painted in 1860, they show scenes from the wedding of Sir Degrevant and his lady Melydor, a popular romantic tale from the early 15th century.

23 SHAKESPEARE'S GLOBE THEATRE EXHIBITION

Address: 21 New Globe Walk, Bankside, SE1 9DT (☎ 020-7902 1500, 💻 shakespearesglobe.com).
Opening hours: Exhibition, daily, 10am to 5pm. See website or telephone for information about tours (times vary). Closed 24-25th December.
Cost: Globe Theatre tour, £13.50 adults, £12 seniors (60+), £11 students, £8 children (5-15), under 5s free, £36 families (up to 2 adults & 3 children). Includes access to exhibition.
Transport: Blackfriars, London Bridge or Southwark tube.
Amenities: Restaurant, bar, shop, wheelchair access.

The first Globe Theatre was built in 1599 by William Shakespeare's company, the Lord Chamberlain's Men. It was destroyed by fire on 29th June 1613, but a second Globe Theatre was built on the same site by the following June and continued till 1642.

👁 DON'T MISS!

To really get a sense of how the Globe worked, it's worth attending a performance. If you don't mind standing with the groundlings, tickets can be purchased for as little as £5, while seats in the galleries start at £10. Contact the box office (☎ 020-7401 9919) or book online.

A modern reconstruction of the Globe, named Shakespeare's Globe, opened in 1997 approximately 750ft (230m) from the site of the original theatre. It's the only building in London permitted to have a thatched roof, and is faithful to the 1599 original in its design. It was founded by the pioneering American actor and director Sam Wanamaker (1919-1993) and is a unique international resource dedicated to the exploration of Shakespeare's work and the playhouse for which he wrote, through performance and education.

The Globe Exhibition & Tour gives you an opportunity to learn more about this fascinating building and Shakespeare. Based beneath the theatre, the exhibition uses modern technology and traditional crafts to explore the life of the Bard, the London where he lived and the theatre for which he wrote. But it's the tours that bring the theatre to life with colourful stories of the 1599 Globe, the reconstruction process and how the 'wooden O' works today. You can stand in the pit, where the 'groundlings' gather to watch the performances, and admire the oak-framed building and its massive stage.

In 2012, work was underway on an indoor Jacobean theatre adjacent to the open-air Globe, allowing plays to take place year-round.

WINCHESTER PALACE & CLINK PRISON MUSEUM

24

Address: Clink Prison Museum, 1 Clink Street, London SE1 9DG (☎ 020-7403 0900, 🖥 clink.co.uk). Winchester Palace ruins are also in Clink Street.

Opening hours: The Clink Prison Museum is open daily, July to September 10am to 9pm; October to June Mon-Fri 10am to 6pm, weekends 10am to 7.30pm. Closed Christmas Day. Ruins of Winchester Palace – unrestricted viewing but no access.

Cost: Clink Prison Museum – £7.50 adults, £5.50 children under 16, students and seniors, £15 families (2 adults and 2 children under 16). Winchester Palace is free.

Transport: London Bridge tube/rail.

Amenities: Wheelchair access.

The graphically-named Clink Street houses two of London's unsung attractions, the remains of Winchester Palace and the Clink Prison Museum. The ruins of the palace – former London residence of the Bishop of Winchester – gaze down majestically over the street, an unexpected rare fragment of history dating back to 1109. It consists mainly of a tall wall topped by an elegant, 13-foot hexagonal rose window dating from the 14th century on 12th-century foundations.

When the bishops moved to Chelsea in the 17th century, the Winchester Palace estate was outside the jurisdiction of the City. Known as the Liberty of the Clink, it became notorious for bull- and bear-baiting – and for brothels. Indeed, the area's prostitutes were known as 'Winchester geese'. The palace was subsequently divided into tenements and warehouses, but was mostly destroyed in a fire in 1814.

The Clink was the bishop's infamous jail (or gaol), in use from 1144 to 1780, and one of England's oldest prisons, if not the oldest. The name is thought to come from the sound of striking metal, either the prison's metal doors as they closed or the rattle of the prisoners' chains; hence the expression 'being in clink'. The prison was burned down in the anti-Catholic riots of 1780 and there's now a museum on the site which tells the history of the prison, policing, punishment and Southwark's colourful past. The exhibits include grisly instruments of torture – you can test the weight of a ball and chain (heavy!). The site is said to be actively haunted.

FOOD & DRINK

Tas Pide: Authentic Turkish pizzas baked in a wood-fired oven. One of the Tas chain (🖥 tasrestaurants. co.uk), it's located in nearby New Globe Street and well worth a visit.

Borough Market: A wide choice of places to eat in the foodies' favourite market.

25 BETHLEM ROYAL HOSPITAL MUSEUM

Address: Monks Orchard Road, Beckenham, BR3 3BX (☎ 020-3228 4227, 🖥 bethlemheritage.org.uk).
Opening hours: Mon-Fri, 9.30am to 4.30pm (archive by appointment) and selected Saturdays (see website). Closed on Bank Holidays and other statutory (NHS) holidays, plus 24th December to 2nd January.
Cost: Free.
Transport: Eden Park or West Wickham rail.
Amenities: Wheelchair access.

The ancient Bethlem Royal Hospital is a psychiatric hospital which was variously known as St Mary Bethlehem, Bethlehem Hospital, Bethlem Hospital and Bedlam. It's recognised as the world's first and oldest institution to specialise in mental illnesses and has been a part of London since 1247, initially as a priory for the sisters and brethren of the Order of the Star of Bethlehem (from where the hospital took its name). The hospital moved to its current home in 1930.

The museum (est. 1970) records the lives and experiences – and celebrates the achievements – of those with mental health problems. It includes items from the hospital's art collection, which specialises in work by artists who suffered from mental health problems, including former Bethlem patients Richard Dadd, William Kurelek, Vaslav Nijinsky and Louis Wain. Other notable exhibits include a pair of statues by Caius Gabriel Cibber, known as *Raving and Melancholy Madness*, which stood at the gates of the 17th-century Bethlem Hospital, as well as 18th- and 19th-century furniture and alms boxes, restraint devices and archive documents dating from the 16th century.

Raving Madness, Caius Gabriel Cibber

26 BLACK CULTURAL ARCHIVES

Address: 1 Othello Close, SE11 4RE (☎ 020-7582 8516, 🖥 bcaheritage.org.uk). The new venue will be at Raleigh Hall, Windrush Square, Brixton, SW9.
Opening hours: Wed, 10am to 12.30pm and 1.30-4.30pm. By appointment only.
Cost: Free.
Transport: Kennington tube.
Amenities: Wheelchair access.

The Black Cultural Archives were founded in 1981 to collect, preserve and celebrate the contributions black people have made to the culture, society and heritage of the UK.

The unique and growing archive collection offers an insight into the history of people of African descent in Britain and includes personal documents, organisational records, rare books and papers, ephemera, photographs and artefacts, oral history testimonies, and objects dating from the 2nd century to the present day.

In 2013, the Archives will be re-born as the UK's National Black Heritage Centre, based at Raleigh Hall in Brixton – a national institution dedicated to commemorating and celebrating the experiences of people of African and African-Caribbean descent in Britain. The new building will enable the public to access the permanent and growing archive collection, and will provide a platform to explore the histories and cultures, familiar and unfamiliar, of black people in the UK. You can follow developments and view some of the collection online via the website.

Erzulie

BRITISH MUSIC EXPERIENCE 27

Address: The O2 Arena, Peninsula Square, SE10 0DX (☎ 020-8463 2000, ⌨ britishmusicexperience.com and theo2.co.uk).
Opening hours: Daily, 11am to 7.30pm. Closed 24-26th and 31st December to 1st January.
Cost: £12 adults, £8 concessions, £6 children aged up to 17, under 5s free.
Transport: North Greenwich tube.
Amenities: The O2 has various restaurants, cafés and bars, wheelchair access.

The British Music Experience (BME) – located in the iconic O2 Arena – is a permanent interactive museum of popular music whose 'mission is to advance the education and appreciation of the art, history and science of music in Britain'. It does this by combining cutting-edge, audio-visual technology and a world-class collection and archive of popular music, including over 3,000 images, 3,000 artist videos, and more than 600 items of artist and music memorabilia, ranging from John Lennon's spectacles to Marc Bolan's guitar.

Opened in 2009, the BME provides a retrospective look at the British music industry since 1944, and features a wide selection of content and experiences, from the classic era defining sounds of The Beatles, Rolling Stones and Dusty Springfield, to stadium filling giants such as The Who and Queen, and more recent crowd-pleasers such as Oasis, Coldplay and the Arctic Monkeys. You can experience classic 'live' performances, learn to dance The Twist and even record your own 'hits' in the Gibson Interactive Studio.

The BME also presents special exhibitions, public events and concerts (see website for information).

28   CAFÉ GALLERY & DILSTON GROVE

> **Address:** Southwark Park, SE16 2UA (☎ 020-7237 1230, 💻 cgplondon.org).
> **Opening hours**: Wed-Sun, noon to 6pm in summer and 11am to 4pm in winter.
> **Cost**: Free.
> **Transport**: Canada Water tube/rail or South Bermondsey rail.
> **Amenities:** Café, wheelchair access.

Collectively called CGP London, this artist-led initiative encompasses two venues in Southwark Park: the purpose built Café Gallery, comprising three interlinked 'white room' spaces and a patio garden, and Dilston Grove (Grade II listed – formerly Clare College Mission Church), which provides a cavernous space for large-scale installations and performance, a reception area and a learning space.

CGP London was founded in 1984 by the Bermondsey Artists' Group with the remit to develop community relationships as a core part of its programme of group and solo exhibitions, workshops and talks.

Artists who have shown at the venues include David Blandy, Mat Collishaw, Suzanne Treister, Richard Wilson, and Pil and Galia Kollectiv. Dilston Grove projects have included Ackroyd & Harvey's seeding of its outside walls with grass and Michael Cross's *Bridge*, a series of steps which rose up and sank down beneath the waterline of the flooded building, allowing observers to feel as if they were walking on water.

29   CHARLTON HOUSE

> **Address:** Charlton Road, Charlton, SE7 8RE (☎ 020-8856 3951,
> 💻 charlton-house.org).
> **Opening hours**: Exhibition area, Mon-Fri, 8.30am to 6pm. Peace Garden, daily 10am to 5pm in summer (dusk in winter). Mulberry Tea Rooms, Mon-Fri 9am to 4pm. The house isn't fully open to the general public, although it can be hired for events.
> **Cost**: Free.
> **Transport**: Charlton rail.
> **Amenities:** Tea rooms, gardens, wheelchair access.

Charlton House is one of London's least-known architectural gems, a magnificent Jacobean mansion improbably situated in unfashionable Charlton. Regarded as Greater London's best-preserved Jacobean house and one of England's finest examples of Jacobean domestic architecture, it commands an impressive site on a hill overlooking lawns and trees at the heart of Charlton village.

Charlton House was constructed between 1607 and 1612 (architect unknown, but thought to be John Thorpe) from red brick with stone dressing, with an 'E'-plan layout. It was built for Sir Adam Newton (who's buried in nearby St Luke's Church), Dean of Durham and tutor to Prince Henry, son of James I and elder brother of the future Charles I. Prince Henry died the year the house was completed. Another famous connection is with Inigo Jones, who it's claimed designed the Orangery, built in 1630.

The house was acquired by Greenwich Council in 1925 and later became a public library and community centre. An exhibition about the history of the house, the magnificent gardens and the tea rooms are open to the public.

CITY HALL ART GALLERY 30

Address: The Queen's Walk, SE1 2AA (☎ 020-7983 4000, 🖥 london.gov.uk/get-involved/exhibitions-other-events).
Opening hours: Mon-Fri, 8.30am to 6pm (Fri, 5.30pm).
Cost: Free.
Transport: London Bridge tube.
Amenities: Café, wheelchair access.

City Hall is a striking building in Southwark on the south bank of the Thames. Designed by Norman Foster, it opened in July 2002. Despite the name, it's nothing to do with the City of London, which has its HQ in the Guildhall, but is the headquarters of the Greater London Authority which represents the 32 boroughs of Greater London. The building has an unusual bulbous shape – described by former mayor Ken Livingstone as a 'glass testicle' – designed to improve energy efficiency, and it incorporates many environmentally-friendly features such as solar panels.

A 1,640ft (500m) helical walkway ascends the full height of the ten-storey building, at the top of which is an exhibition and meeting space called London's Living Room, with an open viewing deck that's occasionally open to the public. The walkway provides views of the interior of the building and is intended to symbolise transparency.

City Hall has a free art gallery which hosts an on-going programme of exhibitions, on topics usually relating to London or created by Londoners (see website for information). There's a café on the lower ground floor.

31 DANSON HOUSE

Address: Danson Park, Bexleyheath, DA6 8HL (☎ 01322-526574,
🖥 bexleyheritagetrust.org.uk/dansonhouse).
Opening hours: Sun-Thu, 10am to 5pm, April to October (see website for exact
dates and times).
Cost: £7 adults, £5 concessions, children under 16 free when accompanied by an
adult. Discount for English Heritage members.
Transport: Bexleyheath rail.
Amenities: Tea room, pub, shop, park, wheelchair access.

Grade I listed Danson House is a Georgian mansion situated in Danson Park (itself Grade II listed) in Bexleyheath. Originally called Danson Hill, the Palladian villa was designed by Sir Robert Taylor (1714-1788), architect to the Bank of England (succeeded by Sir John Soane), and constructed in 1764-67 for sugar merchant and vice-chairman of the British East India Company, Sir John Boyd (1718-1800).

The estate passed through several owners before being acquired by Bexley Urban District Council in 1924. The park opened to the public in 1925, but the house remained uninhabited and was acquired by English Heritage in 1995 in a dangerously dilapidated condition. After a decade of work, it was finally restored, decorated and furnished in its original 18th-century style. The principal floor is sumptuous, with a fine entrance hall, a stunning dining room with the original 18th-century wall paintings, an elegant salon and an opulent library containing a rare George England organ.

The house has a shop and a café with a terrace, while the estate's stable block is now a public house called, aptly, the Danson Stables.

32 DESIGN MUSEUM

Address: 28 Shad Thames, Bermondsey, SE1 2YD (☎ 020-7940 8790,
🖥 designmuseum.org).
Opening hours: Daily, 10am to 5.45pm. Closed 25-26th December. The museum
holds regular events and talks during the evenings (see website for details).
Cost: Exhibitions, £10 adults, £9 concessions, £6 students.
Transport: Tower Hill tube, Tower Gateway DLR or London Bridge tube/rail.
Amenities: Café, shop, wheelchair access.

As a city that's famous for its wealth of creative industries, it's only fitting that London should have a dedicated Design Museum. It's housed in a suitably striking home, a former '40s banana warehouse transformed to resemble a '30s Modernist building, with impressive views of Tower Bridge.

It's a leading centre for contemporary design in every form, from architecture to furniture, graphics to industrial design, and hosts a comprehensive programme of temporary exhibitions which are displayed over two floors and in the 'Design Museum Tank' space by the waterfront. The museum also has a

permanent collection (see
💻 designmuseum.org/collection) of
over 2,000 classic objects – ranging
from a red phone box to a Kalashnikov
AK-47 assault rifle – although they
aren't on permanent display.

The museum stages the annual
Brit Insurance 'Designs of the Year'
exhibition, which explores the most
innovative designs of the previous year
from around the world in architecture,
fashion, furniture, graphics, interactive,
product and transport.

The Blue Print Café on the first
floor has received rave reviews and is a
great vantage point from which to soak
up the river views.

GASWORKS 33

Address: 155 Vauxhall Street, SE11 5RH (☎ 020-7587 5202, 💻 gasworks.org.uk).
Opening hours: Wed-Sun, noon to 6pm.
Cost: Free.
Transport: Oval or Vauxhall tube.
Amenities: Wheelchair access.

Established in 1994, Gasworks
is part of the Triangle Arts Trust
(💻 trianglearts.org), an international
network of artists and organisations
formed in 1982 whose activities include
residencies and workshops. Gasworks
is a contemporary arts organisation

housing 12 artists' studios, a number
of which are filled by non-UK based
artists on an international residency
programme. The aim of the highly
successful programme is the exchange
of ideas and techniques to enable
artists to further the creative direction of
their careers.

Gasworks stages four main projects
a year, as well as a series of small-
scale events, ranging from solo and
thematic exhibitions (by both resident
and non-resident artists) to research-
oriented projects. The most exciting
tend to be the exhibitions by artists
who collaborate with fellow residents
to produce hugely ambitious projects
that use the space to the best of its
potential.

Exhibitions are complemented
by related events including artists'
talks, seminars, screenings and
performances.

34 GOLDEN HINDE

Address: 1 & 2 Pickfords Wharf, Clink Street, SE1 9DG (☎ 020-7403 0123, 🖥 goldenhinde.com).
Opening hours: Daily, 10am to 5.30pm.
Cost: £6 adults, £4.50 concessions and children aged 4-16, £18 families.
Transport: London Bridge tube/rail.
Amenities: Shop, no wheelchair access.

The *Golden Hinde* is a replica of the galleon in which Sir Francis Drake (1540-96) circumnavigated the globe. Drake is now more famous as second-in-command of the English fleet that destroyed the Spanish Armada in 1588, but he was also a notable privateer, authorised by Queen Elizabeth I to attack and loot ships belonging to England's enemies – in effect the Spanish.

In 1577 Drake left Plymouth with five small ships on a voyage which would take him three years; the *Golden Hinde* was the only vessel to complete the voyage, hence her fame. On Drake's return, Elizabeth decreed that the ship should be preserved at Deptford so that the public could visit and celebrate Drake's and England's success. Thus the *Golden Hinde* became Britain's first museum ship although sadly, by the late 17th century she had rotted away.

The replica *Golden Hinde*, a fully working ship, was launched in Devon in 1973 and has since sailed over 140,000 miles, many more than the original. Visits are great fun for children, with regular events such as Pirate Parties – check the website for details and dates.

35 HALL PLACE

Address: Bourne Road, Bexley, DA5 1PQ. (☎ 01322-526574, 🖥 hallplace.org.uk).
Opening hours: **House** – 1st April to 31st October, daily 10am to 5pm; 1st November to 31st March, Mon-Sat 10am to 4pm, Sun and Bank Holidays 11am to 4pm. Closed 24-26th December and 31st December to 1st January. **Gardens** – daily 9am to dusk.
Cost: £7 adults, £5 concessions and under 16s, £20 Families (2 adults and up to 3 children).
Transport: Bexley rail.
Amenities: Restaurant, café, pub, shop, gardens, wheelchair access.

Hall Place (Grade I listed) is a former stately home on a beautiful 160-acre (65ha) estate beside the River Cray on the outskirts of Crayford (Bexley). Dating from around 1537, the Hall was built by wealthy merchant Sir

John Champneys (former Lord Mayor of London) using stone recycled from nearby Lesnes Abbey. The borough of Bexley became the owner of the estate and Hall Place in 1935.

Much of the house that Sir John built still survives. Constructed on a traditional, hierarchical plan, the core consisted of a splendid central great hall with a minstrel's gallery, crossed at one end by a service wing and the other by high status family accommodation, including a parlour and great chamber. The outer walls have a distinctive checkerboard pattern made of flint and rubble masonry, a beautiful example of the Tudor love of pattern. Seventeenth-century additions and improvements include a vaulted Long Gallery and a spectacular Great Chamber with a fine plaster ceiling.

Displays include the house's history and exhibits from Bexley's museum collection, plus contemporary art exhibitions.

LONDON FILM MUSEUM 36

Address: 1st Floor, County Hall, Queens Walk, South Bank, SE1 7PB (☎ 020-7202 7040, 🖳 londonfilmmuseum.com).
Opening hours: Mon-Fri, 10am to 5pm (Thu from 11am), Sat 10am to 6pm, Sun 11am to 6pm. Closed 25th December.
Cost: £13.50 adults, £11.50 concessions (includes local residents), £9.50 child (up to age 15), under 5s free.
Transport: Waterloo tube/rail.
Amenities: Wheelchair access (advance notification required).

The London Film Museum (previously The Movieum) was founded and created by Jonathan Sands in February 2008. It's located in iconic County Hall and dedicated to the silver screen, in particular the British film industry. Some 80 per cent of the museum's collection is from Sands' private archive.

The museum displays an enormous collection of original screen costumes and props from films such as *Superman*, *Star Wars*, *The Italian Job* and *Batman*, as well as the J Arthur Rank gong. There's also a section on how films are made, including information about all the major studios. Permanent exhibitions include Charlie Chaplin – Great Londoner, which traces the life and career of Chaplin, the boy from the London slums who won universal fame with his screen character of the Tramp, while recent temporary exhibitions have included Myths and Legends about the special effects maestro Ray Harryhausen.

The museum receives mixed reviews and is eye-wateringly expensive – perhaps something only for fanatical movie buffs. There's also a branch in Covent Garden.

37 LONDON FIRE BRIGADE MUSEUM

Address: Winchester House, 94A Southwark Bridge Road, SE1 0EG (☎ 020-8555 1200, 🖳 london-fire.gov.uk/ourmuseum.asp).
Opening hours: Guided tours (Mon to Fri, 10.30am and 2pm) must be booked in advance.
Cost: £5 adults, £3 children (under 16), concessions and groups.
Transport: Borough or Southwark tube.
Amenities: Shop, no wheelchair access.

The London Fire Brigade (LFB) museum traces the history of fire-fighting in London from the Great Fire, through two world wars to the present day. The museum is located at Winchester House, former residence of the Brigade's first chief officer, Captain Sir Eyre Massey Shaw (1830-1908), and contains a wealth of historic fire-fighting equipment, including a unique collection of fire engines. There are displays dedicated to the Great Fire and the Blitz, and a reconstruction of a Victorian fire station.

The need for a professional fire service was apparent from 1666, when the Great Fire destroyed 80 per cent of the City. At the time fire-fighters had only leather buckets, axes and water squirts, and the fire wasn't halted until the navy blew up houses in its path.

Following a multitude of ad-hoc fire-fighting arrangements, it wasn't until several large fires – most notably the Palace of Westminster in 1834 and warehouses by the River Thames in 1861 – spurred the government into providing a fire brigade at public expense. In 1865 the Metropolitan Fire Brigade was created, renamed the London Fire Brigade in 1904.

38 LONDON GLASSBLOWING STUDIO & GALLERY

Address: 62-66 Bermondsey Street, SE1 3UD (☎ 020-7403 2800, 🖳 londonglassblowing.co.uk).
Opening hours: Mon-Sat, 10am to 6pm; occasional Sundays (see website).
Cost: Free.
Transport: Borough tube or London Bridge tube/rail.
Amenities: Shop, wheelchair access.

The London Glassblowing studio and gallery was established by Peter Layton in 1976 (in an old factory at Rotherhithe), and was among the first hot-glass studios in Europe. Since 2009, it's been located on vibrant Bermondsey Street, opposite the Fashion and Textile Museum, in a light, spacious gallery ideal for the display of contemporary glass.

Peter Layton is one of the world's most respected glassblowers and has done much to promote glassmaking as an art form. Some glassmakers create technically brilliant pieces and follow a precise pattern, while others – including Layton – produce more abstract works that evolve during the creative process. Layton, whose influences include nature, travel and artists such as David Hockney, is noted for his strong use of colour, organic forms and the sculptural quality of his larger pieces.

Much of the richly coloured glass art on display – most of which is for sale – is Layton's own work, which can be found in museums, galleries and exhibitions across the UK, Europe and the US.

The studio has a schedule of exhibitions (see website for information).

LONDON SEWING MACHINE MUSEUM 39

Address: 292-312 Balham High Road, SW17 7AA (☎ 020-8682 7916, ✉ wimbledonsewingmachinecoltd@btinternet.com).
Opening hours: First Saturday of each month, 2-5pm.
Cost: Free.
Transport: Tooting Bec tube.
Amenities: No wheelchair access.

The London Sewing Machine Museum – part of the Wimbledon Sewing Machine Company (WSMC) – charts the history and evolution of the sewing machine, both domestic and industrial, from 1850 to1950. The small, two-room museum features some 700 different types of machines, accumulated by Thomas Albert Rushton (1900-74), founder of the WSMC. A replica of his first sewing machine shop and workshop can also be seen in the museum.

Exhibits include the first singer No. 1 machine developed in 1855 (the first sewing machine produced by Isaac Merritt Singer), a machine owned by Charlie Chaplin, and a patent machine from America sent over for the Great Exhibition in 1851. The centrepiece is a German machine made for Princess Victoria, the eldest daughter of Queen Victoria, as a wedding gift. The collection also includes industrial machines from the times when there was a flourishing textile trade in the north of England. Although most of the mills and factories have long gone, some of the machines have been saved for posterity by the museum.

40 MORLEY GALLERY

Address: 61 Westminster Bridge Road, SE1 7HT (☏ 020-7450 1826,
🖥 morleycollege.ac.uk/morley_gallery, ✉ gallery@morleycollege.ac.uk).
Opening hours: Check individual exhibitions for opening hours.
Cost: Free.
Transport: Lambeth North tube.
Amenities: Café, wheelchair access.

Morley College is an adult education college founded in the 1880s. Today it has a student population of over 10,000, offering courses in a wide variety of fields including arts, science, languages, drama, dance, music, computing, health and humanities.

Morley Gallery opened in 1968 as part of the Arts Centre in Morley College and is housed in a former pub across the road from the main college building. It hosts a busy programme of public exhibitions, showcasing a wide range of art forms, including painting and drawing, printmaking, sculpture, photography, ceramics, textiles, installation and sound art. The majority of the programme celebrates the creative talents of the staff and students at Morley, in addition to exhibitions by independent artists and members of the local community. Peter Blake and Maggie Hambling are among the major names who have exhibited here.

Morley is home to several artworks created and donated by distinguished artists over the years. Of particular interest are a series of murals painted by Edward Bawden in the early '60s, which depict scenes from Chaucer's *Canterbury Tales* and are unique to Morley.

41 MUSEUM OF CONTEMPORARY ART

Address: 113 Bellenden Rd, SE15 4QY (🖥 mocalondon.co.uk).
Opening hours: Thu-Sat, 2-6pm during exhibitions.
Cost: Free.
Transport: Peckham Rye rail or 12, 36 or 171 bus.
Amenities: Wheelchair access.

The Museum of Contemporary Art (MOCA) – which isn't a museum or gallery in the accepted sense – was founded in 1994 as a project-based museum. It mounted a series of international exhibitions 'presenting unique and challenging contemporary work' incorporating sculpture, video, painting, photography and installation.

In January 2004, MOCA opened a project space in the Bellenden Renewal Area in Peckham to initiate a series of exhibitions. The space offers established and upcoming artists the possibility of making non-commercial work, developing projects over various periods of time to suit both the artist and MOCA. This co-operative style of working means that the project space has no formal exhibition structure and works are in situ when they are ready.

Past projects have included Ristorante Santo Food Turismo celebrating 100 years of Futurism; The Challenger Disaster Re-Visited by artist duo Dash MacDonald and Demitrios Kargotis; and Gradient Change looking at art and science. See website for current and future projects.

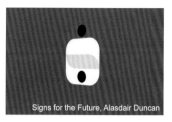

Signs for the Future, Alasdair Duncan

MUSEUM OF CROYDON 45

Address: Level 1, Croydon Clocktower, Katharine Street, Croydon, CR9 1ET (☎ 020-8253 1022, 💻 museumofcroydon.com).
Opening hours: Mon-Sat, 11am to 5pm, including most Bank Holidays (but check before travelling).
Cost: Free.
Transport: East Croydon rail, then Tramlink to George Street.
Amenities: Café, library, wheelchair access.

This appealing local museum is housed within the Croydon Clocktower arts facility – the majestic Clocktower (Grade II listed) is part of the original town hall and library

complex, built in 1892-96. The museum opened in 2006 and showcases historical and cultural artefacts associated with the borough of Croydon. It's an eclectic collection presented in a timeline of five galleries, from 1800 to the present day, with exhibits ranging from a Victorian baby's bottle to a fragment of the Berlin Wall.

The museum's main attraction is the stunning Riesco Collection of Chinese ceramics, donated to the people of Croydon by local businessman Raymond Riesco. The whole collection – numbering some 230 items dating from the pre-Tang period to the Qing dynasty (2,500 BC to the 18th century) – is on permanent display in the Riesco Gallery.

The museum is also home to the Croydon art collection containing over 2,000 paintings, prints and drawings, including prints by Henry Moore and Bridget Riley and paintings by Bengali poet Rabindranath Tagore. It isn't on permanent display – although selections are shown in temporary exhibitions – but can be viewed by appointment.

43 OLD OPERATING THEATRE & HERB GARRET

Address: 9A St Thomas's Street, Southwark, SE1 9RY (☎ 020-7188 2679,
🖳 thegarret.org.uk).
Opening hours: Daily, 10.30am to 5pm. Closed from mid-December to early
January (see website).
Cost: £6 adults, £5 concessions, £3.50 under-16s, £13.90 families (2 adults and up
to 4 children).
Transport: London Bridge tube/rail.
Amenities: Shop, limited wheelchair access.

Tucked away between London
Bridge Station and Guy's Hospital,
the Old Operating Theatre is a museum
of surgical history, evocatively situated
in the garret (roof space – a herb garret
is a place for curing and storing herbs)
of one of the world's oldest surviving
operating theatres (1822). The garret
is located in the (now disused) English
Baroque church of St Thomas's
(ca. 1703) on the original site of St
Thomas's Hospital, which dates back
to the 12th century when it was part of
a monastery.

The rows of raised terraces
encircling the operating theatre
underline the fact that 19th-century
surgery was often performed in
front of an audience of students and
apprentices.

The museum also displays a
collection of objects relating to medical
history and that of St Thomas's and
Guy's hospitals, many of which reveal
the grisliness of medicine before the
age of science. This was a time before
anaesthetics (which weren't an option
until 1847, when ether and chloroform
became available) and surgeons had
to work as quickly as possible, while
sawdust was spread on the floor to
soak up the copious amounts of blood.

44 ROSE THEATRE

Address: 56 Park Street, SE1 9AS (☎ 020-7261 9565, 🖳 rosetheatre.org.uk).
Opening hours: Saturdays 10am to 5pm. See website for information about tours,
open days and productions.
Cost: Visits and open days are free, but donations are welcome.
Transport: London Bridge tube/rail.
Amenities: Wheelchair access.

The Rose was an Elizabethan
theatre built in 1587 by Philip
Henslowe. It was only the fifth purpose-
built theatre in London and the first
on Bankside – an area already rich
in other 'leisure attractions' such as
brothels, gaming dens and bull/bear-
baiting arenas. Although the opening
of the Globe in 1599 signalled the

Rose Theatre's demise, it remains London's most historic theatre, the first Elizabethan theatre on Bankside, and home to many of Shakespeare's and Marlowe's first productions.

Its well-preserved archaeology was discovered in 1989 during exploratory excavation for an office block. At present two-thirds of the original foundations have been excavated, and there are plans to make the site a permanent display as a public educational and historical resource.

In 2007, part of The Rose was opened as a performance space with actors performing plays contemporaneous with the original theatre although productions of more modern plays are also featured (phone or see website for ticket information). The Rose also holds workshops, tours and has free open days throughout the year.

ROYAL PHARMACEUTICAL SOCIETY MUSEUM `45`

Address: 1 Lambeth High Street, SE1 7JN (☏ 020-7572 2211, ▭ rpharms.com/about-pharmacy/our-museum.asp).
Opening hours: Mon-Fri, 9am to 5pm for ground floor displays (no booking necessary). Closed Bank Holidays. Tours Tuesdays and Thursdays (1½-2 hrs – pre-booking necessary).
Cost: Free for ground floor displays. There may be a fee for tours.
Transport: Lambeth North tube or Waterloo tube/rail.
Amenities: Wheelchair access.

The Royal Pharmaceutical Society (RPS) Museum is an absorbing museum founded in 1842 as a scientific collection of *materia medica* for use by pharmacy students. The museum moved to its current site in Lambeth (along with the rest of the RPS) in 1976.

The museum provides a wide range of services and activities for anyone interested in pharmacy. It contains a unique collection of around 45,000 objects covering all aspects of the history of British pharmacy, including traditional dispensing equipment; drug storage containers (including fine 'Lambeth delftware' jars from the 17th and 18th centuries); proprietary 'brand name' medicines dating from the 18th century to the present day; bronze mortars; medical caricatures; and a photo archive.

The ground floor area contains displays on themes of The Evolving Pharmacy and Lambeth's Pharmacy Past, which reveal how pharmacies have changed over time. Other displays focus on unusual medicines, such as 18th-century seahorses and antique equipment used to make and store drugs. There's also a rotating exhibition on the Developing Treatments theme, which focuses on the way that different medical conditions have been treated over time.

46 SOUTH LONDON GALLERY

Address: 65-67 Peckham Road, SE5 8UH (☎ 020-7703 6120,
🖥 southlondongallery.org).
Opening hours: Tue-Sun, 11am to 6pm (Wed and the last Fri of the month, until
9pm). Closed Mondays.
Cost: Free.
Transport: Oval or Vauxhall tube, then 36 or 436 bus. Alight at Peckham Road/
Southampton Way.
Amenities: Café, shop, garden, wheelchair access.

The South London Gallery (or SLG, as it's widely known) is a publicly-funded gallery of contemporary art in Camberwell. Founded in 1891, when it was called the South London Fine Art Gallery, it occupied various locations until moving to its current, purpose-built home constructed of Portland stone and hand-made pressed bricks, much favoured by the Arts and Crafts tradition of the time.

The gallery's permanent collection includes over five hundred 20th-century prints and contemporary works by modern British artists relating to south London (although it isn't on public display). The gallery's profile and visitor numbers have grown in recent decades during which it has staged exhibitions by internationally acclaimed artists such as Gilbert & George, Anselm Kiefer and Sherrie Levine, as well as younger artists such as Gavin Turk, Ann Sofi-Sidén and Tracey Emin – it was the first gallery to display Emin's famous 'tent', entitled *Everyone I Have Ever Slept With 1963-1995*.

In 2010, the gallery opened additional buildings (designed by 6a Architects) which provide new small-scale galleries, an acclaimed café, gardens, and an education and events studio.

47 TOPOLSKI CENTURY GALLERY

Address: 150-152 Hungerford Arches, South Bank, SE1 8XU (☎ 07882-843141,
🖥 topolskicentury.org.uk).
Opening hours: Tours by appointment only.
Cost: Free.
Transport: Waterloo tube/rail.
Amenities: Wheelchair access.

The Topolski Century Gallery is Polish artist Feliks Topolski's monumental painting and a unique eye-witness account of many iconic events and personalities of the 20th century. Topolski was born in Warsaw on 14th August 1907 and studied at the Warsaw Academy of Art from 1927-1932. He came to Britain in 1935 and was a prominent war artist during the Second World War. He was also a fine portraitist and made face-to-face portraits of the leading personalities of the 20th century, including Gandhi, Churchill and Martin Luther King, as well as stage and screen giants such as Edith Evans, Alec Guinness and Laurence Olivier.

In 1975, Topolski began work on the painted panorama he called *Memoir of the Century*, now renamed the *Topolski Century*, which he worked on until his death in 1989. This permanent exhibition is a collection of murals (600ft long and up to 20ft high!) arranged beneath two railway arches, which depicts Topolski's personal record of the 20th century. You can take a virtual tour on the website.

The Topolski Century Gallery offers private tours, educational programmes and events.

TOWER BRIDGE EXHIBITION 48

Address: Tower Bridge Road, SE1 2UP (☎ 020-7403 3761, 🖥 towerbridge.org.uk/tbe).
Opening hours: Daily, April to September, 10am to 6pm; October to March, 9.30am to 5,30pm. Closed 24-26th December and open from 10am on 1st January.
Cost: £8 adults, £5.60 concessions, £3.40 children (5-15), under 5s free, families from £12.50.
Transport: Tower Hill tube.
Amenities: Wheelchair access.

Constructed between 1886 and 1894, Tower Bridge takes its name from the nearby Tower of London (see page 102) and is a combined bascule (a moveable bridge which 'opens' to allow ships to pass through) and suspension bridge. It's an iconic symbol of London and one of the most famous bridges in the world.

The exhibition uses films, photos and interactive displays to explain why and how the bridge was built, while the high-level walkways serve as viewing galleries, offering stunning views of the River Thames and London's landmarks. The East Walkway houses the exhibition Great Bridges of the World, a photographic exhibition featuring over 20 bridges, each representing a ground-breaking feat of engineering.

Visitors can see the original lifting machinery in the Victorian engine rooms, including the steam engines that once powered the bridge bascules (while still operated by hydraulic power, they are now driven by oil and electricity), housed in a building close to the south end of the bridge. You can also experience a virtual bridge lift, which provides a unique view of the bascules being raised.

APPENDICES

APPENDIX A: USEFUL WEBSITES

20/21 British Art Fair (britishartfair.co.uk). Annual event (September) at the Royal College of Art that has been showcasing British art for a quarter of a century.

Aesthetica (aestheticamagazine.com). The UK's leading art, culture and design magazine.

Affordable Art Fair (affordableartfair.com). Annual events at Battersea Park (March) and Hampstead (June) to encourage would-be art investors.

Animal Art Fair (animalartfair.co.uk). View works by many of the greatest contemporary animal artists at this annual event (June) on the Southbank.

Art Angel (artangel.org.uk). Commissions and produces exceptional projects by outstanding contemporary artists throughout the UK.

Art Daily (artdaily.org). The first art 'newspaper' on the net – international coverage.

Art Fund (artfund.org). The national fundraising charity for art. Offers the **National Art Pass** which provides free entry to over 200 UK museums, galleries and historic houses.

Art Info (artinfo.com). Comprehensive international art information from Louise Blouin Media, the world's leading cultural media group. Also publishes *Art+Auction* magazine.

Art, Media, Photography (artmediaphotography.com). A good portal for art lovers with a wealth of links.

Art Newspaper (theartnewspaper.com). The voice of the British art world offering monthly printed and digital versions.

Artnet (artnet.com). Allows you to buy, sell and research fine art online, with a comprehensive auction price database.

ArtLondon.net (artlondon.net). Independent online magazine and blog covering the capital's art scene.

Art Rabbit (artrabbit.com). An open and reactive forum, ArtRabbit connects individuals, artists, galleries, museums and collectors via comprehensive listings and opinion.

Arts Council England (artscouncil.org.uk). Supports a range of activities across the arts, museums and libraries.

Artsline (artsline.org.uk). A disabled led Charity that promotes access for disabled people to arts and entertainment venues.

Asian Art in London (asianartinlondon.com). An annual event for London's leading Asian art dealers, joining together for a series of auctions and (selling) exhibitions during ten days in November.

BBC Arts London (bbc.co.uk/london/entertainment/visual_arts/index.shtml). BBC London's visual arts pages.

Contemporary Art Society (contemporaryartsociety.org). Founded in 1910, the CAS develops public collections of contemporary art in the UK.

Cork Street Open Exhibition (corkstreetopenexhibition.com). The UK's fastest growing independent open exhibition filling two large galleries (in January and August) in Mayfair.

Engage (engage.org). The national association for gallery education that promotes access (to), understanding and enjoyment of visual arts in the UK and worldwide.

English Heritage (english-heritage.org.uk). Manages historic houses and sites throughout the UK and champions and protects the country's historic places.

Evening Standard (standard.co.uk/arts/visual-arts). The *Evening Standard* newspaper's guide to London's visual arts' scene.

Fine Art London (fineartslondon.com). An excellent fine art blog.

First Thursdays (firstthursdays.co.uk) and **Fitzrovia Lates** (fitzrovialates. co.uk). Promote late opening of selected galleries in East London and Fitzrovia (respectively) on the first Thursday or last Thursday (Fitzrovia) of each month.

Frieze London (friezelondon.com). Held in Regent's Park, Frieze is one of London's most important contemporary art events, which in 2012 presented over 170 international galleries and more than 1,000 artists.

Galleries Magazine (galleries.co.uk). Monthly magazine providing comprehensive information about current shows with links to gallery and artist sites.

Londonart (londonart.co.uk). One of the first websites to show and sell art online. Stages pop-up exhibitions around London.

Londonist (londonist.com/tags/arts). News about London's art exhibitions, galleries, museums, fairs and artists.

London Art Fair (londonartfair.co.uk). London Art Fair (January, Business Design Centre, Islington, N1) features over 100 galleries presenting the great names of British art and exceptional contemporary work.

London Art News (coxsoft.blogspot.co.uk). Blog previewing art exhibitions in London.

London Artist Quarter (londonsartistquarter.org). Site run by the Bow Arts Trust (bowarts.org) that supports and promotes art in East London.

London Drum (londondrum.com/events/?cat=4). What's on in London's Art Galleries.

London Museums & Galleries (london-galleries.co.uk). Comprehensive list of London's art galleries, both public and commercial, with website links.

London Net (londonnet.co.uk/ln/guide/about/museums.html). Guide to London's museums.

London Open House (londonopenhouse.org). An annual celebration (September) of London's architecture, offering free access to some 800 buildings over a weekend.

London Pass (londonpass.com). Provides entry to over 55 London attractions and tours, and allows you to avoid the queues.

Londonphile (thelondonphile.com). Exploring London's museums, heritage, architecture and culture.

Love Art London (loveartlondon.com). A membership 'club' that arranges behind the scenes visits to London's art venues, galleries, museums and artists' studios.

Medical Museums (medicalmuseums.org). Information and links to London's museums of health and medicine.

Museum Mile (museum-mile.org.uk). Discover 13 of the city's most extraordinary museums and their equally diverse collections.

Museums Association (museumsassociation.org). Membership organisation for those working in museums, galleries and heritage.

Mutual Art (mutualart.com). An online art information service (launched in 2008) that provides art enthusiasts, collectors and professionals with information about artists, exhibitions, auctions, art fairs, galleries, news and more.

National Trust (thenationaltrust.org.uk). Protects historic houses and their contents, plus a wealth of nature reserves and special sites, and opens them for everyone to enjoy.

New Exhibitions of Contemporary Art (newexhibitions.com). Publishes the bi-monthly *New Exhibitions* magazine, distributed via UK art galleries, museums and art venues.

One Stop Arts (onestoparts.com). Comprehensive information and reviews about London's arts' events, including museums and visual arts.

Royal Academy (royalacademy.org.uk). The UK's leading organisation for artists. The Academy's summer exhibition (June-August) is one of the highlights of the London art year.

Society of London Art Dealers (slad.org.uk). Principal trade association in the UK for dealers in visual art.

South London Art Map (southlondonartmap.com). Guide to South London galleries and also operates tours and hosts a late night opening of galleries on the last Friday of each month.

Spoonfed (spoonfed.co.uk/london/art). News about London art, exhibitions, museums and galleries.

Street Art London (streetartlondon.co.uk). Offers tours of London's street art.

Time Out (timeout.com/london/art). Art reviews and listings of London's best museum and gallery exhibitions.

Trip Advisor (tripadvisor.co.uk). Get the inside track on the places you plan to visit from people who've been there already.

Viewfinder (viewfinder.org.uk). Brings you the latest photography news and previews/reviews of London's top exhibitions and events.

Wallpaper (wallpaper.com). The über-trendy design, fashion and lifestyle magazine with extensive cover of London's arts scene.

Wikipedia (en.wikipedia.org/wiki/list_of_museums_in_london). Wiki's comprehensive information pages for London museums.

SUBJECT INDEX

Art: Oriental

Archaeology

Architecture

Artists, Architects & Writers' Homes

Local History

Medicine

Sport

Theatre & Cinema

Transport

Living and Working in London

ISBN: 978-1-907339-50-9

6th edition

Graeme Chesters

£14.95

Living and Working in London, first published in 2000 and now in its 6th edition, is the most comprehensive book available about daily life – and essential reading for newcomers. What's it really like Living and Working in London? Not surprisingly there's a lot more to life than bobbies, beefeaters and busbys! This book is guaranteed to hasten your introduction to the London way of life, irrespective of whether you're planning to stay for a few months or indefinitely. Adjusting to day to day life in London just got a whole lot simpler!

Where to Live in London

ISBN: 978-1-907339-13-4

David Hampshire & Graeme Chesters

£15.95

Essential reading for newcomers planning to live in London, containing detailed surveys of all 33 boroughs including property prices and rental costs, schools, health services, shopping, social services, crime rates, public transport, parking, leisure facilities, local taxes, places of worship and much more. Interest in living in London and investing in property in London has never been higher, both from Britons and foreigners.

INDEX

H

I/J

K

L

London Sketchbook

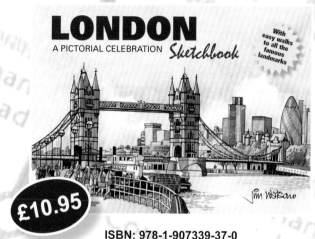

With easy walks to all the famous landmarks

£10.95

ISBN: 978-1-907339-37-0

Jim Watson

A celebration of one of the world's great cities, London Sketchbook is packed with over 200 evocative watercolour illustrations of the author's favourite landmarks and sights. The illustrations are accompanied by historical footnotes, maps, walks, quirky facts and a gazetteer.

Also in this series:

Cornwall Sketchbook (ISBN: 9781907339417, £10.95)
Cotswold Sketchbook (ISBN: 9781907339108, £9.95)
Lake District Sketchbook (ISBN: 9781907339097, £9.95)

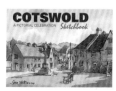

All available at www.survivalbooks.net

PHOTO CREDITS

London's Secrets

£10.95

LONDON'S SECRET PLACES

ISBN: 978-1-907339-92-9, Graeme Chesters & David Hampshire

London is one of the world's leading tourist destinations with a wealth of world-class attractions: amazing museums and galleries, beautiful parks and gardens, stunning palaces and grand houses, and much, much more. These are covered in numerous excellent tourist guides and online, and need no introduction here. Not so well known are London's numerous smaller attractions, most of which are neglected by the throngs who descend upon the tourist-clogged major sights. What *London's Secret Places* does is seek out the city's lesser-known, but no less worthy, 'hidden' attractions.

LONDON'S SECRETS: PUBS & BARS

ISBN: 978-1-907339-93-6, Graeme Chesters

British pubs and bars are world famous for their bonhomie, great atmosphere, good food and fine ales. Nowhere is this more so than in London, which has a plethora of watering holes of all shapes and sizes: classic historic boozers and trendy style bars; traditional riverside inns and luxurious cocktail bars; enticing wine bars and brew pubs; mouth-watering gastro pubs and brasseries; welcoming gay bars and raucous music venues. This book highlights over 250 of the best.
Published Summer 2013.

LONDON'S SECRETS: PARKS & GARDENS

ISBN: 978-1-907339-93-6, David Hampshire

London is one the world's greenest capital cities, with a wealth of places where you can relax and recharge your batteries. Britain is renowned for its parks and gardens, and nowhere has such beautiful and varied green spaces as London: magnificent royal parks, historic garden cemeteries, majestic ancient forests and woodlands, breathtaking formal country parks, expansive commons, charming srna gardens, beguiling garden squares and delightful 'secret' gardens. Not all are secrets, of course, but many of London's most enchanting green spaces are known only to insiders and locals.

So, whether you're a nature lover, horticulturist or keen amateur gardener, or just looking for somewhere for a bit of peace and quiet or a place to exercise or relax, you're sure to find your perfect spot in London. **Published Summer 2013.**